LOOK
TO GOD
AND LIVE

LOOK
TO GOD
AND LIVE

Discourses of MARION G. ROMNEY

Compiled by GEORGE J. ROMNEY

Published by
DESERET BOOK COMPANY
Salt Lake City, Utah

1971

FOREWORD ●

By President Harold B. Lee

The announcement of the appointment of Elder Marion G. Romney as the newest member of the Quorum of the Twelve Apostles at the October 1951 general conference of the Church occasioned no great surprise to most Church members. For nearly eleven years he served as one of the Assistants to the Twelve and had, during that time, directed the far-flung activities of the Church welfare program as the assistant managing director. The membership of the Church had come to know him as a fearless and courageous defender of the faith and possessor of outstanding qualities of leadership.

Few men in our day have come into the council with a broader background than he or with more varied experience and distinguished church and public service preparation for the lifetime calling of an apostle. From serving as a president of a quorum of seventy, he was called to preside as bishop of the Thirty-third Ward of the Liberty (Salt Lake) Stake and later was sustained as the president of the Bonneville Stake.

To those of us who have been privileged to work intimately with him, there has come a deep appreciation for the "Romney traits" in this noble son, as were in others of his forebears as described by an uncle: "a mental and emotional characteristic peculiarly noticeable in the family—an indomitable will, which is re-inforced by a courage and honesty of purpose, admired even by those who disagree with them in matters of judgment."

From the stern discipline of a childhood and youth begun in one of the pioneer outposts of the Church and from the events which followed, one might find at least a partial explanation for the rugged character and the unusual insight and understanding which stamps him immediately as a wise counselor among men and a powerful advocate of the truth.

He was born September 19, 1897, the eldest son and second child of George S. Romney and Artemesia Redd in Colonia Juarez, Chihuahua, Mexico. The Romney and Redd families, along with many other faithful Saints, had been allowed by the Mexican authorities to colonize in northern Mexico in 1885. Here they built their own communities and developed a culture which was very typical of other pioneer Latter-day Saint communities throughout the West during the latter part of the nineteenth century. The *Deseret News* described one such "typical" pioneer community:

They were led by men of faith of whom it was said they never rested; when they tired, they merely changed jobs.

"They were thrifty and industrious.

"They all subscribed to the Church *Deseret News* which was at that time their chief means of communication for these distant communities with the leaders of the Church in Salt Lake City.

"They paid their debts promptly.

"They took care of their own poor."

These Anglo-Mexican Saints in far-off Mexico measured fully to these pioneer standards.

The year 1897, when Marion was born, brought some experiences and tests to the Romney family which were to try their very souls. His father had been a teacher in the schools of Colonia Juarez. A schoolteacher's wages were such as to require additional income from summer employment to take care of the barest necessities of his young family. In the summer of 1897, the father and his brother Miles contracted to sell provisions to a large mining compapny in Cananea in the state of Sonora, Mexico. His mother writes of the disappointments and near tragedy attending this summer's employment: "As summer drew to a close (it was August 1897, only one month before this new baby was to be born), George made preparations for the last trip to the mines. The summer's work had been long and hard, but it had been profitable, for he had earned $1,000.00 in Mexican money. . . . Upon arriving at the mine for this last time, he went immediately to the superintendent and asked if he might get his pay. The superintendent courteously received him and told him that since he was traveling home alone over the lonely mountain route, it would probably be unsafe to carry cash. For this reason, George agreed to accept his payment in the form of a check. Two weeks later when he attempted to cash the check, he learned, to his dismay, that the mine had gone broke and was closed down. The check was not good."

To complicate their financial situation further,

the father had just received a letter from "Box B" which meant a call from the First President for him to serve as a missionary in the Northern States Mission. Those with less faith would have wavered, but not this dedicated, devoted couple. There was no question as to his decision. Eight days after Marion G. was born the father left for his mission where he served for thirty months. Then, as always faithful devoted leaders must have equally devoted wives, and this resourceful, talented young mother with her two infant children rose to the occasion. About these eventful thirty months, the mother wrote: "With no visible means of support . . . we were confident that the Lord would provide for us, too. . . . I worked hard and found great joy in my children. . . . I managed to save about $75.00 from washing and knittings, which I sent to George to help him on his mission."

Inured as the family was to the rigid discipline of near poverty, yet they were always "rich towards God." Their childhood requirements of the pioneer dictum as expressed in simple terms: "Eat it up, Wear it out, Make it do, Do without," may have seemed severe to this young growing son.

In his mature years, as he occupies an important role in the Church welfare program, where "thrift, honesty, and work are to be enthroned in the lives of this people," one could well believe that his early training served to lay the foundations for the service he was to give as the directing head of this great Church welfare program today.

It was in July, 1912 (Marion was in his fifteenth year) during the Mexican Revolution, and because of the danger to the families of the colonists, they were forced to leave for the States.

Many of you who read this brief writing may have heard Elder Romney's recital of the feelings of a young teen-age boy through those stirring events. Here are a few excerpts:

"How well I remember the night in July, 1912, when Father came home from priesthood meeting with word that the decision was made for women, children, and older men to leave the next day for El Paso. I confess that the prospects were exciting and full of romance and adventure. But the soberness of the situation began to register when we were aroused early in the morning following the decision and made ready to leave. . . . Before leaving on our journey to the station, I sat on a chair under the apricot tree at the back of the house while Father cut my hair. As he did so, he told me that he would have to stay home, and I should go with Mother and the children, that I'd have to be the man of the family to take care of her when we got to El Paso.

"About 10 o'clock in the moring we left Juarez in a wagon. Mother and Aunt Lydie and Uncle George sat in the spring seat. Mother's seven children and Uncle George's—I think there were five—were in the back. I was seated on our trunk which carried all the goods we could take because of the crowd that would be on the train. As we drove down Main Street, across the river and down past Dan Skousen's mill, I was facing up the road in the direction from which we had come. Over the flat between Dan Skousen's and San Diego, the rebel army was moving northward. They were not in formation but were straggling along two at a time or in larger groups. Two armed Mexicans, with their large cartridge belts slung over their shoulders and riding their horses with the old-fashioned Mexican saddles with the big horns, stopped us and searched the wagon and Uncle George. They said they were looking for ammunition. They found none, but they did find twenty Mexican pesos on Uncle George, which was all the money we had and upon which we were depending to take care of us when we got into the United States. These twenty pesos they took from him and then permitted us to proceed south. They started north. When they were about 100 yards from the wagon, they turned around, drew their guns from their scabbards and pointed them towards the wagon. As I looked up the barrels of the rifles, they seemed very large to me, and I suppose this was one of the most exciting moments in my life, as I expected that they would shoot. They did not shoot, however; and I lived to tell the story."

Even the harrowing experiences of this rude expulsion from his childhood home was to have a bearing on what is now an apostolic assignment to supervise and preside over all the Mexican and Spanish American Missions and the Central American Mission. He had seen the natives of this land of his birth ground down under the heel of ruthless money-mad conquerors, and their subjugation by a dominant church under the guise of "Christianizing" them. He had seen the uses of cruelty, superstition, and ignorance as tools by which to exploit the natives in an almost unbelievable manner. There has been kindled in him a burning desire to assist in transforming the great nation of Mexico which was once described by Cortez as "a crumpled land of desert and mountains—a magnificent paradox, a land of fabulous wealth and dire poverty," into an independent and self-sustaining people. He is now giving leadership to a tremendous effort of the Church to help these people to throw off the yokes of bondage and to build on a foundation of truth, faith, and independence, to fulfill the prophecies of the ancients. He has had a hand in the organization of a thriving stake and mission in Mexico, with a promise of other stakes and missions to come in that area. Schools are being set up throughout that land under the supervision of Church leaders. Only the testimony of that grateful people will one day bear the full witness of the results of his efforts among those of Mexican birth like his own—a heritage in which he takes great pride.

Their search for financial security and safety after leaving Mexico led them first to El Paso, then to Los Angeles, and again to Oakley, Idaho, and then finally to Rexburg, Idaho. In these places, he worked with his father and Uncle Gaskell Romney as a carpenter, which trade he later turned to his advantage and to the blessing of his family in the building of his several homes.

I first saw Marion G. Romney at Ricks College where he was a star performer both in basketball and football. I saw him then as a "fierce competitor" with a zeal and the energy coupled with a determination which developed him into a fine athlete. Later I was to see these same qualities transferred to his studies in higher education and his successful practice of the law and in his activities in the political field as a state legislator. His call to serve as a missionary after his graduation from high school interrupted what might have developed into an illustrious college athletic career.

In the political field where so much pressure is exerted on men to compromise ideals and principles for expediency, party workers early learned to admire Marion G. Romney's intense loyalty to his own conscience as well as to the advice of his Church leaders whose pronouncements on vital issues affecting the welfare of the nation he accepted as divinely inspired even though it frequently brought him into sharp con-

flict with leaders of his own political party. On one
such occasion when Church leaders in a tersely-worded
editorial had denounced the trends of the political administration then in power, he confided in me something which it might be well if all loyal Church members in public life could emulate: "When I read that
editorial," he told me, "I knew what I should do—but
that wasn't enough. I knew that I must feel right about
following the counsel of the Church leaders and know
that they were right. That took a whole night on my
knees to accomplish." I submit in that statement the
difference between "intelligent" and "blind" obedience.
Marion G. Romney, while never disloyal to authority
over him, could never be rightfully accused of being
"blindly obedient."

Perhaps few, if any, among us is more soundly-
principled in the teaching of gospel truths. Possibly
the secret of his sound doctrine is his knowledge of and
the profound study he has made of the Book of Mormon, which the Prophet Joseph Smith declared to be
"the most correct of any book on earth, and the keystone of our religion, and a man would get nearer to
God by abiding by its precepts, than by any other book"
(*Documentary History of the Church*, Vol· IV, p. 461).
His love for the truths of this great volume of scripture is revealed in an incident which he related in one
of his general conference addresses. I quote briefly:
"I urge you to get acquainted with this great book.
Read it to your children; they are not too young to
understand it. I remember reading it with one of my
lads when he was very young. On one occasion I lay
in the lower bunk and he in the upper bunk. We were
each reading aloud alternate paragraphs of those last
three marvelous chapters of Second Nephi. I heard his
voice breaking and thought he had a cold, but we went
on to the end of the three chapters. As we finished he

said to me, 'Daddy, do you ever cry when you read the Book of Mormon?'

" 'Yes, Son,' I answered. 'Sometimes the Spirit of the Lord so witnesses to my soul that the Book of Mormon is true that I do cry.'

" 'Well,' he said, 'that is what happened to me tonight.'

"I know not all of them will respond like that, but I know that some of them will, and I tell you this book was given to us of God to read and to live by, and it will hold us as close to the Spirit of the Lord as anything I know. Won't you please read it?"

If you would have an example of the sound logic of his thinking on deeply spiritual themes, you have but to read the introductory and concluding paragraphs on the subject of repentance which appeared in an article in the Era many months ago. I quote briefly from that article:

"The Prophet Joseph Smith specified as the first principles and ordinances of the gospel, 'first, Faith in the Lord Jesus Christ; second, Repentance; third, Baptism by immersion for the remission of sins; fourth, Laying on of hands for the gift of the Holy Ghost.'

"These four principles and ordinances form the arch to the entrance of The Church of Jesus Christ of of Latter-day Saints. Compliance with them is the process by which one receives that rebirth of the water and of the Spirit without which, as Jesus taught Nicodemus, a man can neither see nor enter into the kingdom of God. In one sense, repentance is the keystone in that arch. Unless followed by repentance, professed 'faith in the Lord Jesus Christ' is impotent; unless preceded by repentance, baptism is a futile mockery, effecting no remission of sins; and without repenting, no one actually receives the companionship of the Holy Spirit of God, notwithstanding the laying on of hands for the gift of the Holy Ghost."

And then this concluding paragraph: "From the foregoing and many other scriptures, it is clear that repentance is the process by which every person must himself put into operation the plan of mercy on his own behalf, if he would be redeemed from spiritual death. In other words, repentance accomplishes for an individual with respect to his own sins, what the atonement of Jesus Christ did conditionally for the sins of all. Such is the place of repentance in the plan of redemption."

No recital of incidents in his life would be adequate without including reference to the great strength, loyalty, and inspiration of his lovely wife Ida Jensen Romney whom he married September 12, 1924, in the Salt Lake Temple· She has been the kind of companion who has always endeavored to be where Marion and her family needed her when they needed her. Her first two children, an infant daughter and an infant son, brought heartache and sadness. Little Janet lived only six days, and the second child, an infant son, was stillborn.

Their pride and joy is continuing today, however, in the accomplishments of their two splendid sons, Richard and George, who with their beautiful wives and children give promise to Marion and Ida of a continuation of their posterity in the generations to come.

As though by inspiration from a meaningful scripture there came a great comfort when Elder Romney was called to be a General Authority. This was the promise:

"... my son, blessed are you because of your faith in my work.

"Behold, you have had many afflictions ... Nevertheless, I will bless you and your family, yea, your little ones; and the day cometh that they will believe and know the truth and be one with you in my church."

And this devoted couple have full faith that those words were the promise of the Lord to them and theirs.

May the blessings of the Lord continue to strengthen this faithful and humble man of God to the full accomplishment of the mission to which the Lord has called him.

TABLE OF CONTENTS •

PREFACE •

The discourses published in this volume attest to the author's deep and abiding conviction that in the gospel of Jesus Christ is to be found a solution to all the perplexing questions and problems of men and nations.

Generally the discourses respond to a situation, question, or problem existing at the time they were prepared (frequently recalled by head notes).

It is hoped that what is said will help the reader understand the gospel principles discussed and their relevance to the problems involved; that it will help him realize that what is happening in our turbulent times is the result of man's refusal to seek "the Lord to establish his righteousness" (D&C 1:16); that it will help him to know that peace, progress, joy, and happiness may be had and will be had among men when they are sought in God's "own way"; that it will help him orient his own life and inspire him to stay on course by following Alma's charge to his son Helaman: *"Look to God and live"* (Alma 37:47).

It is as easy to give heed to the word of Christ, which will point to you a straight course to eternal bliss, as it was for our fathers to give heed to this compass, which would point unto them a straight course to the promised land.

. . . Just as surely as this director did bring our fathers, by following its course, to the promised land, shall the words of Christ, if we follow their course, carry us beyond this vale of sorrow into a far better land of promise.

. . . The way is prepared, and if we will look we may live forever.

And now, my son, see that ye . . . look to God and live.

Alma 37:44-47

"LOOK TO GOD AND LIVE" •

An address delivered to Brigham Young University student body January 13, 1970.

I have titled these remarks "Look to God and Live." My objective is to encourage and, if possible, inspire us to put complete trust in the Lord—with full purpose of heart to seek him to establish his righteousness. First, I shall indicate something as to the sickness of the society in which we live. Second, I shall call to your attention the proximate cause for that sickness as stated by the Lord. Third, I shall emphasize the remedy which he has prescribed for dealing with it. And fourth, I shall suggest some procedures by which we may reach the goal the Lord has set for us.

THE SICKNESS OF SOCIETY

First, a brief reference to the illness of our society. New Year's Eve I stayed with my grandchildren. This I did because I was somewhat uneasy about their being left with a young baby-sitter until the wee hours of the morning while their parents were welcoming in the new year. To some, my concern seemed unnecessary.

Perhaps it was. Be that as it may, I am convinced that my feeling indicates the spirit of our times.

During the holidays I was told that a middle-aged professor at one of the ivy league universities had said that he did not dare go home after dark from his office to his apartment which was just a block and a half away from the campus.

Last December 19 one of our local newspapers, commenting on the report of the National Commission on the Causes and Prevention of Violence, among other things, said:

Millions of Americans cache arms. They play, study, worship under guard, fleeing the streets at nightfall. Some cry revolution, others mobilize vigilante-like patrols.

Continuing its word picture of civil deterioration, the report continued:

This is a decade which encompassed the assassination of a President, a senator, and a Negro Nobel Prize winner, [a decade] which in its latter half saw ghetto riots involving more than two million persons and resulting in 191 deaths.

It is a time wherein up to one in every 150 Americans yearly commits violent crime, a time in which half the nation's 60 million households possess at least one firearm.

"Violence," decried the commission, "is like a fever in the body politic . . . disfiguring our society . . . making fortresses of portions of our cities . . . dividing our people into armed camps . . . jeopardizing some of our most precious institutions . . . poisoning the spirit of trust and cooperation. . . ."

Commission surveys showed half of the women and one-fifth of the nation's men fear to walk outdoors at night (*Deseret News* [Salt Lake City] December 19, 1969).

No doubt we are all aware of similar reports concerning organized crime, pornography, drugs, unchastity, and other types of moral degeneracy. Current trends, as revealed by these reports, are well known to everybody, and all right-minded people are hoping they can be checked and reversed.

PROXIMATE CAUSE

The commission revealed its opinion as to the cause and the cure in this warning to Americans: Continue to "suffer the violence" or "free all citizens of poverty and social privation." Everyone agrees that poverty and social privation should be eliminated. We ourselves must do all we can to eliminate them. We know, however, that success in such an endeavor would not cure our ills unless that success were accomplished in the Lord's way. Poverty and social privations and other of our ills are not the cause but the consequences of our evil practices.

Concerning the cause, the Lord himself said that his judgments were about to fall upon the inhabitants of the earth because

they have strayed from mine ordinances, and have broken mine everlasting covenant;
They seek not the Lord to establish his righteousness, but every man walketh in his own way, and after the image of his own God, whose image is in the likeness of the world (D&C 1:15-16).

Maybe we can emphasize this by relating President N. Eldon Tanner's statement of an incident which occurred while he was in England. Two of the missionaries were conversing with a minister. They didn't agree on very many things. Finally the minister said, "Well, on this one thing we can agree. We are all trying to serve the Lord." The missionaries replied, "Yes. You in your way and we in his way."

That, in short, is what the Lord says is the trouble with our society. Without seeking the Lord to establish his righteousness, men have from the beginning, over

and over and over again, sought in their own wisdom
to establish a good society. In such efforts they have
always failed, and they are failing now.

LORD'S REMEDY

Having stated the cause, the Lord thus emphasized
the remedy he had already prescribed for dealing with
the malady:

Wherefore [said he], I the Lord, knowing the calamity
which should come upon the inhabitants of the earth, called
upon my servant Joseph Smith Jun., and spake unto him
from heaven, and gave him commandments;

And also gave commandments to others, that they should
proclaim these things unto the world (D&C 1:17-18).

Collectively, the commandments referred to by the
Lord compose the gospel of Jesus Christ. These commandments proclaim the laws by which men may live
in peace, prosperity, and happiness. They prescribe
the rewards which obedience to the law brings, and
they warn of the consequences of disobedience.

Having received the commandments as we have,
we in this dispensation are, by them, put on direct and
specific notice, as have been the peoples of every former
dispensation, that we have an option. The option is
that we can, on the one hand, obey the commandments,
which is just another way of saying obey the eternal
laws of truth, because that is all the commandments of
God are—statements of the eternal laws of truth—and
by these laws Deity himself is bound. We can obey
them and live as God lives, or on the other hand, we can
disregard or defy them and perish.

Alma is the author of our text "Look to God and
Live" (Alma 37:47). About 93 years B.C. he solemnly
charged his son Helaman to "look to God and live." No

man could have been better qualified to give such a charge. In his young manhood Alma himself, while openly and actively defying God, was called to repentance by an angel. Through suffering the torment and the pains of hell he found repentance, however, and received forgiveness. Thereafter, during a lifetime of devoted service, he found the abundant life which comes as a reward for seeking God and striving to establish his righteousness.

Alma further learned that the Jaredites had been utterly destroyed in a fratricidal war brought on by their rejection of the word of God. He had learned from the word of God to their prophets and to the prophets of his own people, from revelation which he himself had received, and from his own experience that the only way he or his people could persist was to look to God.

As chief of state he had learned the limitations of civil and political power. So sure was he that the Nephites, if they would live, must look to God that when he saw them ripening in iniquity, he relinquished his office as chief of state

that he himself might go forth among his people, . . . that he might preach the word of God unto them, to stir them up in remembrance of their duty, and that he might pull down, by the word of God, all the pride and craftiness and all the contentions which were among his people, seeing no [other] way that he might reclaim them [from their wickedness] (Alma 4:19).

Six thousand years of sacred and profane history attest to Alma's wisdom. Every chapter in that history testifies to the fact that uninspired men with all their worldly wisdom cannot build a stable, lasting civilization or bring peace and happiness to individual men. All the evidence teaches that if man would preserve

civilization and live the abundant life, he must look to
God. The experience of generation after generation
has vindicated Nephi's declaration, "Cursed is he that
putteth his trust in the arm of flesh. Yea, cursed is he
that putteth his trust in man" (2 Nephi 4:34).

Nor are the prophets the only ones who have realized that "Except the Lord build the house, they labour
in vain that build it" (Psalm 127:1).

Josephus, the renowned Jewish historian, thus introduces his "Antiquities of the Jews":

> Moses, our legislator, . . . deemed it exceeding necessary,
> that he who would conduct his own life, and give laws to
> others, in the first place should consider the Divine nature,
> . . . [nor did Moses think that] any thing he should write
> [would] tend to the promotion of virtue in his readers: . . .
> unless they be taught first of all, that God is the Father,
> and Lord of all things . . . [It was his—Moses'—conviction
> that] When he had once demonstrated that God was pos-
> sessed of perfect virtue, he supposed that men also ought to
> strive after the participation of it; . . . (*The Works of
> Josephus*, pp. 38-39).

In an exhaustive treatise on *The Good Society*,
Hugh Evander Willis, professor of law emeritus of
Indiana University, argues that Jesus, realizing that
love is the only motive powerful enough to induce men
to exercise the self-control essential to a good society,
"proposed to extend this love to the entire human race
through teaching the fatherhood of God and the brotherhood of man."

The learned author used the word "proposed" because he does not believe in the reality of the fatherhood of God and the brotherhood of man. He expresses
the belief, however, that the love so essential to a good
society can be developed only when men act as if the
doctrine were true. He thus bases his hope for a good
society on the premise that men can be induced to con-

form to the teachings of Jesus without accepting Jesus
for what he claimed to be and what he in fact was and
is—the actual Son of God, the Savior of the world. But
all history and experience, sacred and profane, teach
that the hope for a good society founded on this premise, which is essentially the social gospel nurtured by
millions of professing Christians and other men of good
will, is doomed to fail.

Acceptance of Gospel Essential

The present world crisis has come about precisely
because men have been and now are seeking the fruit
of the gospel, the abundant life for individuals and
peace among nations, without accepting the gospel itself, which requires men to believe in God and his Divine Son and accept them for what they in fact are.

To look to God and keep his commandments is not
an arbitrary command. It is a plea for compliance with
universal law. Happiness, joy, peace, and every other
component of the abundant life for men and peace
among nations must and can only be attained by obedience to the laws upon which they are predicated. Nor
is it unnatural for men to look to God. Inherent in
every man is a spark of divinity which, properly nurtured, inspires him to believe.

He enters mortality enlightened by the Spirit of
Christ, which Spirit enlightens him through the world
so long as he hearkens to it. The Lord himself has said:

And the Spirit [that is, the Spirit of Christ] giveth light
to every man that cometh into the world; and the Spirit enlighteneth every man through the world that hearkeneth to
the voice of the Spirit.

And every one that hearkeneth to the voice of the Spirit
cometh unto God, even the Father (D&C 84:46-47).

PROMPTINGS OF SATAN

The reason men are so remiss in hearkening to the Spirit of Christ is that the promptings of Satan persuade them not to heed its whisperings. This has been the pattern from the beginning. When Adam and Eve received the gospel, which prescribes in detail just how men are to look to God, they

blessed the name of God, and they made all things known unto their sons and their daughters.

And Satan came among them, saying: . . . Believe it not; and they believed it not [You see, we are not very modern today when we deny God. Adam's first children did that.], and they loved Satan more than God. And men began from that time forth to be carnal, sensual, and devilish [when they turned from listening to the guidance of the Spirit] (Moses 5:12-13).

WARNINGS OF THE PROPHETS

Now, from Adam to Noah and beyond, the gospel was taught by father to son. Later on it was revealed to Abraham. Moses received it anew following the long bondage of Israel in Egypt. Jesus, in the meridian of time, taught and demonstrated it. The Jaredites and the Nephites were likewise prophetically instructed.

That men have not enjoyed peace, happiness, and continual progress is, therefore, not because God has failed to make known the way by which these blessings could be had. It is because men have refused to obey the revealed laws upon which these blessings are predicated.

The burden of all the prophets, from Adam to our present prophet, has been to persuade men to look to God and live. Over and over again in every dispensation they have warned of calamities pending because of man's corrupt and sinful ways.

Cain's curse was brought on by his own willful rejection of the counsel of God. The antediluvians brought on the flood in which they perished by rejecting Noah, who taught and pleaded with them for one hundred twenty years. The Jaredites pursued their rebellious course to their utter destruction in defiance of the teachings and warnings of their prophets. Following the same course, the Nephites suffered great destruction at the time of Christ's crucifixion.

All of this endless tragedy, carnage, and sorrow could have been avoided. All of these peoples could have existed in peace and prosperity had they been willing to look to God. Jesus expressed the pathos of it all when, envisioning the impending fate of the city, he cried out:

O Jerusalem, Jerusalem, thou that killest the prophets, and stonest them which are sent unto thee, how often would I have gathered thy children together, even as a hen gathereth her chickens under her wings, and ye would not!

Behold, your house is left unto you desolate.

For I say unto you. Ye shall not see me henceforth, till ye shall say, Blessed is he that cometh in the name of the Lord (Matthew 23:37-39).

THE EFFICACY OF LOOKING TO GOD

Certainly the overall picture portrayed by history of the decline and fall of civilizations is a gloomy one. There are, however, two bright spots in the record— accounts which conclusively demonstrate the efficacy of looking to God.

The most recent one concerns the Book of Mormon people who survived the cataclysm which occurred in America incident to Christ's crucifixion. The record says that by A.D. 36 these survivors (they were a minority; those who couldn't be brought to listen had gone

their way in the cataclysm) were "all converted unto
the Lord" and this was the result:

There were no contentions and disputations among them,
and every man did deal justly one with another.

And they had all things common among them; therefore
there were not rich and poor, bond and free, but they were
all made free, and partakers of the heavenly gift.

They did walk after the commandments which they had
received from their Lord and their God continuing in fasting
and prayer, and in meeting together oft both to pray and to
hear the word of the Lord.

And there were no envyings, nor strifes, nor tumults,
not whoredoms, nor lying, nor murders, nor any manner of
lasciviousness; and surely there could not be a happier people
among all the people who had been created by the hand of
God.

They were in one, the children of Christ, and heirs to
the kingdom of God (4 Nephi 2, 3, 12, 16, 17).

Now this blissful condition prevailed among them
for nearly 200 years, and then, sad to say, at the beginning of the third century

there began to be among them those who were lifted up in
pride, such as wearing of costly apparel, and all manner of
fine pearls, and of the fine things of the world.

And from that time forth they did have their goods and
their substance no more common among them.

And they began to be divided into classes; and they began
to build up churches unto themselves to get gain, and began to
deny the true church of Christ (4 Nephi 24-26).

Continuing on in their corrupt ways, the Nephites
as a people, by the end of the fourth century, were
annihilated in internecine conflict.

The other account has a happier ending. It concerns the saints spoken of in the scriptures as the
people of Enoch. In the day of war and bloodshed
among their contemporaries, these people "built a city
that was called the City of Holiness, even Zion" (Moses
7:19). So circumspect were they in looking to God and

keeping his commandments that the Lord himself came and dwelt among them, and

the fear of the Lord was upon all nations, so great was the glory of the Lord, which was upon his people. And the Lord blessed the land, and they were blessed upon the mountains, and upon the high places, and did flourish.

And the Lord called his people Zion, because they were of one heart and one mind, and dwelt in righteousness; and there was no poor among them.

And lo, Zion, in process of time, was taken up into heaven (Moses 7:17, 18, 21).

While there have been men and women in every dispensation who have faithfully looked to God to the end of their mortal lives, Enoch's Zion as an organized society is the only community of record in which all members have persisted in looking to God. All other societies have sooner or later succumbed.

OUR TOTAL SOCIETY IN JEOPARDY

Now, keeping in mind the foregoing references to the past, let us resume for a moment our consideration of the present situation. In my view, the issues we must now see clearly are (1) the direction in which our society is headed and (2)the course we individually should follow.

As I see it, our total society is now in jeopardy. Unless we can reverse current trends, we shall shortly be experiencing some of the more serious predicted consequences of our sinful ways. Here is one prediction which ought to wake us up. It was spoken by the Lord in March 1829:

A desolating scourge shall go forth among the inhabitants of the earth, and shall continue to be poured out from time to time, if they repent not, until the earth is empty, and the inhabitants thereof are consumed away and utterly destroyed by the brightness of my coming.

Behold, I tell you these things, even as I also told the people of the destruction of Jerusalem; and my word shall be verified at this time as it hath hitherto been verified (D&C 5:19, 20).

Now we do not glory in this prospect. We hope we are in error (at least I do) in our appraisal of present world conditions. The scriptures, however, are not mine. They are not ours. They were spoken by the Lord. And of them he himself said:

Search these commandments, for they are true and faithful, and the prophecies and promises which are in them shall all be fulfilled.

What I the Lord have spoken, I have spoken, and I excuse not myself; and though the heavens and the earth pass away my word shall not pass away, but shall all be fulfilled, whether by mine own voice or by the voice of my servants, it is the same (D&C 1:37, 38).

LOVE THE LORD AND SERVE HIM

For us as individuals the course is crystal clear. By precept and example we should do all that lies within our power to take the message of the gospel, the Lord's solution to our problems, to the peoples of the earth and inspire them to look to him and live. For every individual in this world there is yet an option, and it is still open. But whatever others may do, let us not personally be diverted from our course. Let us "be not faithless, but believing" (John 20:27).

Let us so long as we live continue to "seek . . . the Lord to establish his righteousness" (D&C 1:16). Let us prove worthy to live with him eternally in the heavens. Let us not be deceived by the learning and sophistries and the wickedness of this world. Let us not forget that God lives, that we are his children, that his purpose is to bring us to immortality and eternal life. Let us always remember and keep in mind that all man

has learned and accomplished, together with all that he
will yet learn and accomplish in mortality, is as a drop
in the ocean compared to the knowledge and works of
God. Let us remember that in the light of God's knowledge, and he knows all things, still his instruction to
us—against that total knowledge—is that, above all
else, the one thing of most importance to us is to love
the Lord our God with all our heart, soul, mind, and
strength.

Let us be constantly aware that we are living in
the last gospel dispensation; that Satan has marshaled
all his forces for war; that he is making his final pre-
millennium struggle for our individual souls and for
the souls of all men. Let us realize that the conflict we
are now in will be accelerated to such intensity "that
every man that will not take his sword against his
neighbor must needs flee unto Zion for safety" (D&C
45:68).

Let us understand that The Church of Jesus Christ
of Latter-day Saints is the literal kingdom of God in
the earth; that neither defectors from within nor enemies from without can stay its progress. It is here to
stay and to triumph. In the words of Moroni, "The
eternal purposes of the Lord shall roll on, until all his
promises shall be fulfilled" (Mormon 8:22).

Righteousness in the end is to prevail in this dispensation. So said the Lord himself in his reply to
Enoch's query,

Wilt thou not come again upon the earth?
[He said] As I live, even so will I come in the last days,
in the days of wickedness and vengeance.
And the day shall come that the earth shall rest, but before that day the heavens shall be darkened, and a veil of
darkness shall cover the earth; and the heavens shall shake,
and also the earth; and great tribulations shall be among the

children of men, but my people will I preserve. [The Lord is here talking to Enoch, long before the flood, concerning our day, the last gospel dispensation. He continued]

And righteousness will I send down out of heaven [Think of angel Moroni and the other messengers from heaven who came to the Prophet Joseph Smith!] ; and truth will I send forth out of the earth, to bear testimony of mine Only Begotten; his resurrection from the dead; yea, and also the resurrection of all men [Think of the Book of Mormon and its testimony of Christ!] ; and righteousness and truth will I cause to sweep the earth as with a flood [Think of the missionaries as they go out today and as they will go out in greater numbers in the immediate future, sweeping the earth as with a flood of truth and righteousness!], to gather out mine elect from the four quarters of the earth, unto a place which I shall prepare, an Holy City, that my people may gird up their loins, and be looking forth for the time of my coming; for there shall be my tabernacle, and it shall be called Zion, a New Jerusalem.

And the Lord said unto Enoch: Then shalt thou and all thy city meet them there, and we will receive them into our bosom, and they shall see us.

And there shall be mine abode, and it shall be Zion, which shall come forth out of all the creations which I have made; and for the peace of a thousand years the earth shall rest (Moses 7:59-64).

It is Zion, as portrayed in this scripture, for which we are preparing ourselves and which we shall yet build, which has held the righteous on course in all dispensations. It will so hold us if we keep it in view and individually commit ourselves to meet Alma's charge to "look to God and live."

To these truths I bear solemn witness in the name of Jesus Christ. Amen.

GOD REVEALS HIMSELF •

An address delivered at general conference October 1, 1967, a time at which the satanic doctrine "God Is Dead" was being widely heralded.

THE "UNKNOWN GOD"

I would like to begin my remarks this afternoon by quoting the scripture which Paul spoke on Mars' Hill in Athens. As he stood among the people, he said,

Ye men of Athens, I perceive that in all things ye are too superstitious.

For as I passed by, and beheld your devotions, I found an altar with this inscription, To the Unknown God. Whom therefore ye ignorantly worship, him declare I unto you (Acts 17:22, 23).

As I now address you on three types of evidence through which God has revealed himself, I invite you to join with me in a prayer that the Holy Spirit will bear witness to the truth and importance of what is said.

THE ORDERLINESS OF THE UNIVERSE

The three types of proof to which I refer are, first, the orderliness of the universe; second, the testimony of eyewitnesses; third, the witness of the Holy Spirit.

As to the orderliness of the universe and its probative evidence, the psalmist exclaimed, "The heavens
declare the glory of God; and the firmament sheweth
his handywork" (Psalm 19:1).

In 1887 the English physicist Lord Kelvin wrote,
"If you think strongly enough you will be forced by
science to the belief in God."

Countless scientists have confirmed this judgment.

Dr. Henry Eyring, our own world-renowned scientist, has said that the two most famous modern math-
ematicians, Sir Isaac Newton, the Englishman, and
Carl Friederick Gauss, the German, were both believers "in an allwise Creator of the universe . . ." (Henry
Eyring, *The Faith of a Scientist*, p. 74).

He has further said that

in the autumn of 1957, in Houston, Texas, the Welch Foundation invited the top nuclear physicists and chemists from all
over the world to a symposium. At a dinner, twelve of the
most distinguished were seated at a table. . . . Mr. Malone,
a trustee of the foundation, said, "Dr. Eyring, how many of
these gentlemen believe in a Supreme Being?" I answered
"I don't know but I'll ask."
    . . . Twelve people were asked and every one said "I be-
lieve." All of these students of the exact sciences—two of
them Nobel Prize winners—saw in the universal order about
them evidence for a Supreme Being (Ibid., p. 147).

Dr. Thomas J. Parmley, another of our own eminent scientists, has eloquently written:

The moon and stars in the night sky, one hundred million
suns with their attendant planets, space, oceans, earth and
nature, the flight of a bird, the wonder of a flower, the intri-
cate design and unbelievable coordination of the human body,
all of these and countless other creations proclaim the handiwork of God ("Proclaim the Handiwork of God," *Instructor*,
July 1967, p. 272).

The Lord gave his own personal witness that the orderliness of the universe is probative evidence of his existence, in these words:

The earth rolls upon her wings, and the sun giveth his light by day, and the moon giveth her light by night, and the stars also give their light, as they roll upon their wings in their glory, in the midst of the power of God.

Behold, all these are kingdoms, and any man who hath seen any or the least of these hath seen God moving in his majesty and power (D&C 88:45, 47).

Myriads of people are persuaded by the universal order about them that there is a divine power, a God, presiding over and controlling the universe. This conclusion is correct and comforting as far as it goes, but it is not enough. The honest, believing, inquiring soul wants to know about the nature and personality of God. This vital information God has provided in the testimony of the prophets to whom he has revealed himself.

THE TESTIMONY OF WITNESSES

In Eden God revealed himself to Adam and Eve. They carried with them from the Garden a personal knowledge of him (James E. Talmage, *Articles of Faith*, p. 30). There they had seen, heard, and talked with him. They knew from personal association that they were his offspring, created in his image. These truths they taught to their posterity.

Noah not only learned about the personality and nature of God from his father, Lamech, who had learned from the lips of Adam; he also

held direct communication with God and lived to instruct ten generations of his descendants. Then followed Abraham, who also enjoyed personal communion with God. . . .

Unto Moses the Lord made Himself known, not alone from behind the curtain of fire and the screen of clouds, but by face to face communion . . . [Moses] beheld "the similitude" of God (Ibid., pp. 31-32).

Jesus in his mortal ministry, being, as Paul said, "the express image of his [Father's] person" (Hebrews 1:3), was a true and complete revelation of the person and nature of God. This he confirmed to Philip when he said, "He that hath seen me hath seen the Father" (John 14:9).

Even though these testimonies of Jesus and the ancient prophets concerning the person and nature of God are clear and convincing, the Lord does not require us to rely upon them alone. He has never required the people of one age to rely upon the records of the past alone. At the beginning of every dispensation he has revealed himself anew. The revelation which he gave of himself in this day and which is binding upon us today, came in this manner:

In the spring of 1820, disturbed by the conflicting claims of the contending churchmen, Joseph Smith, Jun., desiring to know which of all the sects was right, found privacy in a grove near his home. There he kneeled and called upon God in humble, fervent prayer. As he did so, a pillar of light descended upon him from above.

When the light rested upon me [he said] I saw two Personages, whose brightness and glory defy all description, standing above me in the air. One of them spake unto me, calling me by name and said, pointing to the other—*This is My Beloved Son. Hear Him!* (Joseph Smith 2:17).

Later on the Prophet said of these "two personages": "The Father has a body of flesh and bones as tangible as man's; the Son also; [to this he added] but the Holy Ghost has not a body of flesh and bones, but is a personage of Spirit" (D&C 130:22).

He said further: "When the Savior shall appear [and for this appearance we are now preparing] we shall see him as he is. We shall see that he is a man like ourselves" (D&C 130:1).

THE POWER OF THE SPIRIT

Nor does Joseph Smith stand alone as the only modern witness to whom the Father and the Son have revealed themselves. Making record of an experience that they had together February 16, 1832, Sidney Rigdon joined with the Prophet in this magnificent testimony:

By the power of the Spirit our eyes were opened and our understandings were enlightened, so as to see and understand the things of God—
We beheld the glory of the Son, on the right hand of the Father, and received of his fulness; . . .
And now, . . . this is the testimony, . . . which we give of him: That he lives!
For we saw him, even on the right hand of God; and we heard the voice bearing record that he is the Only Begotten of the Father (D&C 76:12, 20, 22, 23).

Some months later Oliver Cowdery, a third witness, joined the Prophet in this testimony concerning an experience that they had as they bowed in solemn and silent prayer at the pulpit in the Kirtland Temple:

The veil was taken from our minds, and the eyes of our understanding were opened.
We saw the Lord standing upon the breastwork of the pulpit, before us; . . .
His eyes were as a flame of fire; the hair of his head was white like the pure snow; his countenance shone above the brightness of the sun; and his voice was as the sound of the rushing of great waters, even the voice of Jehovah saying:
I am the first and the last; I am he who liveth I am he who was slain; I am your advocate with the Father (D&C 110:1-4).

Now the revelations that God has given of himself have in every age been intended and given for the benefit of all men, not just for those chosen servants who received the revelation. Even as he gave them, he declared: "The voice of the Lord is unto the ends of the earth, that all that will hear may hear" (D&C 1:11).

God has from the beginning seen fit to place a knowledge of himself within the reach of all men. We who are his present witnesses are but discharging our responsibility when we bring these testimonies of the prophets and our own testimonies as to the form and nature of God to your attention.

To the extent we do bring them to your attention, the responsibility passes from us to you to determine the credibility of the witnesses and their testimonies. Let no man underestimate the importance of his decision concerning this matter. To know God and his Son Jesus Christ is life eternal. Without such knowledge no man can be saved. And the only way to get it is to obtain a personal witness to the truth of the revelations which God the Father and Jesus Christ, his Son, have given of themselves.

THE WITNESS OF THE HOLY GHOST

This brings us to a consideration of our third and last source of evidence to which I shall refer: the witness of the Holy Ghost.

The Holy Ghost is the third member of the Trinity. He is, as has already been said, a personage of Spirit (D&C 130:22). One of his functions is to bear witness of the Father and the Son to the honest, believing truth seeker.

THE POWER BY WHICH TRUTH IS MADE KNOWN

In harmony with the Lord's promises, every soul who will acquaint himself with the testimonies of the prophets concerning God and then ask Him "in the name of Christ, . . . with a sincere heart, with real intent, having faith in Christ" if these testimonies are true will receive a manifestation "by the power of the Holy Ghost" that they are true (Moroni 10:4).

It is not easy to explain to the uninitiated how this witness comes. Speaking about it to Nicodemus, Jesus said, "The wind bloweth where it listeth, and thou hearest the sound thereof, but canst not tell whence it cometh, and whither it goeth: so is every one that is born of the Spirit" (John 3:8).

When the witness comes, however, it is very real and powerful. He whose desire to know the living God is strong enough to induce him to follow the prescribed course can and will get the witness for himself. Then he will understand what the Lord was saying in these scriptures. However, he who does not so seek will never understand these scriptures, nor the revelations which God has given of himself.

SURE KNOWLEDGE

One who receives the witness of the Holy Ghost has a sure knowledge that God lives; that he is our Father in heaven; that Jesus Christ is our elder brother in the spirit and the Only Begotten of the Father in the flesh, our Savior and Redeemer. Such a one knows that the universal order in the heavens above, in the earth beneath, and in the waters under the earth, all give evidence that God lives; he knows that the testimonies of the prophets concerning the Father, Son, and Holy Ghost are accurate and true. Secure in this knowledge, his life has purpose. The gospel of Jesus Christ becomes for him what Paul said it is, "the power of God unto salvation" (Romans 1:16).

Now, as for myself, the Holy Ghost has borne and continues to bear witness to me that the words of the prophets are true. I know that God lives, that he is my Father, and that Jesus Christ is my Redeemer and that he spoke the truth when he said, "It shall come to pass that every soul who forsaketh his sins and cometh unto me, and calleth on my name, and obeyeth my voice and keepeth my commandments, shall see my face and know that I am" (D&C 93:1).

To the reality of this promise, I bear solemn witness in the name of Jesus Christ. Amen.

GIFTS OF THE SPIRIT ●

An address delivered at general conference April
1956. At the time the minds of the people were
being agitated by fantastic claims by purported
faith-healers over radio and television and
through the press.

Because of the great interest evidenced by the public in, and some resulting confusion from, certain so-called supernatural manifestations such as telecast healings, hypnotic performances, and the doctrine of reincarnation, I thought it might be appropriate for me to take as my text for these remarks the seventh Article of Faith, which reads: "We believe in the gifts of tongues, prophecy, revelation, visions, healing, interpretation of tongues, etc."

You can get the message I would like to give you in more detail than I will have time to give it here if you will read the 46th section of the Doctrine and Covenants and an editorial written by the Prophet Joseph Smith in 1842 titled "Try the Spirits," which you will find in volume four of *History of the Church*, page 571. It is also printed in *Teachings of the Prophet Joseph Smith*, compiled by our beloved President Joseph Fielding Smith, beginning on page 202.

GIFTS OF THE SPIRIT, CHARACTERISTICS OF THE
CHURCH OF CHRIST

The gifts named in the seventh Article of Faith
quoted above are enjoyed through the Holy Ghost.
These gifts have always been a distinctive characteristic of the Church of Jesus Christ. As a matter of fact,
without the gift of revelation, which is one of the gifts
of the Holy Ghost, there would be no Church of Jesus
Christ. This is apparent from the obvious fact that in
order for his Church to exist there must be a society of
people who individually have testimonies that Jesus is
the Christ. According to Paul, such testimonies are
revealed only by the Holy Ghost, for said he, "No man
can [know] that Jesus is the Lord, but by the Holy
Ghost" (1 Corinthians 12:3).

In the 46th section of the Doctrine and Covenants
the Lord lists such knowledge as one of the gifts of the
Holy Ghost. "To some [he says] it is given by the Holy
Ghost to know that Jesus Christ is the Son of God"
(D&C 46:13). Everyone who has a testimony of Jesus
has received it by revelation from the Holy Ghost.

Wherever and whenever revelation is operative,
manifestations of other gifts of the Holy Ghost are
prevalent. This has been so in all dispensations. It began with Father Adam who, having obeyed, repented,
and called upon God in the name of the Son,

was caught away by the Spirit of the Lord, and was carried
down into the water, and was laid under the water, and was
brought forth out of the water.
And thus he was baptized, and the Spirit of God
descended upon him, and thus he was born of the Spirit
(Moses 6:64, 65).

And in that day the Holy Ghost fell upon him and he
began to prophesy (Ibid., 5:9, 10).

The prophets from Adam to Malachi all enjoyed gifts of the Spirit. To Abraham was shown in vision the spirits of men as they were in the spirit world ere this earth rolled into being or ere "the morning stars sang together, and all the sons of God shouted for joy" (Job 38:7). In the days of Moses, Aaron's rod became a serpent, the waters of Egypt were turned to blood, for the Israelites a dry passage was provided through the Red Sea, and in the desert water burst from the solid rock to quench their thirst. In the days of the prophets, the widow's son was raised from the dead, fire came down from heaven to consume Elijah's sacrifice in his contest with the priests of Baal, and the leprous Naaman was instantly healed by following the instructions of Elisha.

Jesus exercised power over all things. He healed the sick, restored the lame, gave sight to the blind, cast out devils, and raised the dead. He turned water into wine, cursed the barren fig tree, stilled the storm, and walked upon the sea. He miraculously fed the four and the five thousand and provided the tribute money.

Among the gifts of the Spirit manifest in the apostolic church, Paul lists wisdom, knowledge, faith, healing, working of miracles, prophecy, discerning of spirits, diverse kinds of tongues, and the interpretation of tongues. The New Testament records numerous examples of the manifestation of these gifts.

Among the Jaredites and Nephites the manifestations of these gifts were likewise prevalent. Mormon testified that they would not cease, except for unbelief, "so long as time shall last, or the earth shall stand, or there shall be one man upon the face thereof to be saved" (Moroni 7:36).

Unfortunately, however, and because of unbelief, they have at times temporarily ceased both in the old world and in the new. For more than fifteen centuries, so far as our records reveal, no mortal man enjoyed them. Then finally came that glorious event in 1820 when, by the appearance of the Father and the Son, this awful darkness was put to flight and the return of these gifts of the Spirit heralded.

The Prophet Joseph Smith translated the Book of Mormon by the gift of the Holy Ghost. The direction to him to organize the Church came in like manner. Within a year from the organization of the Church, the Lord set forth in a revelation the gifts which were to be enjoyed by the restored Church. He named all those listed by Paul, to which were added the following:

> To some it is given by the Holy Ghost to know that Jesus Christ is the Son of God, and that he was crucified for the sins of the world.
> To others it is given to believe on their words, that they also might have eternal life if they continue faithful.
> And again, to some it is given by the Holy Ghost to know the differences of administration. . . .
> And . . . to some to know the diversities of operations, whether they be of God (D&C 46:13-16).

In 1839 the Prophet Joseph told Mr. Van Buren, then president of the United States, that possession of the gift of the Holy Ghost was the characteristic which distinguished the restored Church from other religions of the day.

I know that the gifts of the Holy Ghost are in the Church today. Every faithful Latter-day Saint knows that they are. As Sister Romney and I left this building at the close of one of the conference meetings yesterday, a faithful sister was waiting at the door for us. She called our attention to an administration received by her some three years ago at a stake conference in California. She, with cancer, and her family, all fasting, sought for her a blessing. She reported yesterday that she is well. No evidence of her former affliction remains. Presently she is a stake missionary.

Yes, all the gifts of the Holy Spirit are in the Church today.

NOT ALL SUPERNATURAL MANIFESTATIONS ARE GIFTS OF THE SPIRIT

According to the statement in the revelation on spiritual gifts, "it is given by the Holy Ghost to some to know the diversities of operations, whether they be of God, . . . And to others the discerning of spirits" (D&C 46:16, 23). From this it appears that there are some apparently supernatural manifestations which are not worked by the power of the Holy Ghost. In fact, there are many such. The world today is full of counterfeits. It has always been so. Away back in the days of Moses when Aaron's rod became a serpent, Pharaoh's wise men, sorcerers, and magicians "cast down every man his rod, and they became serpents" (Exodus 7:11, 12). Isaiah warned against seeking "unto them that have familiar spirits, and unto wizards that peep, and that mutter" (Isaiah 8:19).

Jesus, in his great Sermon on the Mount, stated that

not every one that saith unto me, Lord, Lord, shall enter into the kingdom of heaven; . . .

Many will say to me in that day, Lord, Lord, have we not prophesied in thy name? and in thy name have cast out devils? and in thy name done many wonderful works?

And then will I profess unto them, I never knew you: depart from me, ye that work iniquity (Matthew 7:21-23).

Before the end of 1830, the very year in which the restored Church was organized, some of the leading brethren were deceived as to the source of certain spiritual manifestations.

> To our great grief [wrote the Prophet Joseph], . . .
> Satan had been lying in wait to deceive, and seeking whom
> he might devour. Brother Hiram Page had in his possession
> a certain stone, by which he had obtained certain "revelations"
> concerning the upbuilding of Zion, the order of the Church,
> etc., all of which were entirely at variance with the order
> of God's house, as laid down in the New Testament, as well as
> in our late revelations (*History of the Church* 1:109-110).

In a revelation given in answer to the Prophet's prayer concerning the matter, the Lord said to Oliver Cowdery: "Thou shalt take thy brother, Hiram Page, between him and thee alone, and tell him that those things which he hath written from that stone are not of me and that Satan deceiveth him" (D&C 28:11).

The Saints were cautioned by the Lord to walk uprightly before him, doing all things with prayer and thanksgiving, that they might "not be seduced by evil spirits, or doctrine of devils, or the commandments of men" (D&C 46:7).

These citations not only sustain the proposition that there are counterfeits to the gifts of the Spirit, but they also suggest the origin of the counterfeits. However, we are not required to rely alone upon their implications, plain as they are, for the Lord states specifically that some of the counterfeits are of men, and others of devils   (D&C 46:7).

Some of these counterfeits are crude and easily detected, but others closely simulate true manifestations of the Spirit. Consequently, people are confused and deceived by them. Without a key, one cannot distinguish between the genuine and the counterfeit. The Egyptians could not tell the difference between the power through which Moses and Aaron worked and that by which the magicians worked. On the day of Pentecost the non-believers did not recognize that the apostles were speaking in tongues by the power of the Spirit; on the contrary, they concluded that they were drunken with new wine. The Savior himself said "There shall also arise false Christs, and false prophets, and shall show great signs and wonders, insomuch, that, if possible, they shall deceive the very elect, who are the elect according to the covenant" (Joseph Smith 1:22). Now those "who are the elect according to the covenant" are members of the Church; so we ourselves are on notice to beware.

DISTINGUISHING BETWEEN MANIFESTATIONS OF THE SPIRIT AND COUNTERFEITS

This brings us to our most important consideration. Believing as we do in all the gifts named in the 46th section of the Doctrine and Covenants, and knowing that there are counterfeits to them, how are we to distinguish between the true and the false, the genuine and the counterfeit?

The Apostle John gave to the saints in his day the following test:

Beloved, believe not every spirit, but try the spirits whether they are of God: because many false prophets are gone out into the world.

Hereby know ye the Spirit of God: Every spirit that confesseth that Jesus Christ is come in the flesh is of God:

And every spirit that confesseth not that Jesus Christ is come in the flesh is not of God (1 John 4:1-3).

This was a good test for them. It will not, however, do for us. The reason is given by the Prophet Joseph as follows:

Did not the Apostle speak the truth? Certainly he did—but he spoke to a people who were under the penalty of death, the moment they embraced Christianity; and no one without a knowledge of the fact would confess it, and expose themselves to death (*History of the Church* 4:580).

The Prophet Joseph, having recited some of the workings of evil spirits in his day, said:

A man must have the discerning of spirits before he can drag into daylight this hellish influence and unfold it unto the world in all its soul-destroying, diabolical, and horrid colors; for nothing is a greater injury to the children of men than to be under the influence of a false spirit when they think they have the Spirit of God. Thousands have felt the influence of its terrible power and baneful effects. Long pilgrimages have been undertaken, penances endured, and pain, misery and ruin have followed in their train; nations have been convulsed, kingdoms overthrown, provinces laid waste, and blood carnage and desolation are habiliaments in which it has been clothed (*History of the Church* 4:573).

Without attempting an exhaustive discussion of this question, I shall take the liberty to suggest three simple tests which, if applied, will prove of great value in making the distinction.

First, determine whether the alleged supernatural manifestation is edifying. If it is not, then it is not of God, because spiritual gifts are given for the edification of God's people.

Paul, writing to the Corinthian saints concerning spiritual gifts, instructed them to "let all things be done unto edifying" (1 Corinthians 14:26). And of those who would speak in tongues, he said, "If there be no interpreter, let him keep his silence in the church" (1 Corinthians 14:28).

And as to prophecy, he added, "The spirits of the prophets are subject to the prophets. For God is not the author of confusion, but of peace" (1 Corinthians 14:32, 33). He compared the speaking in tongues without a clear interpretation thereof to a trumpet giving forth an uncertain sound, at which no one would know whether to prepare for the battle.

There are [he wrote] so many kinds of voices in the world, . . .

Therefore if I know not the meaning of the voice, I shall be unto him that speaketh a barbarian, and he that speaketh shall be a barbarian unto me (1 Corinthians 14:10, 11).

That the Saints of the infant Church in this dispensation be not deceived, the Lord pleaded with them to keep in mind that the purpose of spiritual gifts was to benefit those who loved him and kept his commandments. They were not to be given as signs to those who would consume them upon their lusts.

Second (this pertains particularly to purported supernatural healings), find out whether the purported healer follows the divinely established procedure— that is, does he do as Jesus did when he laid hands upon the sick and healed them (Mark 6:5), and as his apostles did when, at his direction, "they went out, and preached that men should repent. And . . . cast out many devils, and anointed with oil many that were sick, and healed them" (Mark 6:12, 13). The pattern which prevailed in the apostolic church, and which has been prescribed anew by revelation in this day (D&C 42:43, 44), is set out by James as follows:

Is any sick among you? Let him call for the elders of the church; and let them pray over him, anointing him with oil in the name of the Lord.

And the prayer of faith shall save the sick, and the Lord shall raise him up; and if he have committed sins, they shall be forgiven him (James 5:14, 15).

Third, find out whether the worker of the purported miracle has himself received the gift of the Holy Ghost through the prescribed ordinances. If he has

not, then his works, whatever they may be, are not the
manifestations of the Holy Spirit. This is a key test
because, as we have already pointed out, the gifts of
the Spirit are given by the power of the Holy Ghost.
Without the gift of the Holy Ghost, the manifestations
of his gifts may not be enjoyed. The Prophet Joseph
Smith states this foundation doctrine as follows:

> We believe in the gift of the Holy Ghost being enjoyed
> now, as much as it was in the Apostles' days; we believe that
> it [the gift of the Holy Ghost] is necessary to make and to
> organize the Priesthood, that no can can be called to fill any
> office in the ministry without it: we also believe in prophecy,
> in tongues, in visions, and in revelations, in gifts, and in
> healings; and that these things cannot be enjoyed without the
> gift of the Holy Ghost (*History of the Church* 5:27).

Thus, one who has never received the gift of the Holy
Ghost cannot possibly work miracles by his power.

We know that there is but one way to obtain the
gift of the Holy Ghost. That way is through the prescribed ordinances of baptism by immersion for the
remission of sins and the laying on of hands for the
gift of the Holy Ghost. The Apostle Paul's procedure
emphasizes the indispensability of the ordinances:

> [Coming to] Ephesus: and finding certain disciples,
> He said unto them, Have ye received the Holy Ghost
> since ye believed? And they said unto him, We have not so
> much as heard whether there be any Holy Ghost.
> And he said unto them, Unto what then were ye baptized?
> And they said, unto John's baptism.
> Then said Paul, John verily baptized with the baptism of
> repentance saying unto the people, that they should believe
> on him which come after him, that is, on Christ Jesus.
> When they heard this, they were baptized in the name
> of the Lord Jesus.
> And when Paul had laid his hands upon them, the Holy
> Ghost came on them; and they spake with tongues, and
> prophesied (Acts 19:2-6).

These gifts of the Spirit they could not possibly have exercised until after they had received the gift of the Holy Ghost through compliance with the proper ordinances. Such has been the procedure for receiving the gift of the Holy Ghost from the days of Father Adam. We quoted at the beginning of these remarks the procedure by which he received it. That procedure was precisely the same as that followed by Paul in bestowing it. Such will always be the procedure, for God established it.

Baptism [said the Prophet Joseph] is a holy ordinance preparatory to the reception of the Holy Ghost; it is the channel and key by which the Holy Ghost will be administered.

The gift of the Holy Ghost by the laying on of hands, cannot be received through the medium of any other principle than the principle of righteousness, for if the proposals are not complied with, it is of no use, but withdraws (*History of the Church* 3:379).

Now, righteous men bearing the holy priesthood of the living God and endowed with the gift of the Holy Ghost, who are magnifying their callings (and such are the only men upon the earth with the right to receive and exercise the gifts of the Spirit), will do so circumspectly and in all humility. They will not spectacularly advertise their divine power, nor boast about it. Neither will they display it for money. Of this you may be sure.

TESTS FOR SPECIAL CLAIMS AND DOCTRINES

Now, the Prophet gave other tests applicable to special claims and doctrines, of which the following two are typical:

1. He made it clear that there is never more than one man on the earth at a time authorized to receive revelations for the Church. This principle answered the claims of the purported peepstone revelations.

2. Of an interview with a Mr. Matthias, the Prophet wrote:

He said that he possessed the spirit of his fathers, that he was a literal descendant of Matthias, the Apostle, who was chosen in the place of Judas that fell; that his spirit was resurrected in him; and that this was the way or scheme of eternal life—this transmigration of soul or spirit from father to son.

I told him [said the Prophet] that his doctrine was of the devil (*History of the Church* 2:307).

He thus removed all doubt with respect to the fallacious doctrine of "transmigration of souls or spirits," currently referred to as reincarnation.

In conclusion I again call attention to the statement of the Prophet Joseph Smith already quoted that "a man must have the discerning of spirits before he can drag into daylight this hellish influence and unfold it unto the world in all its soul-destroying, diabolical, and horrid colors." Or after all, the things of God can be understood only by the Spirit of God. The gift of discernment of spirits is the sure solution of this knotty problem. Seek after this gift, brethren and sisters, and after its kindred gifts—knowledge, wisdom and "to know the diversities of operations, whether they be of God"—and not after sensational and miraculous signs and wonders. Remember that

unto the bishop of the church, and unto such as God shall appoint and ordain to watch over the church and to be elders unto the church, are to have it given unto them to discern all those gifts lest there shall be any among you professing and yet be not of God.

And it shall come to pass that he that asketh in Spirit shall receive in Spirit;

That unto some it may be given to have all those gifts, that there may be a head, in order that every member may be profited thereby (D&C 46:27-29).

Finally:

Be virtuous and pure; be men of integrity and truth; keep the commandments of God; and then you will be able more perfectly to understand the difference between right and wrong—between the [gifts] of God and the things of men; and your path will be like that of the just, which shineth brighter and brighter unto the perfect day (*History of the Church* 5:31).

God grant that it may be so, I humbly pray in the name of Jesus Christ. Amen.

If ye shall ask with a sincere heart, with real intent, having faith in Christ, he will manifest the truth of it unto you, by the power of the Holy Ghost.

And by the power of the Holy Ghost ye may know the truth of all things.

Moroni 10:4, 5

TESTIMONY AND HOW TO GAIN ONE •

An address delivered to Brigham Young University student body March 24, 1953.

WHAT A TESTIMONY IS

There are many types of testimonies, and testimonies to many things. The testimony I have in mind discussing today is an abiding, living, moving conviction of the truths revealed in the gospel of Jesus Christ.

One aspect of such a testimony is a settled conviction that there is a personal God—"an exalted man" was the phrase the Prophet Joseph used in describing Him—and that He is our Heavenly Father.

A second aspect of such a testimony is a belief in God's plan of salvation, with Jesus Christ as the central figure.

Another essential to such a testimony is to believe the Prophet's account of his first vision; that in it he saw God, our Eternal Father, and Jesus Christ, His Son; that they stood before him and conversed with him and that he conversed with them.

Still another requisite is an acceptance of the fact that the Book of Mormon came forth in the manner the

Prophet Joseph said it did; that Moroni delivered to him the plates of gold upon which the ancient record was inscribed and that he, the Prophet, made the translation by the gift and power of God.

One must also be convinced that the Prophet received from heavenly beings all the principles, ordinances, and priesthood power required to enable men to gain exaltation in the celestial presence of God; that The Church of Jesus Christ of Latter-day Saints is the repository of such principles, ordinances, and priesthood powers.

One who has such a testimony accepts the truth that the keys to the kingdom of God have been held by every man who has presided over the Church, from the Prophet Joseph to and including our present prophet.

One of the most important things about such a testimony, and one of the most difficult to obtain, is a conviction that the living prophet is just as much a prophet as was Joseph Smith, Jr.

For some people it is much easier to accept ancient prophets than to accept living prophets. This was true in the days of Jesus. He charged the scribes and Pharisees with being hypocrites because they built tombs of the dead prophets and killed the living prophets (see Matthew 23:29-34).

The possession of a sure testimony is the most valuable possession a person can have. It gives him the knowledge, the hope, and the assurance that he himself can, through obedience to the laws and ordinances of the gospel, become a partaker of all the promised blessings.

It is always an uplift to me to hear a person bear his testimony. I remember the times I have thrilled as I

have listened to President Grant bear his testimony.
When he used to close conference, he would say:

> I know as I know that I live that God lives, that Jesus
> is the Christ the Son of the living God, the Redeemer of the
> world, and that Joseph Smith was a prophet of the true and
> the living God, and that Mormonism, so-called, is in very deed
> the plan of life and salvation (*Conference Report*, Oct. 1934,
> p. 132).

I never heard him say these words without getting a
tingling feeling up and down my spine.

TESTIMONIES RECEIVED BY THE HOLY GHOST

Such a testimony is not produced by the learning
of the world. It does not come through philosophizing
nor from studying what men who do not have a testimony say. Here is an example of what men have come
to when they, without the guidance of the Spirit, have
tried to explain some of the great truths we have just
been considering. Concerning the nature of God, they
have said:

> There is but one living and true God, everlasting; without
> body, parts or passions; of infinite power, wisdom and good-
> ness; the maker and preserver of all things, both visible and
> invisible; and in the unity of this Godhead there are three
> persons of one substance, power and eternity—the Father,
> Son, and the Holy Ghost (Church of England Thirty-nine
> Articles).

Compare this babble with the Prophet Joseph
Smith's statement: "The Father has a body of flesh
and bones as tangible as man's; the Son also; but the
Holy Ghost has not a body of flesh and bones, but is a
personage of Spirit" (D&C 130:22).

Here is another example of where men get to when
they revise the scriptures without the inspiration of
the Spirit.

Isaiah, in predicting the birth of Christ, said, "Behold a *virgin* [italics added] shall conceive, and bear a son, and shall call his name Immanuel" (Isaiah 7:14). When Isaiah used the word *virgin*, he was saying that a woman who had not known a man should bear a son.

The modern translators say, "Behold a *young woman* [italics added] shall conceive and bear a son, and shall call his name Immanuel" (Isaiah 7:14, Holy Bible Revised Standard Version, 1952). You see, they do not believe that Christ was divine, so it doesn't make any difference to them whether they say a *young woman* or a *virgin*.

A testimony comes through the power of the Holy Ghost. Every person who ever had a testimony, received it through the inspiration of the Holy Spirit. As the Prophet Joseph Smith said, the Holy Ghost is a personage of Spirit. He is a member of the Godhead. As such, one of his assignments is to bear witness to believers that Jesus is the Christ.

Paul taught in his day "that no man can [know] that Jesus is the Lord but by the Holy Ghost" (1 Corinthians 12:3; see also *Teachings of the Prophet Joseph Smith*, p. 223).

President Grant used to tell about the experience of Senator Beveridge from Indiana, who spent a summer vacation interviewing eminent divines. One of his questions had to do with the personality of God:

"Do you believe in God the Father, God a person, God a definite and tangible intelligence—not a congeries of laws floating like a fog through the universe; but God, a person in whose image you were made? Don't argue; don't explain; but is your mind in a condition where you can answer yes or no?"

Not a minister answered "yes," but they all gave a lot

of explanations to the effect that we could not be sure about such things. . . .

The next question was: "Yes or no: do you believe that Christ was the Son of the living God, sent by Him to save the world? I am not asking whether you believe that He was inspired in the sense that the great moral teachers are inspired—nobody has any difficulty about that. But do you believe that Christ was God's very Son, with a divinely appointed and definite mission dying on the cross, and raised from the dead—yes or no?"

Again, not a single minister answered "Yes" (Heber J. Grant, "Three Questions," *Improvement Era*, July 1940, p. 394).

They could not answer yes because they did not have a witness from the Holy Ghost.

If we should ask you students here today, and you men and women here on the stand, how many of you know that Jesus is the Christ, many of you would answer yes. And how do you know? You know because the Holy Spirit has borne witness to you.

How a Witness from the Holy Ghost Comes

Sometimes this knowledge comes to a person of a sudden. He gets it at a certain time, and he knows that he so received it.

Let me tell you an experience had by the girl who later became my wife. At one time she was a member of a stake Sunday School board. As such, it was her responsibility to instruct teachers in a union meeting class. The lesson for a particular session was the Prophet's vision of the Father and the Son. She was aware that in that class there would be a graduate from the University of Idaho who was not a Latter-day Saint and who did not believe the gospel. It occurred to her that the account of the Father and the Son coming to the Prophet Joseph Smith would not be accepted by this educated, refined, and lovely woman. Thinking about it, she became greatly disturbed. She was not sure that she herself knew it was true. She was so distraught that she sought out her mother and weepingly said, "Mother, I can't give this lesson. I don't know that Joseph Smith had that vision. The woman will laugh at me and ridicule me."

Her mother was not an educated woman, but she did have a testimony. She said to her daughter, "You know how the Prophet got the vision, don't you?"

"Yes," answered her daughter, "he got it by praying to God for wisdom."

"Why don't you try that?" said mother to her daughter.

Her daughter went to her room and tried it; she wrestled with God, as did Enos. The result was she went to that union meeting and gave the lesson convincingly, with power beyond her natural abilities.

How could she do it? Well, the Holy Spirit came to her in response to her inquiry. She received a burning within her soul. She knew that Joseph Smith had seen the vision as well as Joseph Smith knew it. She hadn't seen just the same things with her eyes that the Prophet saw, but she had the same knowledge. She knew from his description what he had seen, and she had a witness from the Holy Ghost that his account was true.

Sometimes a testimony comes to a person slowly, over an extended period of time. I do not remember of a testimony coming to me as suddenly as it did to my wife. I cannot remember when I did not have a testimony. It has, of course, been strengthend through the years.

CHANGES WROUGHT BY TESTIMONIES

But whether a testimony comes of a sudden or whether it comes by degrees, it does something to a person. One is different after he receives a testimony than he was before he received one. Good men, great men, are different. Peter was different. When Jesus spoke of his approaching crucifixion, Peter said he would die with him. In response, Jesus said to Peter, "Before the cock crow twice, thou shalt deny me thrice" (Mark 14:30).

When they took Christ into custody, Peter, following a distance behind, went to the place where Jesus was being indicted. As he sat among the spectators,

a certain maid beheld him . . . and earnestly looked upon him, and said, This man was also with him.

And he denied him, saying, Woman, I know him not.

And after a little while another saw him, and said, Thou art also of them. And Peter said, Man, I am not.

And about the space of one hour after another confidently affirmed, saying, Of a truth this fellow also was with him: for he is a Galilaean.

And Peter said, Man, I know not what thou sayest. And immediately, while he yet spake the cock crew.

And the Lord turned, and looked upon Peter. And Peter remembered the word of the Lord, how he had said unto him, Before the cock crow, thou shalt deny me thrice.

And Peter went out, and wept bitterly (Luke 22:56-62).

But that was not the end for Peter. When, on the day of Pentecost, the Holy Ghost fell on him and the rest of the apostles, they received testimonies. Thereafter Peter and John went up to the temple and healed a lame man—that is, in the name of Jesus they exercised the power of the priesthood, and God healed the man at their request. The people gathered around and made a great to-do about the miracle. The Jewish leaders became concerned lest they should lose their following. They therefore took Peter and John into custody and told them not to preach and teach any more in the name of Christ. These rulers had the power to put them to death, as they put Christ to death. But Peter was different now. When they told him and John not to preach any more, Peter said, "Whether it be right in the sight of God to hearken unto you more than unto God, judge ye. For we cannot but speak the things which we have seen and heard" (Acts 4:19, 20). He had a testimony then.

The experiences of Alma and Paul are also examples of how testimonies change men.

My father used to tell me that the difference between a man when he has a testimony and when he does not have one is the difference between a living, growing tree and a dry stump. I am sure he was right.

How to Get a Testimony

I think Jesus gave the answer as to how to go about getting a testimony as well as it has ever been given. As he taught in the temple at the Jewish Feast of Tabernacles, the Jews, although they were even then plotting his death, marveled at his teachings and said,

How knoweth this man letters, having never learned?
Jesus answered them, and said, My doctrine is not mine, but his that sent me.
If any man will do his will, he shall know of the doctrine, whether it be of God, or whether I speak of myself (John 7:16, 17).

This statement points the way so clearly and simply that even "warfaring men, though fools," need "not err therein" (Isaiah 35:8).

It is obvious that the first step toward getting a testimony is to learn the will of the Father. This can be done by studying the word of God and obeying his commandments as they are learned. Study the scriptures; study the teachings of the prophets; study the Book of Mormon, Doctrine and Covenants, Pearl of Great Price, and Bible. Read the teachings of the modern prophets, the life of the Prophet Joseph. Learn and obey!

There is no shortcut to a testimony. There are not two ways. There is only one way. The Lord revealed that sure and certain way when he said:

> Oliver Cowdery, verily, verily, I say unto you, that assuredly as the Lord liveth, who is your God and your Redeemer, even so surely shall you receive a knowledge of whatsoever things you shall ask in faith, with an honest heart, believing that you shall receive a knowledge. . . .
>
> Yea behold, I will tell you in your mind and in your heart, by the Holy Ghost, which shall come upon you and which shall dwell in your heart.
>
> Now, behold, this is the spirit of revelation (D&C 8:1-3).

Everyone who sincerely prays with real desire to know concerning what he has learned about the gospel will receive a witness in his mind and in his heart by the Holy Ghost, as the Lord said to Oliver. And, as the Lord said, this witness shall dwell in his heart. And it shall dwell in his heart forever if he retains his faith by (1) repenting of his sins, (2) being baptized, (3) receiving the gift of the Holy Ghost by the laying on of hands, and (4) continuing to obey the principles of the gospel to the end of his mortal life.

MY TESTIMONY

I have a witness in my soul to the truth of all the principles I enumerated when I began this little talk. I know that God lives and that Jesus Christ lives. I shall not be more certain when I stand before them to be judged of my deeds in the flesh. The Holy Ghost has revealed these truths to me. I know that God can hear prayers; he has heard mine on many occasions. I have received direct revelation from him. I have had problems which it seemed I could not solve, and I have suffered in facing them until it seemed that I could not go farther if I did not have a solution to them. After praying and on many occasions fasting for a day each week over long periods of time, I have had answers revealed to my mind in finished sentences. I have heard the voice of the God in my mind and I know his words.

May God bless you, brothers and sisters, that you may all enjoy the great gift of a testimony of the gospel. The Prophet Joseph Smith said that men could not be saved in ignorance. He did not have in mind, however, that a man could not be saved in ignorance of some foreign language nor in ignorance of some field of science. (I would not cast any reflection upon learning; all learning is good. I urge you to get just as much as you can in this university, and when you are through here if you want to go on in special fields of learning, go where you can get more learning. It is all important. But none of it will give you a knowledge of those things which the Prophet had in mind when he said that man could not be saved in ignorance.) The knowledge one must have to be saved is that which comes with a testimony of the truthfulness of the gospel of Jesus Christ, including all the principles that it teaches. It can be had; I know many of you have it. God bless you that you may all get it and that you will continue faithful in it to the end of your lives, for unto those who get it and continue faithful to the end all the promises are given.

I leave my blessing with you in the name of Jesus Christ. Amen.

When I the Lord had spoken these words unto my disciples, they were troubled.

And I said unto them: Be not troubled, for, when all these things come to pass, ye may know that the promises which have been made unto you shall be fulfilled.

D&C 45:34, 35

THE COURAGE OF FAITH •

I have titled these remarks "The Courage of Faith." My thesis is that courage born of faith will dispel trouble born of fear. My text is the 45th section of the Doctrine and Covenants.

When the disciples of Jesus were troubled by his description of the turmoil through which we are now passing, he sought to calm their souls by calling their attention to the glories that would follow.

I can think of no better way to inspire in us the courage of faith required to calm our souls as we live through these troubled times than to recall what Jesus said about them and the counsel he gave his apostles.

That we live in the predicted period when "perilous times shall come" is common knowledge. Every day we hear such questions as What is going to happen next? Will things get better for us? or will they get worse? Will the Church escape? or will we all be subjected to violence and bloodshed?

These questions are reminiscent of the query repeated in the days of Isaiah: "Watchman, what of the night? Watchman, what of the night?" To this query, the watchman replied, "The morning cometh, and also the night" (Isaiah 21:11, 12).

This was essentially what Jesus said to his disciples as he responded to their question "What shall be the sign of thy coming, and of the end of the world?" (Matthew 24:3).

The morning will come with the advent of the Savior. The night, which is even now upon us, to precede the morning and, true to the adage "The darkest hour is just before the dawn," the present darkness in the world will continue to increase as it seeks to obscure the light which is already heralding the dawn.

We Latter-day Saints should not—and we cannot if we would—ignore our plight. We must not, however, let the wickedness and commotion of the world engulf or confuse us. This is not the time for us to panic. It is a time for sober, thoughtful, resolute commitment. It is the time for us to demonstrate the courage of our faith; the time for us to implement the Savior's challenge to be *in* the world but not *of* the world.

By the prophets in all ages we have been warned and forewarned of what is now transpiring and of what will follow. That we might be prepared to cope with and surmount our present difficulties, the Savior himself foretold our present predicament and outlined the future in clear and simple language. The instructions he gave were, in his view, of such significance and importance to us that he has had a record of them preserved in three separate scriptures—the Bible, the Pearl of Great Price, and the Doctrine and Covenants.

In the Bible much of what he said is recorded in the 24th chapter of Matthew. In the Pearl of Great Price it is recorded in the Writings of Joseph Smith,

chapter 1. In the Doctrine and Covenants, from which
I shall quote, it is recorded in the 45th section.

The background for Christ's prophetic account of
the sequence of events to occur in this last dispensation
is given by Dr. Talmage in his great book *Jesus the
Christ*:

In the course of His last walk from Jerusalem back to the
beloved home at Bethany, Jesus rested at a convenient spot on
the Mount of Olives, from which the great city and the magnificent temple were to be seen in fullest splendor, illumined
by the declining sun in the late afternoon of that eventful
April day. As He sat in thoughtful revery He was approached
by Peter and James, John and Andrew, of the Twelve, and to
them certainly, though probably to all the apostles He gave instruction, embodying further prophecy concerning the future
of Jerusalem, Israel, and the world at large. His fateful prediction—that of the temple buildings not one stone would be
left upon another—had caused the apostles to marvel and fear;
so they came privately requesting explanation. "Tell us," they
said, "when shall these things be? and what shall be the sign
of thy coming and of the end of the world?" (p. 569).

I shall not here recite what he said about the impending destruction of Jerusalem which was, forty
years later, fulfilled. I shall, however, quote rather
extensively from what he said about the signs of his
second coming and the end of the world.

Concerning these signs, some of which are now
and have been visible for a century and a half and
which will culminate at his coming, he said,

When the times of the Gentiles is come in, a light shall
break forth among them that sit in darkness, and it shall be
the fulness of my gospel [It is clear from this statement that
the restoration of the gospel signaled the coming in of the
times of the gentiles.];

But [continued the Savior] they [that is, the gentiles that
sit in darkness] receive it not; for they perceive not the light,
and they turn their hearts from me because of the precepts of
men [The fulfillment of this prediction that "they turn their

hearts from me because of the precepts of men" is everywhere painfully evident today.].

And in that generation [our present generation in which men are turning their hearts away from Christ] shall the times of the Gentiles be fulfilled.

And there shall be men standing in that generation [the generation in which the times of the gentiles shall be fulfilled] that shall not pass until they shall see an overflowing scourge; for a desolating sickness shall cover the land.

But my disciples shall stand in holy places, and shall not be moved; but among the wicked, men shall lift up their voices and curse God and die.

And there shall be earthquakes also in divers places, and many desolations; yet men will harden their hearts against me, and they will take up the sword, one against another, and they will kill one another.

And now [said the Savior to Joseph Smith as he repeated to him what he had said to his disciples], when I the Lord had spoken these words unto my disciples, they were troubled.

And I said unto them: Be not troubled, for, when all these things shall come to pass ye may know that the promises which have been made unto you shall be fulfilled (D&C 45:31-35).

Jesus was here indicating that their faith in the promised blessing incident to his second advent should calm the troubled souls of his disciples. Today we can get like comfort and courage by keeping in mind the events which will accompany his second coming.

Faith in promised blessings has always been the anchor to which the saints have moored their faith.

President Brigham Young said it was their vision of Zion as it would be in its glory which sustained the Saints as they crossed the plains. Paul said that Jesus himself "endured the cross" for the "joy that was set before him" (Hebrews 12:2).

Be not troubled [said the Lord to his disciples], for, when all these things shall come to pass, ye may know that the promises which have been made unto you shall be fulfilled.

[Then, speaking more specifically of events to occur in this last dispensation, he said:] And when the light shall begin to break forth [that is, when the gospel is restored, as it was through the Prophet Joseph Smith], it shall be with them like unto a parable which I will show you—

Ye look and behold the fig-tree, and ye see them with your eyes, and ye say when they begin to shoot forth, and their leaves are yet tender, that summer is now nigh at hand;

Even so it shall be in that day when they shall see all these things, then shall they know that the hour is nigh.

And it shall come to pass that he that feareth me shall be looking forth for the great day of the Lord to come, even for the signs of the coming of the Son of Man. [We are looking for these signs today, and we are seeing some of them, as he predicted we would. But to continue with his words:]

And they shall see signs and wonders, for they shall be shown forth in the heavens above, and in the earth beneath.

And they shall behold blood, and fire and vapors of smoke.

And before the day of the Lord shall come, the sun shall be darkened, and the moon be turned into blood, and the stars fall from heaven.

And the remnant shall be gathered unto this place [He was on the Mount of Olives.]:

And then they shall look for me, and behold, I will come; and they shall see me in the clouds of heaven, clothed with power and great glory; with all the holy angels; and he that watches not for me shall be cut off.

But before the arm of the Lord shall fall, an angel shall sound his trump, and the saints that have slept shall come forth to meet me in a cloud.

Wherefore, if ye have slept in peace blessed are you; for as you now behold me and know that I am, even so shall ye come unto me and your souls shall live, and your redemption shall be perfected; and the saints shall come forth from the four quarters of the earth. [We are assured by these words that, whether we die before he comes or live on in mortality, we shall be with him and rejoice at his coming if we had the courage of our faith.]

[And] then shall the arm of the Lord fall upon the nations.

And then shall the Lord set his foot upon this mount [the Mount of Olives], and it shall cleave in twain, and the earth shall tremble, and reel to and fro, and the heavens also shall shake.

And the Lord shall utter his voice, and all the ends of the earth shall hear it; and the nations of the earth shall mourn, and they that have laughed shall see their folly.

And calamity shall cover the mocker, and the scorner shall be consumed; and they that have watched for iniquity shall be hewn down and cast into the fire.

And then shall the Jews look upon me and say: What are these wounds in thine hands and in thy feet?

Then shall they know that I am the Lord; for I will say unto them: These wounds are the wounds with which I was wounded in the house of my friends. I am he who was lifted up. I am Jesus that was crucified. I am the Son of God.

And then shall they weep because of their iniquities; then shall they lament because they persecuted their king.

And then shall the heathen nations be redeemed. . . .

And Satan shall be bound, that he shall have no place in the hearts of the children of men.

And at that day, when I shall come in my glory, shall the parable be fulfilled which I spake concerning the ten virgins.

For they that are wise and have received the truth, and have taken the Holy Spirit for their guide, and have not been deceived—verily I say unto you, they shall not be hewn down and cast into the fire, but shall abide the day. ["They that are wise and have received the truth" are they who, when they hear the gospel, accept it. They who "have taken the Holy Spirit for their guide and have not been deceived" are they who have not only had the gift of the Holy Ghost bestowed upon them, but who have thereafter so lived by faith as to have received the guidance of the Holy Ghost to such an extent that they have not been deceived. Such are they who, whether resurrected or living in mortality, shall abide the day of Christ's second coming.]

And the earth [the Lord continued] shall be given unto them for an inheritance; and they shall multiply and wax strong, and their children shall grow up without sin unto salvation.

For the Lord shall be in their midst, and his glory shall be upon them, and he will be their king and their lawgiver (D&C 45:35-59).

The message of the foregoing scripture is of such importance to the inhabitants on the earth that Jesus not only gave it to his disciples on the Mount of Olives, but he also quoted it for our benefit to Joseph Smith March 7, 1831. To the truth of it, I bear my witness. I know that he who gave it was and is the Son of God, the Creator, the Lord and Redeemer of the earth and the inhabitants thereof. He knows, and knew from the beginning, all things. The words he spoke are ultimate truth.

I bear witness that the fulness of the everlasting gospel is in the earth. The predicted light has broken forth. Many other of the predicted signs of Christ's coming have been given. Others are now visible. The rest are imminent.

The powers of Satan are combined; they are exerting maximum pressure against the work of God, but they shall not stay it.

God is not dead. He is at the helm. His power— his priesthood—is in the earth; his programs are on schedule; his "eternal purposes . . . shall roll on, until all his promises shall be fulfilled" (Mormon 8:22).

We are most fortunate to have the foregoing great message of Jesus concerning our times and to know that it is true. If we have the courage of our faith, we shall "conquer Satan, and . . . escape the hands of the servants of Satan that do uphold his work" (D&C 10: 5). We shall be at peace with ourselves during these troublous times and be with the Savior at his coming.

God grant that we may so live as to enjoy the promised blessings, I humbly pray.

BEWARE CONCERNING YOURSELVES •

An address delivered by request at priesthood session of general conference October 8, 1960, to counter apostate claims to priesthood authority purportedly derived through sources that bypassed the First Presidency of the Church.

For my text I have chosen the 43rd verse of the 84th section of the Doctrine and Covenants. It reads: "And I now give unto you a commandment to beware concerning yourselves, to give diligent heed to the words of eternal life."

The Lord gave the brethren this charge immediately following his explanation of the priesthood and the oath and covenant which is entered into between him and each recipient of the Melchizedek Priesthood:

Which priesthood continueth in the church of God in all generations, and is without beginning of days or end of years.

And the Lord confirmed the priesthood also upon Aaron and his seed, throughout all their generations, which priesthood also continueth and abideth forever with the priesthood which is after the holiest order of God.

. . . This greater priesthood administereth the gospel and holdeth the key of the mysteries of the kingdom even the key of the knowledge of God.

Therefore, in the ordinances thereof, the power of godliness is manifest.

And without the ordinances thereof, and the authority of the priesthood, the power of godliness is not manifest unto men in the flesh (D&C 84:17-21).

The Lord promises in the oath and covenant that

whoso is faithful unto the obtaining these two priesthoods of which I have spoken, and the magnifying their calling, are sanctified by the Spirit unto the renewing of their bodies.

They become the sons of Moses and of Aaron and the seed of Abraham, and the church and kingdom, and the elect of God.

And also all they who receive this priesthood receive me, saith the Lord;

For he that receiveth my servants receiveth me (D&C 84:33-36).

The word *servants* as used in in this statement ("He that receiveth my servants receiveth me") includes the Lord's representatives in the various presiding offices of the priesthood—general, regional, priesthood quorum, stake, mission, ward, branch, etc. It behooves us to keep this in mind when we are tempted to disregard their counsel and direction. To his apostles in the land of Jerusalem, Jesus said:

He that receiveth a prophet in the name of a prophet shall receive a prophet's reward; and he that receiveth a righteous man in the name of a righteous man shall receive a righteous man's reward.

And whoever shall give to drink unto one of these little ones a cup of cold water only in the name of a disciple, verily I say unto you, he shall in no wise lose his reward (Matthew 10:41, 42).

But back to the covenant of the priesthood:

He that receiveth me receiveth my Father;

And he that receiveth my Father receiveth my Father's kingdom; therefore all that my Father hath shall be given unto him.

And this is according to the oath and covenant which belongeth to the priesthood.

Therefore, all those who receive the priesthood, receive this oath and covenant of my Father, which he cannot break, neither can it be moved (D&C 84:37-40).

Now I am tempted to comment on this covenant at length, but since it is not the heart of my message, I shall here say only that, as I understand it, all of us who have received the Melchizedek Priesthood are bound by this covenant with our Heavenly Father to magnify our callings in the priesthood. On condition that we do so, the Father promises to make us equal with him in the sense that

all that my Father hath shall be given unto him. . . .

For whoso breaketh this covenant after he hath received it, and altogether turneth therefrom, shall not have forgiveness of sins in this world nor in the world to come (D&C 84:38, 41).

When I first began to seriously think about this statement, I wondered if it would not have been better for me never to have received the priesthood, if failing to magnify my callings in it would mean I would never receive forgiveness in this world nor in the world to come. As I pondered over this and the next verse, which reads, "And wo unto all those who come not unto this priesthood" (D&C 84:42), I finally came to the conclusion that I was on the horns of a dilemma—that my only hope was to receive the priesthood and magnify my callings in it.

It was against this background that the Lord said,

And I now give unto you [bearers of the priesthood] a commandment to beware concerning yourselves, to give diligent heed to the words of eternal life.

For you shall live by every word that proceedeth forth from the mouth of God (D&C 84:43, 44).

Having explained the covenant of the priesthood and clearly set forth the awesome consequences of magnifying or breaking it, the Lord knew that the brethren needed to be alerted to the opposition arrayed against them. He himself was well acquainted with it. He knew that, although the Church had been organized but thirty months, Satan was already marshaling his forces against the priesthood. Satan, likewise, knew the power of the priesthood. Ever since, and before, the war in heaven, he has sought to overthrow and usurp it. As a result of the conflict he there precipitated, he was cast out of heaven.

Banishment from heaven did not, however, end his attack on the priesthood of God. Before the Fall, in the Garden of Eden he pursued his nefarious work. He continued it after the Fall. When Adam and Eve, having received the gospel, taught it to their children, Satan came among them saying, "Believe it not; . . . they loved Satan more than God. And men began from that time forth to be carnal, sensual, and devilish" (Moses 5:13).

When the presence of God withdrew from Moses following the great revelation he gave of himself to Moses, "Satan came tempting him, saying: Moses, son of man, . . . I am the Only Begotten, worship me" (Moses 1:12, 19).

He sought to deceive the Savior. You will all remember how he tempted Jesus in the wilderness, on the pinnacle of the temple, and on the high mountain.

Satan has sought in all ages to deceive the sons of God who have received the priesthood. Nor has he been entirely unsuccessful. In all past dispensations he has finally succeeded in deceiving them to the extent that he has driven the priesthood from the earth.

Now we know he is not going to drive the priesthood from the earth in this dispensation, because the

Lord has said it is here to stay until the Savior comes. But there is no guarantee that he will not deceive a lot of men who hold the priesthood. His objective is still to deceive every one of us he can and to drive the priesthood from the earth. Satan is very real. His power is very real. His influence is felt everywhere. He literally stalks the earth. "The powers of darkness prevail upon the earth, . . . and, behold, the enemy is combined" (D&C 38:11, 12).

You no doubt heard what President McKay said in his opening address yesterday morning about the power of the evil one trying to deceive and deprive men of their agency. Free agency is the principle against which Satan waged his war in heaven. It is still the front on which he makes his most furious, devious, and persistent attacks. That this would be the case was foreshadowed by the Lord when he said to Moses:

> That Satan, whom thou hast commanded in the name of mine Only Begotten, is the same which was from the beginning, and he came before me, saying—Behold, here am I, send me, I will be thy son, and I will redeem all mankind, that one soul shall not be lost, and surely I will do it; wherefore give me thine honor. [His plan was to save us all by depriving us of free agency and subjecting us to his will.]
>
> But, behold [continued the Lord], my Beloved Son, which was my Beloved and Chosen from the beginning, said unto me—Father, thy will be done, and the glory be thine forever.
>
> Wherefore, because that Satan rebelled against me, and sought to destroy the agency of man, which I, the Lord God, had given him, and also, that I should give unto him mine own power [Priesthood is God's power. That is what Satan is after—power. He wants it in the form of dictatorship.]; by the power of mine Only Begotten, I caused that he should be cast down.
>
> And he became Satan, yea, even the devil, the father of all lies, to deceive and to blind men and to lead them captive at his will even as many as would not hearken unto my voice (Moses 4:1-4).

You see, at the time he was cast out of heaven, his objective was (and still is) to deceive and to blind men, and to lead them captive at his will. This he effectively does to as many as will not hearken unto the voice of God. His main attack is still on free agency. When he can get men to yield their agency, he has them well on the way to captivity.

We who hold the priesthood must beware concerning ourselves that we do not fall into the traps he lays to rob us of our freedom. We must be careful that we are not led to accept or support in any way any organization, cause, or measure which, in its remotest effect, would jeopardize free agency, whether it be in politics, government, religion, employment, education, or any other field. It is not enough for us to be sincere in what we support. We *must* be right!

As to Satan's direct attack upon the restored Church and its priesthood, you will remember this account of the Prophet as to what happened in the Sacred Grove as he knelt to pray:

> I had scarcely done so, when immediately I was seized upon by some power which entirely overcame me, and had such an astonishing influence over me as to bind my tongue so that I could not speak. Thick darkness gathered around me, and it seemed to me for a time as if I were doomed to sudden destruction.
> But, exerting all my powers to call upon God to deliver me out of the power of this enemy which had seized upon me, and at the very moment when I was ready to sink into despair and abandon myself to destruction—not to an imaginary ruin, but to the power of some actual being from the unseen world, who had such marvelous power as I had never before felt in any being (Joseph Smith 2:15, 16).

During the Kirtland days some of the leaders of the Church were deceived and fought the Prophet right up until the end of his life. Among them you will remember Bennett and the Laws. Even the Three Witnesses were deceived. You know, of course, what happened after the Prophet was gone and Brother Brigham took over. Lyman Wight and many of the others, strong men who stood by the Prophet, were deceived and left the Church.

And so it has gone through the years. Today is no exception. We have people now who yield to the temptations and follow the counterfeits of Satan.

A paramount consideration for us bearers of the priesthood today is, how may we combat these on-slaughts of Satan? How can we distinguish between his counterfeits and divine truth?

I have already indicated that many organizations, causes, and measures may be tried by applying the test of free agency.

1. *Does it purport to originate in the wisdom of men, or was it revealed from heaven?* If it originated in the wisdom of men it is not of God. Remember what the Savior said to Nicodemus, "Except a man be born again, he cannot see . . . [nor] enter . . . the kingdom of God" (John 3:3, 5). He also said, "My doctrine is not mine, but his that sent me" (John 7:16). Even Jesus himself did not purport to originate gospel doctrine. One cannot arrive at truth by reason alone. We have already heard this theme developed in this conference. I need not stress it further.

In the Book of Mormon the prophet Jacob said:

O that cunning plan of the evil one! O the vainness and the frailties, and the foolishness of men! When they are learned they think they are wise, and they hearken not unto the counsel of God, for they set it aside, supposing they know of themselves, wherefore, their wisdom is foolishness and it profiteth them not. And they shall perish.

[Then he adds this lovely sentence:] But to be learned
is good if they hearken unto the counsels of God (2 Nephi
9:28, 29).

You are all acquainted with Paul's great doctrine
that the things of God are understood by the power of
God and that the things of men are understood by the
wisdom of men: "But the natural man receiveth not
the things of the Spirit of God: for they are foolishness
unto him: neither can he know them, because they are
spiritually discerned" (1 Corinthians 2:14).

We never need to be deceived by the learning of
the world. We can always with safety reject those
doctrines which are founded in the wisdom of men.

2. *Does the teaching bear the proper label?* You
will remember that when his Nephite disciples inquired
of Jesus what they should call the church, he

said unto them: Verily, verily, I say unto you, why is it that
the people should murmur and dispute because of this thing?

Have they not read the scriptures, which say ye must
take upon you the name of Christ, which is my name? For
by this name shall ye be called at the last day;

And whoso taketh upon him my name and endureth to
the end, the same shall be saved at the last day.

Therefore, whatsoever ye shall do, ye shall do it in my
name; therefore ye shall call the church in my name; and
ye shall call upon the Father in my name that he will bless
the church for my sake.

And how be it my church save it be called in my name?
For if a church be called in Moses' name then it be Moses'
church; or if it be called in the name of a man it be the
church of a man; but if it be called in my name then it is
my church, if it so be that they are built upon my gospel
(3 Nephi 27:4-8).

From the foregoing it is perfectly plain that if any
teaching purporting to be from Christ comes under any
label other than that of Jesus Christ, we can know it
is not of God.

3. The last phrase of the above quotation gives us the third test: "But if it be called in my name then it is my church, if it so be that they are built upon my gospel." *The teaching must not only come under the proper label, but it must also conform to the other teachings of the gospel of Jesus Christ.*

4. Now the fourth and last test I shall mention is: *Does it come through the proper Church channel?* We read in the 42nd section of the Doctrine and Covenants:

Again, I say unto you, that it shall not be given to any one to go forth to preach my gospel, or to build up my church, except he be ordained by some one who has authority, and it is known to the church that he has authority and has been regularly ordained by the heads of the church (D&C 42:11).

In the light of this divinely established order, how can any man accept the doctrine of authority from some secret source unknown to the Church?

The Lord has made it crystal clear that one's authority must come through the established order of the Church and that the president of the Church stands at the head of that order. The Lord has placed him there:

The duty of the President of the office of the High Priesthood [he said] is to preside over the whole church, and to be like unto Moses [Now one of Moses' greatest callings was to be a lawgiver, to declare the word of God. Only the president can declare the doctrines of the Church.]—

[The revelation continues:] Behold, here is wisdom; yea, to be a seer, a revelator, a translator, and a prophet, having all the gifts of God which he bestows upon the head of the church (D&C 107:91, 92).

In the revelation the Lord gave to the Prophet in answer to his inquiry about the stone which Hiram Page had, he said (speaking of the president of the Church):

Wherefore, meaning the church, thou shalt give heed
unto all his words and commandments which he shall give
unto you as he receiveth them, walking in all holiness before
me;

For his word ye shall receive, as if from mine own mouth,
in all patience and faith. [Such is the obligation of this
priesthood with respect to our present prophet, seer, and
revelator.] . . .

By doing these things the gates of hell shall not prevail
against you; yea, and the Lord God will disperse the powers
of darkness from before you, and cause the heavens to shake
for your good, and his name's glory (D&C 21:4-6).

Now, brethren, if we will keep these things in
mind, we shall not be deceived by false teachings. I
remember years ago when I was a bishop I had President Grant talk to our ward. After the meeting I drove
him home. At that time there was a great deal of criticism against the president of the Church because of a
front-page editorial some of you may remember. We
talked about it. When we arrived at his home I got out
of the car and went up on the porch with him. Standing by me, he put his arm over my shoulder and said,
"My boy, you always keep your eye on the president of
the Church, and if he ever tells you to do anything, and
it is wrong, and you do it, the Lord will bless you for
it." Then with a twinkle in his eye he said, "But you
don't need to worry. The Lord will never let his mouthpiece lead the people astray."

I have thought much about this statement. I remember that counselors in the presidency have been
deceived. I remember that members of the Twelve have
been deceived and left the Church. And men in every
other council in the Church have been deceived, and,
according to President Grant (and I believe him),
there never will be a president of this Church who will
lead the people astray.

We need not be led astray, my brethren. The

safest way for each of us to avoid being led astray is to magnify our priesthood. We should go on our knees, each one of us, morning and evening and plead with Almighty God to keep us in the way of magnifying our callings in this great priesthood. We should live righteously. We should resist every temptation of lust. When we harbor lustful thoughts and participate in lustful practices, we cannot see these great principles clearly, and we get into the dark.

If, in addition to living righteously, we will study and learn what the Lord has said and apply the tests I have suggested, we shall never go astray. God help us, I pray, that we shall remain true and faithful ourselves and help all of the members of the Church to see clearly, thereby placing themselves among those who, taking the Holy Spirit for their guide, are not deceived but look to God and live. That it may be so, I humbly pray, in the name of Jesus Christ. Amen.

Surely the Lord God will do nothing, but he revealeth his secret unto his servants the prophets.

Amos 3:7

REVELATION AND HOW IT COMES •

An address delivered at general conference April 6, 1964.

I would like to say a few things this afternoon about revelation, which underlies all that God has done in the earth with his children. I invite you to join your prayers with mine that while I speak you and I may both enjoy the spirit of revelation. That we do so is imperative, because to talk about revelation without the spirit of revelation would be an exercise in futility.

FIRST, THE PRINCIPLE

Prayer is the means by which men communicate with God. Revelation, as used in these remarks, is the means by which God communicates with men.

Revelation is indispensable to an understanding of the gospel of Jesus Christ. The very nature of the gospel is such that, without the active and constant operation of the principle of revelation, it cannot be understood nor could it be had.

The gospel deals with total truth—"knowledge of things as they are, and as they were, and as they are to come" (D&C 93:24).

Such truth is not to be had through man's ordinary learning processes. His sensory powers are calculated and adapted to deal only with the things of this telestial earth. Without revelation, man's intellect is wholly inadequate for the discovery of the ultimate truth with which the gospel deals.

Paul spoke of this to the Corinthians when he said:

My speech and my preaching was not with enticing words of man's wisdom, but in demonstration of the Spirit and of power:

Your faith should not stand in the wisdom of men, but in the power of God. . . .

For what man knoweth the things of a man, save the spirit of man which is in him? even so the things of God knoweth no man, but the Spirit of God (1 Corinthians 2:4, 5, 11).

The spirit of revelation turns the key which opens the mind and spirit of man to an understanding of the gospel. There is no other approach to such knowledge. Thinkers have philosophized, poets have dreamed, and scientists have experimented; but only God speaks with a sure knowledge of all truth.

Some years ago I listened to a lecturer who argued long and deviously and came to the conclusion that there was no such thing as religious knowledge. Within his premise he was right. He had no religious knowledge, and he could not obtain any because he had ruled out revelation.

It is my witness to you, however, that by the power of God truth concerning the eternal verities with which the gospel deals has been in the past, is now being, and will in the future continue to be communicated to men from heaven by revelation. Revelation is the governing law of conduct—the age-old established rule of action or principle—by which God communes with men.

NATURE OF REVELATION

Since revelation is by nature spiritual, man, to receive it, must be spiritually born again.

You will recall how earnestly Jesus sought to put this point over to Nicodemus, repeatedly telling him that except a man be born again he could neither see nor enter the kingdom of God.

Man is a dual being. He is composed of a spirit and a body of flesh and bones. His body came into being with his entrance into this world of mortality. His spirit as an individual person was begotten unto God in the spirit world. Through a long period of growth and development, each person's spirit came to know God and spiritual things, including the gospel, obedience to which is a prerequisite to attaining eternal life. Men, however, enter mortality spiritually blind. Never in this life do they recover memory of premortal spiritual things. What they here learn of them must be revealed anew.

One of God's purposes in granting men mortal life is that they might be tested "to see if they will do all things whatsoever the Lord their God shall command them; . . . they who keep their second estate [meaning this mortal estate] shall have glory added upon their heads for ever and ever" (Abraham 3:25, 26).

Since attaining this glory is conditioned upon obedience to the laws and ordinances of the gospel and since men come into life ignorant of these principles and ordinances, justice demands that they be given opportunity to learn about them. God, being not only just but merciful, provided revelation as the means by which man may be so advised.

He also saw to it that men were so constituted that by the proper exercise of the moral agency, with which he also endowed them, it would be natural for them to respond to revelation. Otherwise, it would not be just to hold them accountable for their failure to respond thereto.

I know the scriptures say that "the natural man is an enemy of God" (Mosiah 3:19), and so he is when he rejects the promptings of the Spirit and follows the lusts of the flesh. But he is not an enemy to God when he follows the promptings of the Spirit.

I firmly believe that, notwithstanding the fact that during their mortal lives men do not remember anything about their premortal experiences, there still persists in the spirit of every human soul a residuum from his premortal life which instinctively responds to the voice of the Spirit of Christ until and unless, in the exercise of his own free agency, he rejects it. In the 84th section of the Doctrine and Covenants, the Lord says that

whatsoever is truth is light, and whatsoever is light is Spirit, even the Spirit of Jesus Christ.

And the Spirit giveth light to every man that cometh into the world; and the Spirit enlighteneth every man through the world, that hearkeneth to the voice of the Spirit (D&C 84:45, 46).

MANIFESTATIONS OF REVELATION

Revelation comes to men in an unlimited number of ways. Three separate mediums are mentioned in the first recorded account of revelation—the spoken word, the visitation of angels, and the power of the Holy Ghost. As a consequence of his transgression,

Adam was cast out from God's presence. But he was not forsaken. As he and Eve toiled and prayed, *"they heard the voice* of the Lord from the way toward the Garden of Eden, . . . And after many days an *angel of the Lord appeared* unto Adam, . . . And in that day the *Holy Ghost fell upon Adam*, which beareth record of the Father and the Son, . . ." (Moses 5:4, 6, 9; italics added).

The spoken word has been heard on many occasions. Moses heard it from the burning bush; Samuel, in the temple. The Nephites heard the voice of the unseen Jesus.

As to the visitation of angels, we have many examples. One which moves me as much as any is the record in the third chapter of Ether of the appearance of Jesus in his spirit body to the brother of Jared.

You will remember how, as Alma was traveling from Ammonihah to Aaron, an angel appeared to him and said, referring to the time of Alma's conversion, "I am the same angel that appeared to you before" (Alma 8:15).

We read in the 110th section of the Doctrine and Covenants about the visitation of Moses, Elias, and Elijah to the Prophet and Oliver.

Another manifestation of revelation is the unspoken word, a good illustration of which is given us by Enos. He says, "While I was thus struggling in the spirit, behold, the voice of the Lord came into my mind again, saying: . . ." (Enos 10). Then he tells us what the voice of the Lord put in his mind. This is a very common means of revelation. It comes into one's mind in words and sentences. With this medium of revelation I am personally well acquainted.

Another medium is an impelling impulse of the nature received by the Prophet when he read James 1:5. "Never [he said] did any passage of scripture come with more power to the heart of man than this did at this time to mine. It seemed to enter with great force into every feeling of my heart" (Joseph Smith 2:12).

Another means is dreams—Jacob's ladder, for example, Joseph's dream of the sheaves, Pharaoh's dream of the lean and fat years. There was Nebuchadnezzar's dream, Daniel's dream, Lehi's dream. Joseph, the husband of Mary, was warned in a dream to take Mary and Jesus into Egypt.

Another medium of revelation is visions. You know about Nephi's vision, the Prophet's great vision recorded in the 76th section of the Doctrine and Covenants, and President Joseph F. Smith's vision of work for the dead in the spirit world.

Flashes of ideas that come into one's mind represent another type of manifestation of revelation. Listen to this statement by the Prophet Joseph:

A person may profit by noticing the first intimation of the spirit of revelation; for instance, when you feel pure intelligence flowing into you, it may give you sudden strokes of ideas, so that by noticing it, you may find it fulfilled the same day or soon; (i.e.) those things that were presented unto your minds by the Spirit of God, will come to pass; and thus by learning the Spirit of God and understanding it, you may grow into the principle of revelation, until you become perfect in Christ Jesus (*Teachings of the Prophet Joseph Smith* p. 151).

One of the most familiar types of revelation the Lord explained in great detail to Oliver Cowdery in the 6th, 8th, and 9th sections of the Doctrine and Covenants.

This kind of revelation we can all live by. If we will follow the prescribed formula and become sensitive to the whisperings of the Spirit as it enlightens our minds, quickens our understandings, and speaks peace to our souls, we need not make serious mistakes in our lives.

The foregoing are but some of the means of revelation.

In connection with this principle of revelation, the Prophet Joseph Smith further said:

We consider that God has created man with a mind capable of instruction, and a faculty which may be enlarged in proportion to the heed and diligence given to the light communicated from heaven to the intellect. The nearer man approaches perfection, the clearer are his views, and the greater his enjoyments, till he has overcome the evils of his life and lost every desire for sin; and like the ancients, arrives at that point of faith where he is wrapped in the power and glory of his Maker and is caught up to dwell with him.

In qualifying to receive revelation, as in all righteousness, Jesus is our great exemplar. He so qualified himself that he received through revelation a fulness of the glory of the Father.

With respect to this point, John the Beloved bore this witness:

I beheld his glory, as the glory of the Only Begotten of the Father, . . .
And I, John, saw that he received not of the fulness at the first, . . .
But continued from grace to grace, until he received a fulness; . . .
And I, John, bear record that he received a fulness of the glory of the Father (D&C 93:11-13, 16).

To me, among the most inspiring passages of all scripture is the following comment of Jesus on this testimony of John's, which, as you will remember, was dictated to the Prophet by the Savior:

> I give unto you these sayings that you may understand and know how to worship, and know what you worship, that you may come unto the Father in my name, and in due time receive of his fulness.
> For if you keep my commandments you shall receive of his fulness, and be glorified in me as I am in the Father; therefore, I say unto you you shall receive grace for grace (D&C 93:19, 20).

Now this is Christ's promise to the Prophet, and it is His promise to us. However, "no man receiveth a fulness unless he keepeth his commandments. [But] he that keepeth his commandments receiveth truth and light, until he is glorified in truth and knoweth all things" (D&C 93:27, 28). We receive a little revelation; we obey it—we receive a little more; obey it—and repeat the cycle over and over again.

This is the pattern by which the promise of the first paragraph of this great revelation may be obtained. As you now listen to this promise, let your souls be filled with hope. "Verily, thus saith the Lord: It shall come to pass that every soul who forsaketh his sins and cometh unto me, and calleth on my name, and obeyeth my voice, and keepeth my commandments, shall see my face and know that I am" (D&C 93:1).

In these remarks I have, as you of course have noted, omitted any reference to revelation in connection with the great advances of science in our age. This I have done deliberately. I know that all men live and learn by the light of the Spirit of Christ; I know that all progress in science and other fields of secular learning is made possible by the Light of Christ. I do not, however, think that our distinctive message about revelation lies in such fields of learning, but rather in the field of religion.

Our message is that we are living in the great and last dispensation of the gospel of Jesus Christ; that God has opened the heavens anew; that by direct revelation, through the means we have been considering, he has revealed himself, restored his gospel, and set up his Church with power and authority to preach the gospel and administer the saving ordinances thereof; and that he is now, today, continuing to direct by revelation his great program for the blessing and the salvation of the human race.

Our great mission is to declare this message with such simple clarity and inspired conviction that men of all lands will hearken, investigate, and prayerfully seek until, through personal revelation to themselves, they obtain a saving witness for themselves. That we may successfully discharge this mission, I humbly pray in the name of Jesus Christ. Amen.

Wednesday, 8 [February 1843]—This morning, I . . . visited with a brother and sister from Michigan, who thought that "a prophet is always a prophet"; but I told them that a prophet was a prophet only when he was acting as such.

Joseph Smith in *History of the Church* 5:265

HOW TO KNOW WHEN A PROPHET IS SPEAKING AS A PROPHET •

An address delivered at Ricks College devotional February 24, 1970.

Recently a young lady student came seeking an interview. She wanted to know how she could tell when a prophet is speaking as a prophet. This question arose in an institute class in which the statement of the Prophet Joseph Smith that a prophet is a prophet only when he is acting as such (*History of the Church* 5: 265) had been discussed.

A few days later a perplexed young man came questioning the recent restatement of the First Presidency of the Church concerning who can be given the priesthood.

These two incidents, and the discussions they provoked, underscore the great importance of one's knowing how to recognize inspired statements of prophets and other teachers.

Because you are students, as were the two young folks above referred to, it occurred to me that you might also be interested in the questions. I have therefore decided to say to you some of the things I said to them.

At the outset I informed them that the sure way to know when a prophet is speaking as a prophet—or whether the statement of the First Presidency concerning who may receive the priesthood or, for that matter, the gospel truth in any statement, teaching, or practice by anybody or from any source whatever—is by the power of the Holy Ghost.

Since the Holy Ghost reveals gospel truth and since we cannot discern such truth unless he reveals it to us, I am sure we can, with profit, give serious consideration to the manner in which such revelation comes. To begin with, it is comforting to know that all members of The Church of Jesus Christ of Latter-day Saints have had the gift of the Holy Ghost bestowed upon them. It is also comforting to know that all men may, by obedience to the required principles and ordinances, have the gift of the Holy Ghost bestowed upon them.

Very early in this dispensation—a year before the Church was organized, in fact—the Lord identified and explained certain manifestations of the power of the Holy Ghost, which he said was "the spirit of revelation" (D&C 8:2, 3).

On April 5, 1829, Oliver Cowdery went to the home of Joseph Smith and proffered his services in bringing forth the Book of Mormon. On the 7th of April, two days following his arrival, he began to write as the Prophet translated the Book of Mormon record. Before long, however, Oliver "became anxious to learn . . . the will of the Lord concerning . . . his connection with the work then coming forth" (B. H Roberts, *Comprehensive History of the Church* 1:120). Whereupon, at Oliver's request, the Prophet inquired of the Lord.

Before he went to see the Prophet, Oliver had boarded at the home of the Prophet's parents for a short period. He learned from them and from his conversations with David Whitmer, who knew the Smiths, and he developed such an intense interest that he had secretly inquired of the Lord as to the truth of what he had heard about the Prophet. In response to his prayer, he had received a manifestation from the Lord that Joseph's account of the gold plates was true. It was against this background, of which Joseph knew nothing, that the Lord spoke through the Prophet to Oliver:

Verily, verily, I say unto thee, blessed art thou for what thou hast done; for thou hast inquired of me, and behold, as often as thou hast inquired thou hast received instruction of my Spirit. If it had not been so, thou wouldst not have come to the place where thou art at this time.

Behold, thou knowest that thou hast inquired of me and I did enlighten thy mind; and now I tell these things that thou mayest know that thou has been enlightened by the Spirit of truth;

Yea, I tell thee, that thou mayest know that there is none else save God that knowest thy thoughts and the intents of thy heart. [It seems most remarkable to me that the Lord should talk to Oliver in this manner through one who had no knowledge of his secret prayer and the guidance of the Spirit he had received.]

I tell thee these things as a witness unto thee—that the words or the work which thou hast been writing are true. . . .

[Then, as a final emphasis, the Lord adds:] Verily, verily, I say unto you, if you desire a further witness, cast your mind upon the night that you cried unto me in your heart, that you might know concerning the truth of these things.

Did I not speak peace to your mind concerning the matter? [This is one way, and perhaps the most common way, in which the Holy Ghost reveals the truth to a person.] What greater witness can you have from God?

And now, behold, you have received a witness; for if I have told you things which no man knoweth have you not received a witness? (D&C 6:14-17, 22-24).

Following receipt of these instructions, the Prophet wrote in his journal that Oliver "had kept the circumstance" referred to in the revelation "entirely secret, and had mentioned it to no one; so that after this revelation was given, he knew that the work was true, because no being living knew of the thing alluded to in the revelation, but God and himself" (*History of the Church* 1:37).

In this same revelation, the Lord also said to Oliver Cowdery, "Behold, I grant unto you a gift, if you desire of me, to translate, even as my servant Joseph" (D&C 6:25).

Oliver soon became anxious to receive and exercise the promised gift. Whereupon the Lord, through the Prophet, gave another revelation in which he confirmed his promise to Oliver and explained that the translations he could receive would come into his mind and heart by the power of the Holy Ghost, which, said the Lord, is the spirit of revelation. Listen now to the words of the revelation:

Oliver Cowdery, verily, verily, I say unto you, that assuredly as the Lord liveth, who is your God and your Redeemer, even so surely shall you receive a knowledge of whatsoever things you shall ask in faith, with an honest heart, believing that you shall receive. . . .

Yea, behold, I will tell you in your mind and in your heart, by the Holy Ghost, which shall come unto you and which shall dwell in your heart.

Now, behold, this is the spirit of revelation; behold, this is the spirit by which Moses brought the children of Israel through the Red Sea on dry ground.

Therefore, this is thy gift; apply unto it.   (D&C 8:1-4).

Unfortunately for Oliver Cowdery, he never did properly "apply unto it." In his attempt to exercise the gift, he failed. He was, of course, disappointed and had a disposition to complain. The Lord, therefore, in another revelation, explained the reason for his failure.

Behold, I say unto you, my son, that because you did not translate according to that which you desired of me, . . .

It is not expedient that you should translate at this present time.

And, behold, it is because that you did not continue as you commenced, when you began to translate, that I have taken away this privilege from you. . . .

Behold, you have not understood; you have supposed that I would give it unto you, when you took no thought save it was to ask me.

But, behold, I say unto you, that you must study it out in your mind; then you must ask me if it be right, and if it is right I will cause that your bosom shall burn within you; therefore, you shall feel that it is right.

But if it be not right you shall have no such feeling, but you shall have a stupor of thought (D&C 9:1, 3, 5, 7-9).

There is much for us to learn in these early revelations. The truths they teach have universal application. They teach us that the Holy Ghost is the spirit of revelation. From them we learn that instruction by the power of the Holy Ghost is indeed a reality. We further learn something about how such instruction is received. Listen again to some of the language the Lord used:

I did enlighten thy mind (D&C 6:15).

Did I not speak peace to thy mind concerning the matter? (D&C 6:23).

I will tell you in your mind and in your heart, by the Holy Ghost, which shall come upon you and which shall dwell in your heart. Now, behold, this is the spirit of revelation (D&C 8:2, 3).

We learn also from these early revelations that instruction by the Spirit comes only to those who earnestly seek it. It is not received by the light-minded, the

giddy, the immoral, nor by those whose minds are sur-
feited with the things of this world. It is not received
by the lazy, the indolent and slothful, nor by the unbelievers.

Note the Lord's reference to Oliver Cowdery's
attitude at the time he first received knowledge by
revelation: "Cast your mind upon the night that you
cried unto me in your heart, that you might know concerning the truth of these things" (D&C 6:22).

Oliver was earnestly praying, pleading for light.
Consider also the condition under which he was to receive further knowledge through revelation:

Oliver Cowdery, verily, verily, I say unto you, that assuredly as the Lord liveth, who is your God and your Redeemer, even so surely shall you receive a knowledge of whatsoever things you shall ask in faith, with an honest heart,
believing that you shall receive . . . (D&C 8:1).

To believe that we shall receive the things we pray
for, as promised by the Lord, takes a lot of faith. On
an occasion when some of the early brethren failed to
receive a promised blessing, the Lord said to them:

Ye endeavored to believe that ye should receive the
blessing which was offered unto you; but behold verily I
say unto you there were fears in your hearts, and verily this
is the reason that ye did not receive (D&C 67:3).

The attainment of such faith is not beyond our
reach, however. The Prophet Joseph Smith had it when
he went into the Sacred Grove to find out which of all
the churches was right. Nephi had it when he went into
Jerusalem to get the brass plates.

We Latter-day Saints must develop such faith and
get the spirit of revelation so that we can feel within
ourselves and know when a prophet speaks as a prophet
and when others speak by the power of the Holy Ghost.

We must be able to get for ourselves the witness that when the First Presidency issues a statement on Church doctrine or practices, they speak for the Lord by the power of the Holy Ghost. On this point President Brigham Young once said:

You may know whether you are led right or wrong, as well as you know the way home; for every principle God has revealed carries its own convictions of its truth to the human mind, and there is no calling of God to man on earth but what brings with it the evidences of its authenticity (*Journal of Discourses* 9:149).

Further on in the same address he cautioned the Saints not to let their confidence in their leaders keep them from inquiring

for themselves of God whether they are led by Him, I am fearful they settle down in a state of blind self-security, trusting their eternal destiny in the hands of their leaders with a reckless confidence that in itself would thwart the purposes of God in their salvation, and weaken that influence they could give to their leaders, did they know for themselves, by the revelations of Jesus, that they are led in the right way. Let every man and woman know, by the whispering of the Spirit of God to themselves, whether their leaders are walking in the path the Lord dictates, or not. . . .

Let all persons be fervent in prayer, until they know the things of God for themselves and become certain that they are walking in the path that leads to everlasting life (*Journal of Discourses* 9:150).

Moroni promised this kind of knowledge concerning the Book of Mormon to all who would ponder in their hearts the things which were therein written and then "ask God, the Eternal Father, in the name of Christ, if these things are not true." Hear the words of his promise:

And if ye shall ask with a sincere heart with real intent, having faith in Christ, he will manifest the truth of it unto you, by the power of the Holy Ghost. [He then adds this all-inclusive and most significant promise:]

And by the power of the Holy Ghost ye may know the truth of all things (Moroni 10:3-5).

I bear you my witness that these teachings and promises are true. If we follow them, they will bring us to a knowledge of all truth. I have personally put Moroni's promise to the test and have learned for myself that the Book of Mormon is true. Through following the same pattern, I have learned the truth of many things.

By consistently seeking the guidance of the Holy Spirit of revelation in the manner prescribed in the revelations we have been considering, and living by them, we shall be able to tell when a prophet is speaking as a prophet and correctly understand the statements of the First Presidency of the Church.

To learn to live by the spirit of revelation is of first importance. Only those who do so will be prepared for the second advent of the Savior. Speaking of that glorious occasion, the Lord said:

At that day, when I shall come in my glory, . . . they that are wise and have received the truth, and have taken the Holy Spirit for their guide, and have not been deceived —verily I say unto you, they shall not be hewn down and cast into the fire, but shall abide the day (D&C 45:56, 57).

That we may all so qualify, I humbly pray.

I told the brethren that the Book of Mormon was the most correct of any book on earth, and the keystone of our religion, and a man would get nearer to God by abiding by its precepts, than by any other book.

Joseph Smith in *History of the Church* 4:461

THE KEYSTONE OF OUR RELIGION •

An address delivered at general conference October 1970.

The Prophet Joseph Smith wrote in his diary for November 28, 1841:

I spent the day in the council with the Twelve Apostles at the house of President Young, conversing with them upon a variety of subjects. . . . I told the brethren that the Book of Mormon was the most correct of any book on earth, and *the keystone of our religion,* and a man would get nearer to God by abiding by its precepts, than by any other book (*History of the Church* 4:461; italics added).

Whatever else it implies, this statement is amply justified by the fact that acceptance of the Book of Mormon is almost tantamount to acceptance of the restored gospel. The authenticity of the book and the restoration of the gospel rest upon the same two fundamentals—the fact of modern revelation and the fact that Joseph Smith was a prophet of God. These two verities are inseparably connected in their relationship to the Book of Mormon and the restored gospel. To accept one is to accept the other.

When he retired to bed on the night of September 23, 1823, Joseph Smith was deeply concerned about his

standing with the Lord. This, in prayer and supplication, he sought to determine. While praying, he was
visited by Moroni, a personage sent from the presence
of God, who told him that

there was a book deposited [in nearby Cumorah], written
upon gold plates, giving an account of the former inhabitants
of this continent, and the sources from whence they sprang.
He also said that the fullness of the everlasting Gospel was
contained in it, as delivered by the Savior to the ancient inhabitants; also that there were two stones in silver bows . . .
deposited with the plates; . . . and that God had prepared
them for the purpose of translating the book (*History of the
Church* 1:12).

In this interview with Moroni, the Prophet received his first concept of the Book of Mormon.

From this night until the book was published, Joseph was constantly guided from heaven in obtaining,
caring for, and translating the sacred record. Confirm-
ing His own participation in bringing forth the Book
of Mormon, the Lord, in August 1830, said to the
Prophet: "I . . . sent [Moroni] unto you to reveal the
Book of Mormon, containing the fulness of my everlasting gospel." (D&C 27:5).

In the preface to the Doctrine and Covenants, the
Lord said that he called upon "Joseph Smith, Jun., and
spake to him from heaven and gave him commandments" that he might "have power to translate through
the mercy of God, by the power of God, the Book of
Mormon" (D&C 1:17, 29).

The Lord also told the Three Witnesses that the
Prophet had "translated the book," and added, "as
your Lord and your God liveth it is true" (D&C 17:6).

As the Prophet proceeded with the translation, he
learned many great and marvelous truths. He learned
that the concept of the book originated in the mind of

the Lord himself—that both the source material for the record and the engravings which he was translating were prepared by righteous men as they were directed by the Lord.

He learned that, under the guidance of the Lord, the gathering of source material for the book began as early as 2200 B.C. when the Lord commanded the brother of Jared "to go down out of the mount from the presence of the Lord, and write the things which he had seen" (Ether 4:1). He learned that the record thus begun was continued by commandment of the Lord until the end of the Jaredite era; that the complete Jaredite record miraculously came into the hands of Moroni who, about A.D. 400 abridged it into the short record we know as the book of Ether. He learned that the things in this short abridgment were written by Moroni upon the plates he, Joseph, was translating, because, according to Moroni's own words, "the Lord hath commanded me to write them," and Moroni continues:

I have written upon these plates the very things which the brother of Jared saw;

[And the Lord] commanded me that I should seal them up; and he also hath commanded that I should seal up the interpretation thereof; wherefore I have sealed up the interpreters, according to the commandment of the Lord (Ether 4: 4, 5).

Similar direction was given concerning the Nephite records:

The Lord commanded me [said Nephi], wherefore I did make plates of ore that I might engraven upon them the record of my people. . . . And this have I done, and commanded my people what they should do after I was gone (1 Nephi 19:1-4).

Thus, pursuant to divine command and direction, the comprehensive record on the large plates of Nephi, from which Mormon made his abridgment, was kept for nearly a thousand years.

Jesus himself edited part of that record. During his post-resurrection ministry among the Nephites, he instructed them to write the things he had taught them. He also reminded them that they had not made record of the prophecy of his servant Samuel the Lamanite to the effect that at the time of His resurrection many saints should arise from the dead. When he drew this to their attention, his disciples remembered the prophecies and their fulfillment. (Jesus commanded that it should be written; therefore, it was written according as he commanded.)

From the title page of the Book of Mormon, the Prophet learned that one of the two purposes of the book was "the convincing of the Jew and the Gentile that Jesus is the Christ."

For the accomplishment of this purpose, the book is from beginning to end a witness for Christ. Its first chapter contains an account of a vision in which Lehi beheld Jesus descending out of the midst of heaven in luster above the noonday sun (1 Nephi 1:9). Its last chapter concludes with Moroni's great exhortation to come unto Christ and be perfected in him, with this assurance:

And if ye shall deny yourselves of all ungodliness and love God with all your might, mind and strength, then is his grace sufficient for you, that by grace ye may be . . . sanctified (Moroni 10:32, 33).

Numerous and great are the stirring testimonies which illuminate the 500 pages between these chapters.

I bear you my witness that I have obtained for myself a personal knowledge that the Book of Mormon is all the Prophet Joseph said it is; that from it radiates the spirit of prophecy and revelation; that it teaches in plain simplicity the great doctrine of salvation and the principles of righteous conduct calculated to bring men to Christ; that familiarity with its spirit and obedience to its teachings will move every contrite soul to fervently pray with David, "Create in me a clean heart, O God; and renew a right spirit within me" (Psalm 51:10).

One's soul is lifted above the sordid things of this world and soars in the realm of the divine as in spirit he stands with the brother of Jared on Mount Shelem in the presence of the premortal Redeemer and hears him say:

Behold, I am he who was prepared from the foundation of the world to redeem my people. Behold, I am Jesus Christ. . . . In me shall all mankind have light, and that eternally, even they who shall believe on my name; . . .

Seest thou that ye are created after mine own image? Yea, even all men were created in the beginning after mine own image.

Behold, this body which ye now behold, is the body of my spirit; and man have I created after the body of my spirit; and even as I appear unto thee to be in the spirit will I appear unto my people in the flesh (Ether 3:14-16).

One's soul is likewise lifted as in spirit he mingles with the multitude "round about the temple . . . in the land Bountiful," who, as Mormon said,

were marveling and wondering one with another, and were showing one to another the great and marvelous change which had taken place.

And . . . also conversing about this Jesus Christ of whom the sign had been given concerning his death.

And it came to pass that while they were thus conversing one with another, they heard a voice as if it came out of heaven; . . . and it was not a harsh voice, neither was it a loud voice; nevertheless, and notwithstanding it being a small voice it did pierce them that did hear to the center, insomuch that there was no part of their frame that it did not

cause to quake; yea, it did pierce them to the very soul, and
did cause their hearts to burn.

. . . and it said unto them:

Behold my Beloved Son, in whom I am well pleased, in
whom I have glorified my name—hear ye him.

. . . and behold, they saw a Man descending out of heav-
en; and he was clothed in a white robe; and he came down and
stood in the midst of them; and the eyes of the whole multitude were turned upon him, and they durst not open their
mouths, even one to another, and wist not what it meant, for
they thought it was an angel that had appeared unto them.

And it came to pass that he stretched forth his hand and
spake unto the people saying:

Behold, I am Jesus Christ, whom the prophets testified
shall come into the world.

And behold, I am the light and the life of the world (3
Nephi 11:1-11).

No one can read Alma's resumé of the experiences
of his father with the saints who joined the church at
the waters of Mormon; of the Lord's mercy and long-
suffering in bringing them out of their spiritual and
temporal captivity; of how, by the power of the Holy
Spirit, they were awakened from the deep sleep of
death to experience a mighty change wrought in their
hearts—no one, I say, can contemplate this marvelous
transformation without yearning to have a like change
wrought in his own heart.

And no one can answer for himself the following
questions which Alma put to his brethren:

Have ye spiritually been born of God?

Have ye received his image in your countenances? Have
ye experienced this mighty change in your hearts?

Do ye exercise faith in the redemption of him who created
you? Do you look forward with an eye of faith, and view
this mortal body raised in immortality, and this corruption
raised in incorruption, to stand before God to be judged according to the deeds which have been done in the mortal body?

I say unto you, can you imagine to yourselves that ye
hear the voice of the Lord saying unto you, in that day: Come

unto me ye blessed, for behold, your works have been the works of righteousness upon the face of the earth?

Have ye walked, keeping yourselves blameless before God? Could ye say, if ye were called to die at this time . . . that ye have been sufficiently humble? That your garments have been cleansed and made white through the blood of Christ (Alma 5:14-16, 27).

I say, no one with the spirit of the Book of Mormon upon him, can honestly answer to himself these soul-searching questions without resolving to so live that he can answer them in the affirmative on that great day to which each of us shall come. I leave you my humble testimony that the Prophet knew whereof he spoke and uttered divine truth when he "told the brethren that the Book of Mormon was the most correct book of any book on earth, and the keystone of our religion, and a man would get nearer to God by abiding by its precepts, than by any other book."

I urge you, my brethren and sisters and friends, all of you who hear my voice, to become familiar with the teachings and spirit of the Book of Mormon, the keystone of our religion. Its teachings and its spirit will lead us to Christ and eternal life. To this I bear solemn witness in the name of Jesus Christ. Amen.

He that exercises no faith unto repentance is exposed to the whole law of the demands of justice; therefore only unto him that has faith unto repentance is brought about the great and eternal plan of redemption.

Alma 34:16

PLACE OF REPENTANCE IN THE PLAN OF SALVATION •

An article published in Improvement Era *March 1956.*

The Prophet Joseph Smith specified as the first principles and ordinances of the gospel, "first, Faith in the Lord Jesus Christ; second, Repentance; third, Baptism by immersion for the remission of sins; fourth, Laying on of hands for the gift of the Holy Ghost" (Fourth Article of Faith).

These four principles and ordinances form the arch to the entrance of The Church of Jesus Christ of Latter-day Saints. Compliance with them is the process by which one receives that rebirth of the water and of the Spirit without which, as Jesus taught Nicodemus, a man can neither see nor enter into the kingdom of God. In one sense, repentance is the keystone in that arch. Unless followed by repentance, professed faith in the Lord Jesus Christ is impotent; unless preceded by repentance, baptism is a futile mockery, effecting no remission of sins; and without repenting, no one actually receives the companionship of the Holy Spirit of God, notwithstanding the laying on of hands for the gift of the Holy Ghost.

In this attempt to discover and define the place of repentance in the plan of redemption, I have been confirmed in my persuasion that it is most difficult to separate the principles of the gospel from each other and treat them one at a time. However, an attempt to do so, as our late beloved and able Elder Albert E. Bowen has so eloquently said,

is proper enough as a device for facilitating examination and analysis—making it easier to talk about. It is a common resort of the human mind which cannot always compass the whole until it has become familiar with the parts and these gradually have shaped themselves into relation with each other and are seen to fit into one pattern. Truth, presumably, is one whole, but the human mind does not grasp the entirety. We break it up into segments and nibble at them in apparent isolation from each other. Finally, with greater familiarity we begin to see relationships and begin putting the segments together. But we never really understand the separate fragments until we begin to see them as parts of the whole (Albert E. Bowen, *The Church Welfare Plan*, p. 41).

With this statement in mind, you will understand why, as we proceed in our consideration of the place of repentance in the plan of redemption, we shall frequently have under consideration other principles of the gospel, particularly the atonement, with which repentance is inextricably involved.

Repentance has to do with releasing men from spiritual death. It has nothing to do with the universal resurrection spoken of by Paul when he said, "Since by man came death, by man came also the resurrection of the dead. For as in Adam all die, even so in Christ shall all be made alive" (1 Corinthians 15:21, 22; see also Romans 5:18).

Spiritual death means banishment from God. It was the first death which passed upon Adam. It will be the last death to pass upon the still unrepentant at the days of final judgment. It is infinitely more far-reaching and terrible than physical death.

Perhaps it will assist us to understand spiritual death if we keep in mind that God is perfect; that he and all who associate with him are spotless; that no unclean thing can dwell in his presence. Jesus said, "No unclean thing can enter into his kingdom" (3 Nephi 27:19).

This earth is a battleground where two mighty contending forces struggle for the souls of men. All mortals who come to accountability, as they react to the play of these forces upon them, yield in some measure to the temptations of evil. Thereby they become stained with sin. Thus stained, they are unclean and therefore unfit for the society of God and are, as a consequence, banished from his presence. Such is the penalty imposed upon them by the law of justice.

Herein (that is, in the banishment of men from the presence of God) lies the necessity for the plan of redemption. For without some means being provided for payment of the penalty which the law of justice imposes upon men for transgressing the law of righteousness (that is, some means other than banishment from the presence of God) men would remain spiritually dead forever. Awful would be their situation.

Jacob says that without the plan of redemption "the first judgment which came upon man must needs have remained to an endless duration . . . our spirits must become subject to that angel who fell from before the presence of the Eternal God, and became the devil to rise no more" (2 Nephi 9:7, 8).

You see, the devil is spiritually dead for all time. So far as repentance is concerned, he has reached the point of no return.

Without the plan of redemption, of which repentance is a vital part, as we shall hereafter see, "our spirits," Jacob continues, "must have become like unto him, and we become devils, angels to a devil, to be shut out from the presence of our God, and to remain with the father of lies, in misery, like unto himself" (Ibid., 9:9).

Then contemplating the escape provided for us in the plan of redemption, Jacob continues, "O how great the goodness of our God, who prepareth a way for our escape from the grasp of this awful monster; yea, that monster, death and hell, which I call the death of the body, and also the death of the spirit" (Ibid., 9:10).

As already intimated, the purpose of the plan of redemption was to provide a means to meet the demands of justice in some way other than by leaving men forever banished from the presence of God. Now the demands which justice made for releasing men from spiritual death were heavy, but they could not be robbed. They had to be met.

One of those demands was that men's sins be atoned for. Man, being within the grasp of the demands of justice, could not make the required atonement. So far as he was concerned, he was forever bound. By the exercise of his own will, he had incurred the penalty of the broken law, and he could not, by himself alone, remove the penalty. He had to be rescued by someone other than himself or remain forever spiritually dead.

The required atonement had to be made by someone upon whom spiritual death had not passed, someone over whom the demands of justice had no claim.

Such a one could be none other than a god—a god who, endowed with free agency, would in mortality submit himself to the temptations of Satan without once yielding thereto in any particular.

Because man had fallen, said Jacob, "they were cut off from the presence of the Lord. Wherefore, it must needs be an infinite atonement—save it should be an infinite atonement . . . the first judgment which came upon man must needs have remained to an endless duration" (Ibid., 9:6, 7).

On the same point, Alma explains that as

the fall had brought upon all mankind a spiritual death as well as a temporal, that is, they were cut off from the presence of the Lord, it was expedient that mankind should be reclaimed from this spiritual death. . . .

And thus we see that all mankind were fallen, and they were in the grasp of justice; yea, the justice of God, which consigned them forever to be cut off from his presence.

And now, the plan of mercy could not be brought about except an atonement should be made; therefore God himself atoneth for the sins of the world, to bring about the plan of mercy to appease the demands of justice, that God might be a perfect, just God, and a merciful God also (Alma 42:9, 14, 15).

In the spirit world, when this matter of an atonement was under consideration, Jesus volunteered to make it. If you will indulge me for a moment, I should like to give you, in the words of the late Apostle Orson F. Whitney, his description of the circumstances under which Jesus' proffer was made:

In solemn council sat the Gods;
    From Kolob's height supreme,
Celestial light blazed forth afar
    O'er countless kokaubeam;
And faintest tinge, the fiery fringe
    Of that resplendent day,
"Lumined the dark abysmal realm
    Where earth in chaos lay.

Silence. That awful hour was one
    When thought doth most avail;
Of words unborn the destiny
    Hung trembling in the scale.
Silence self-spelled, and there arose,
    Those kings and priests among,
A power sublime, than whom appeared
    None nobler 'mid the throng.

A stature mingling strength with grace,
    Of meek though godlike mien;
The glory of whose countenance
    Outshone the noonday sheen.
Whiter his hair than ocean spray,
    Or frost of alpine hill.
He spake;—attention grew more grave,
    The stillness e'en more still.

"Father!" the voice like music fell,
    Clear as the murmuring flow
Of mountain streamlet trickling down
    From heights of virgin snow.
"Father," it said, "since one must die,
    Thy children to redeem
From spheres all formless now and void,
    Where pulsing life shall teem;

"And mighty Michael foremost fall
    That mortal man may be;
And chosen saviour Thou must send,
    Lo, here am I—send me!
I ask, I seek no recompense,
    Save that which then were mine;
Mine be the willing sacrifice,
    The endless glory Thine!

"Give me to lead to this lorn world,
    When wandered from the fold,
Twelve legions of the noble ones
    That now Thy face behold;
Tried souls, 'mid untried spirits found,
    That captained these may be,
And crowned the dispensations all
    With powers of Deity.

"Who blameless bide the spirit state,
    Clothe them in mortal clay,
The stepping-stone to glories all,
    If man will God obey,
Believing where he cannot see,
    Till he again shall know,
And answer give, reward receive,
    For all deeds done below.

"The love that hath redeemed all worlds
    All worlds must still redeem;
But mercy cannot justice rob—
    Or where were Elohim?
Freedom—man's faith, man's work, God's grace—
    Must span the great gulf o'er;
Life death, the guerdon or the doom,
    Rejoice we or deplore."

Still rang that voice, when sudden rose
    Aloft a towering form,
Proudly erect as lowering peak
    'Lumed by the gathering storm;
A presence bright and beautiful,
    With eye of flashing fire,
A lip whose haughty curl bespoke,
    A sense of inward ire.

"Send me!"—coiled 'neath his courtly smile
"And none shall hence, from heaven to earth,
    That shall not rise again.
My saving plan exception scorns.
    Man's will?—Nay, mine alone.
As recompense, I claim the right
    To sit on yonder Throne!"

Ceased Lucifer. The breathless hush
    Resumed and denser grew.
All eyes were turned; the general gaze
    One common magnet drew.
A moment there was solemn pause—
    Listened eternity,
While rolled from lips omnipotent
    The Father's firm decree:

"Jehovah, thou my Messenger!
    Son Ahman, thee I send;

And one shall go thy face before,
  While twelve thy steps attend.
And many more on that far shore
  The pathway shall prepare,
That I, the first, the last may come,
  And earth my glory share.

"After and ere thy going down,
  An army shall descend—
The host of God, and house of him
  Whom I have named my friend.
Through him, upon Idumea
  Shall come all life to leaven,
The guileless ones, the sovereign sons,
Throned on the heights of heaven.

"Go forth, thou Chosen of the Gods,
  Whose strength shall in thee dwell!
Go down betime and rescue earth,
  Dethroning death and hell.
On thee alone man's fate depends,
  The fate of beings all.
Thou shalt not fail, though thou art free—
  Free, but too great to fall.

"By arm divine, both mine and thine,
  The lost thou shalt restore,
And man redeemed, with God shall be,
  As God forevermore.
Return, and to the parent fold
  This wandering planet bring
And earth shall hail thee Conqueror,
  And heaven proclaim thee King."

'Twas done. From congregation vast,
  Tumultuous murmurs rose;
Waves of conflicting sound, as when
  Two meeting seas oppose.
'Twas finished, But the heavens wept,
  And still their annals tell
How one was choice of Elohim
  O'er one who fighting fell.

Pursuant to his divine appointment, received in
that great council, Jesus in due time came to earth as

the literal Son of Elohim and the virgin Mary. He endured the temptations of Satan but he never once yielded to them. "He suffered temptations but gave no heed unto them" (D&C 20:22; see also Mosiah 15:5). He endured the indignities and cruelty of men. The pain he endured in Gethsemane and on the cross was sufficient to pay the penalty imposed by the demands of justice, sufficient to atone for all the sins of all men who ever had lived or ever would live in mortality upon the earth.

The intensity of his suffering was beyond the ken of men. No mortal has ever understood it; none ever will, for it is beyond human comprehension. We do know, however, that it was of terrible intensity, for of Gethsemane Luke wrote:

> He kneeled down, and prayed,
> Saying, Father, if thou be willing, remove this cup from me: nevertheless not my will, but thine, be done.
> And there appeared an angel unto him from heaven, strengthening him.
> And being in an agony he prayed more earnestly; and his sweat was as it were great drops of blood falling down to the ground (Luke 22:41-44).

Speaking of that same suffering eighteen hundred years later, Jesus said to the Prophet Joseph Smith:

> Which suffering caused myself, even God, the greatest of all, to tremble because of pain, and to bleed at every pore, and to suffer both body and spirit—and would that I might not drink the bitter cup, and shrink—
> Nevertheless, glory be to the Father, and I partook and finished my preparations unto the children of men (D&C 19:18, 19).

This was the awful price demanded by the justice of God and paid by Jesus to put into effect the plan of mercy—that is, the gospel plan of redemption through which men may escape from spiritual death.   In this manner Jesus literally bought us with his blood. Paul twice says, "Ye are bought with a price" (1 Corinthians 6:20; 7:23), and Peter charges "false teachers" with "denying the Lord that bought them" (2 Peter 2:1). His blood was drawn from him in blood sweat, the most torturous manner in which it could be spilt. From every beneficiary of the plan of redemption, Jesus merits everlasting praise, honor, and gratitude.

By his atonement, Jesus accomplished two things: (1) he overcame mortal death, and (2) he put into effect the plan of redemption from spiritual death.

By atoning for the fall of Adam, he overcame death and brought about the resurrection. As has already been pointed out, the benefits of this aspect of his atonement are extended to every creature to whom death came as a result of Adam's fall. The Lord indicates the scope of its application in the following quotation from the 29th section of the Doctrine and Covenants:

And the end shall come, and the heaven and the earth shall be consumed and pass away, and there shall be a new heaven and a new earth.

For all old things shall pass away, and all things shall become new, even the heaven and the earth, and all the fulness thereof, both men and beasts, the fowls of the air, and the fishes of the sea;

And not one hair, neither mote, shall be lost, for it is the workmanship of mine hand (D&C 29:23-25).

The working out of that part of the atonement which brought about the resurrection was a great act of mercy by the Redeemer. It is matched only by the second aspect of his atonement. However, so far as the beneficiaries of universal resurrection are concerned, the bringing of it about was for them an act of justice, not of mercy only. This is so because mortal death came to them not as a penalty for their own sins, but as a consequence of the fall of Adam. Therefore, it was but justice to them that their bodies should be raised from the grave.

Since by the fall of Adam came death (that is, mortal death—death of the body), so by the atonement of Christ comes the resurrection. One is as wide in its scope as the other. The resurrection is universal and unconditional as a matter of justice to the beneficiaries thereof.

As has already been said, the second aspect of Christ's atonement was the putting into effect of the law of mercy, the plan of redemption whereby men may be cleansed from the stain of their own sins and thereby freed from spiritual death. With respect to this aspect of the atonement, the circumstances differ from those attending the first. The difference arises in the origin of spiritual death.

As we have seen, spiritual death is the penalty for men's own sins and not for the transgression of Adam, as was the case in temporal death. Men, in the exercise of their own free agency, voluntarily break the laws of righteousness, the penalty for which is spiritual death. They therefore have no such claim upon justice for relief from spiritual death as they have for relief from temporal death. So far as men are concerned, Christ's atonement for their individual sins was entirely beyond the scope of justice—it was an act of pure mercy. It seems to me that, if possible (particularly since it was an act beyond the power of men to do for themselves), we owe our Redeemer an even deeper debt of gratitude for this aspect of his atonement than we do for bringing about the resurrection.

Because men's transgressions are voluntary acts of their own, Jesus did not, by his atonement, remove the stain thereof unconditionally. He merely did for men, with respect to the remission of their sins, what they themselves could not do, that which they were powerless to do. Specifically, he put into effect the plan of redemption whereby they may secure forgiveness upon the condition that they will do what they can do to bring themselves within reach of that plan. He left with them the responsibility to meet this condition.

This requirement is in full harmony with the laws of justice, for in addition to the atonement which Christ made for the sins of men. justice itself requires, as part of the price for their release from spiritual death, that men do what they can do for themselves. This they must do before they can profit from the atonement which Christ has conditionally made for them. For, as Nephi put it, we are saved by the grace of Christ only after we have done "all we can do" (2 Nephi 25:23).

This, then, brings us to repentance. For it is repentance which both mercy and justice require of men as a condition for their participation in the plan of redemption. The very intent of Christ's sacrifice, according to Amulek, was "to bring about the bowels of mercy, which overpowereth justice, and bringeth about means unto men that they may have faith unto repentance" (Alma 34:15).

From this and companion scriptures, it is clear that our ability to repent, as well as the efficacy of our repentance, comes as a gift from the Redeemer. It is one of the fruits of his atonement. This gift men reject at their peril. Unless they exercise it, they remain spiritually dead, just as dead as if there had been no redemption made. For it takes repentance to bring one within reach of the atoning blood of Jesus Christ and thereby secure to himself the full benefits of the plan of redemption. In this manner, and only in this manner, does "mercy . . . satisfy the demands of justice, and encircles them in the arms of safety, while he that exercises no faith unto repentance is exposed to the whole law of the demands of justice; therefore only unto him that has faith unto repentance is brought about the great and eternal plan of redemption" (Ibid., 34:16).

So testifies Amulek, while Abinadi (Mosiah 16: 15), Amulek (Alma 11:41), Alma (Ibid., 12:18), Samuel the Lamanite (Helaman 14:18), and Mormon (Moroni 7:38) all testify that the unrepentant "remain as though there had been no redemption made, except it be the loosing of the bands of death" (Alma 11:41).

Jesus taught this principle at the time he told of his suffering, as above quoted.

I command you to repent [he said to Martin Harris through the Prophet Joseph], lest I smite you by the rod of my mouth, and by my wrath, and by my anger, and your sufferings be sore—how sore you know not, . . . yea, how hard to bear you know not. For behold, I God, have suffered these things for all that they might not suffer if they would repent; But if they would not repent they must suffer even as I" (D&C 19:15-17).

On a later occasion he said, "Behold, my blood shall not cleanse them if they hear me not" (Ibid., 29: 17). This statement he made following a warning to the wicked who he said would not repent. Later on in the same revelation he said that those who would not believe would be raised in immortality unto "eternal damnation; for they cannot be redeemed from their spiritual fall, because they repent not" (Ibid., 29:43, 44).

These quotations call to mind the great summary of his gospel which Jesus gave to the Nephites as he drew near to the close of his ministry among them:

Behold [said he], I have given unto you my gospel, and this is the gospel which I have given unto you—that I came into the world to do the will of my Father, because my Father sent me.

And my Father sent me that I might be lifted up upon the cross; and after that I had been lifted up upon the cross, that I might draw all men unto me, that as I have been lifted up by men even so should men be lifted up by the Father, to stand before me, to be judged of their works whether they be good or whether they be evil.

And for this cause have I been lifted up; therefore, according to the power of the Father I will draw all men unto me, that they may be judged according to their works.

And it shall come to pass, that whoso repenteth and is baptized in my name shall be filled; and if he endureth to the end, behold, him will I hold guiltless before my Father at that day when I shall stand to judge the world.

And he that endureth not unto the end, the same is he that is also hewn down and cast into the fire, from whence they can no more return, because of the justice of the Father.

And this is the word which he hath given unto the children of men. And for this cause he fulfilleth the words which he hath given, and he lieth not but fulfilleth all his words.

And no unclean thing can enter into his kingdom; therefore nothing entereth into his rest save it be those who have washed their garments in my blood, because of their faith, and the repentance of all their sins, and their faithfulness unto the end.

Now this is the commandment: Repent, all ye ends of the earth, and come unto me and be baptized in my name, that ye may be sanctified by the reception of the Holy Ghost, that ye may stand spotless before me at the last day.

Verily, verily, I say unto you, this is my gospel (3 Nephi 27:13-21).

From the foregoing and many other scriptures, it is clear that repentance is the process by which every person must himself put into operation the plan of mercy on his own behalf if he would be redeemed from spiritual death. In other words, repentance consummates for an individual, with respect to his own sins, what the atonement of Jesus Christ did conditionally for the sins of all. Such is the place of repentance in the plan of redemption.

If ye will repent and harden not your hearts, immediately shall the great plan of redemption be brought about unto you.

Alma 34:31

REPENTANCE AND FORGIVENESS •

An address delivered at general conference October 1955.

Among the many things for which I am thankful is the sanctifying process of repentance. I am grateful to the Lord Jesus Christ who, through the atonement he wrought, gave us the gift of repentance. I am grateful that he was willing voluntarily to give his life for us. That is literally what he did. He did not have to give it; he did not have to die. Because he was the Son of God, he was not subject to the fall, as were men. Within him was power to live forever. "I lay down my life for the sheep," he said. "No man taketh it from me, but I lay it down of myself. I have power to lay it down, and I have power to take it again" (John 10:15, 18). He inherited power over death from his divine Father.

It took a person with power over death to pay the debt to justice to bring men forth in the resurrection. It took a sinless one, a god, even the sinless Son of God, to satisfy the demands of justice for men's sins. They themselves could not make an atonement which would either bring about their resurrection or pay for their sins and bring about their spiritual rebirth.

And so, I repeat, I am grateful for my Redeemer —grateful that he paid the debt and brought about the means of repentance so that by repenting of my transgressions I can bring my soul within the reach of his atoning blood and thereby be cleansed of sin. For, after all, it is by the grace of Christ that men are saved, after all they can do. The thing they can and must do is repent. I love the doctrine of repentance.

During the past few months I have seen the need of it—oh, how I have seen the need of it. I have seen missionaries, Saints, and nonmembers of the Church in far-off lands sorrowing with a godly sorrow for sin. I have heard them say, "Oh, Brother Romney, do you think there is any hope for me, any chance for me to get even on the bottom rung of the gospel ladder?"

And as I have witnessed their sorrowing, I have remembered the sorrowing of repentant men in the days of old; Zeezrom, for example, whose soul, after he realized what he had done in opposing the ministry of Alma and Amulek, "began to be harrowed up under a consciousness of his own guilt; yea, he began to be encircled about by the pains of hell." So severe were his sufferings that he "lay sick at Sidom, with a burning fever, which was caused by the great tribulations of his mind on account of his wickedness" (see Alma 14 and 15). And Alma, who said of the suffering he endured for seeking to destroy the church of God:

I was racked with eternal torment, for my soul was harrowed up to the greatest degree and racked with all my sins. Yea, I . . . was tormented with the pains of hell; . . . with inexpressible horror, . . . even with the pains of a damned soul (see ibid., 36).

But then I also remembered the rest which came into their souls when, through repentance, they found forgiveness. "Yea, I say unto you," said Alma to his son Helaman, that as "there could be nothing so exquisite and so bitter as were my pains," so "on the other hand, there can be nothing so exquisite and sweet as was my joy" (Ibid., 36:21).

And so I was comforted and encouraged those who confided in me, and I encourage all sorrowing, repentant men to be comforted—comforted by the experience of Alma and by Paul's assurance that " . . . godly sorrow worketh repentance to salvation . . ." (2 Corinthians 7:10). Today, as well as in days of old, there is hope; there is peace; there is rest in Christ for all whose godly sorrow brings them to the repentance which worketh salvation. Forgiveness is as wide as repentance. Every person will be forgiven for all the transgressions of which he truly repents. If he repents of all of his sins, he shall stand spotless before God because of the atonement of our Master and Savior, Jesus Christ. While he that exercises no faith unto repentance remains "as though there had been no redemption made, except it be the loosing of the bands of death" (Alma 11:41). Such is the gist of God's merciful plan of redemption.

My brothers and sisters, there are many among us, those whose distress and suffering are unnecesarily prolonged because they do not complete their repentance by confessing their sins. You will recall the following words of the Savior, "I command you to repent, . . . and that you confess your sins, lest you suffer these punishments of which I have spoken" (D&C 19:20).

In another revelation he said, "By this ye may know if a man repenteth of his sins—behold, he will confess them and forsake them" (Ibid., 58:43).

Repeatedly he says that he forgives the sins of those who confess their sins with humbleness of heart, "who have not sinned unto death" (see ibid., 61:2; 64:7). And adds, "He who has repented of his sins, the same is forgiven, and I, the Lord, remember them no more" (Ibid., 58:42).

But how are we to fulfil this commandment? To whom are we to confess our sins? In the 59th section of the Doctrine and Covenants the Lord, with other directions concerning his holy day, says,

Remember that on this, the Lord's day, thou shalt offer thine oblations and thy sacraments unto the Most High, confessing thy sins unto thy brethren, and before the Lord (Ibid., 59:12).

I would assume that we are to confess all our sins unto the Lord. For transgressions which are wholly personal, affecting none but ourselves and the Lord, such confession would seem to be sufficient.

For misconduct which offends another, confession should also be made to the offended one and his forgiveness sought.

Where one's transgressions are of such a nature as would, unrepented of, put in jeopardy his right to membership or fellowship in the Church of Jesus Christ, full and effective confession would, in my judgment, require confession by the repentant sinner to his bishop or other proper presiding Church officer—not that the Church officer could forgive the sin (this power rests in the Lord himself and those only to whom he specifically delegates it), but rather that the Church, acting through its duly appointed officers, might with full knowledge of the facts take such action with respect to Church discipline as the circumstances merit.

One, having forsaken his sins and, by proper confession, cleared his conduct with the Lord, with the people he has offended, and with the Church of Jesus Christ, where necessary, may with full confidence seek the Lord's forgiveness and go forth in newness of life, relying upon the merits of Christ.

Let us in this manner clear for righteous living the decks of our own lives and get on our way to eternal life. Only by so doing can we rid ourselves of those guilty feelings of unworthiness, depression, fear, uncertainty, and self-condemnation which block our upward climb. So long as we put off either the forsaking or confessing of our sins, just so long do we delay the day of our redemtpion.

> Let not the past hang heavy as a millstone to thy heels,
> To drag thee downward as each upward impulse to thy
>   nobler self appeals;
> But as the joyous butterfly from its chrysalistic shell
>   breaks free,
> So from the past must thou rise jubilant, thine own true
>   self to be.

This we may do today if we will. Amulek assures us that

if [we] repent and harden not [our] hearts, immediately shall the great plan of redemption be brought about unto [us] (Alma 34:31).

And President Joseph F. Smith spoke these comforting words:

None of the children of the Father who are redeemed through obedience, faith, repentance, and baptism for the remission of sins, and who live in that redeemed condition, and die in that condition, are subject to Satan. . . . They are absolutely beyond his reach just as little children are who die without sin (*Gospel Doctrine,* p. 570).

God grant that it may be so with us all, I humbly pray in the name of Jesus Christ, our Redeemer. Amen.

Return unto me and repent of your sins, and be converted, that I may heal you.

3 Nephi 9:13

COVERSION •

An address delivered at general conference October 4, 1963.

Perhaps the most frequently asked question today is, Do quick baptisms stay as active in the Church as when more time was taken? My observation is that activity among so-called quick baptisms is about the same as it is among those born to Church members in the stakes.

From the time of Father Adam until today, some people have been baptized almost immediately upon hearing the gospel. Others have investigated long and studiously. So far as I know, the Lord has never fixed a time limit. The only prerequisite he has prescribed is conversion.

Webster says the verb *convert* means "to turn from one belief or course to another"; that *conversion* is "a spiritual and moral *change* attending a *change* of belief with conviction." As used in the scriptures, *converted* generally implies not merely mental acceptance of Jesus and his teachings, but also a motivating faith in him and in his gospel—a faith which works a transformation, an actual *change*, in one's understanding of life's meaning and in his allegiance to God—in interest, in thought, and in conduct. While conversion may be accomplished in stages, one is not really converted in the full sense of the term unless and until he is at heart a new person. *Born again* is the scriptural term.

In one who is wholly converted, desire for things inimical to the gospel of Jesus Christ has actually died, and substituted therefor is a love of God with a fixed and controlling determination to keep his commandments. Paul told the Romans that such a one would walk in newness of life.

Know ye not [he said], that so many of us as were baptized into Jesus Christ were baptized into his death?

Therefore we are buried with him by baptism into death: that like as Christ was raised up from the dead, . . . even so we also should walk in the newness of life (Romans 6:3, 4).

Peter taught that by walking in this newness of life one escapes "the corruption that is in the world through lust," and by developing within himself faith, virtue, knowledge, temperance, patience, godliness, brotherly kindness and charity he becomes a partaker "of the divine nature."

One who walks in newness of life is converted. On the other hand, says Peter, "He that lacketh these things is blind, and cannot see afar off, and hath forgotten that he was purged from his old sins" (2 Peter 1:1-9). Such a one is not converted, even though he may have been baptized.

There is a striking example of the change wrought by conversion in Mormon's account of King Benjamin's farewell address. This sermon was so powerful that as Benjamin delivered it the multitude fell to the earth, for

they . . . viewed themselves in their own carnal state, . . . And they all cried aloud . . . O have mercy, and apply the atoning blood of Christ that we may receive forgiveness of our sins, and our hearts may be purified; for we believe in Jesus Christ, the Son of God (Mosiah 4:2).

Observing their humility, King Benjamin continued:

Believe in God; believe that he is, and that he created all things, . . . believe that he has all wisdom, and all power, both in heaven and in earth;

Believe that ye must repent of your sins and forsake them, and humble yourselves before God; and ask in sincerity of heart that he would forgive you; and now if you believe all these things see that ye do them (Mosiah 4:9, 10).

When he had concluded, he inquired as to whether they believed his words.

And they all cried . . . Yea, we believe all thy words . . . and also, we know of their surety and truth, . . .

[And why were they so confident?] Because [as they said] . . . the Spirit of the Lord . . . has wrought a mighty change in us, or in our hearts that we have no more disposition to do evil, but to do good continually. . . .

And [they continued] we are willing to enter into a covenant with our God to do his will, and to be obedient to his commandments in all things . . . all the remainder of our days (Mosiah 5:2, 5).

Notwithstanding the fact that these people seem to have been converted rather quickly from a disposition to do evil to a determination to do good continually all the remainder of their days, they nevertheless evidently fully met the conditions prescribed by the Lord for baptism when he said:

All those who humble themselves before God, and desire to be baptized, and come forth with broken hearts and contrite spirits, and witness before the church that they have truly repented of all their sins, and are willing to take upon them the name of Jesus Christ, having a determination to serve him to the end, and truly manifest by their works that they have received of the Spirit of Christ unto the remission of their sins, shall be received by baptism into his church (D&C 20:37).

That the Prophet Joseph Smith applied these instructions strictly is apparent from his entry in his diary of July 5, 1835: "Michael H. Barton tried to get into the Church, but he was not willing to confess and forsake all his sins—and he was rejected" (*History of the Church* 2:235).

Had Mr. Barton obtained membership in the Church in his then unrepentant state, it would have availed him nothing, no matter how much he knew about the gospel, because he was not converted.

From some of the Savior's sayings, it would seem that there might even be people in high places whose conversion is not complete. For example, conversing with his apostles at his last supper, he said to Peter,

Simon, Simon, behold Satan hath desired to have you, that he may sift you as wheat:
But I have prayed for thee, that thy faith fail not: and when thou art converted, strengthen thy brethren (Luke 22:31, 32).

From this it would appear that membership in the Church and conversion are not necessarily synonymous. Being converted, as we are here using the term, and having a testimony are not necessarily the same thing either. A testimony comes when the Holy Ghost gives the earnest seeker a witness of the truth. A moving testimony vitalizes faith—that is, it induces repentance and obedience to the commandments. Conversion, on the other hand, is the fruit of, or the reward for, repentance and obedience. (Of course, one's testimony continues to increase as he is converted.)

Conversion is effected by divine forgiveness which remits sins. The sequence is something like this: An honest seeker hears the message. He asks the Lord in prayer if it is true. The Holy Spirit gives him a witness. This is a testimony. If one's testimony is strong enough, he repents and obeys the commandments. By such obedience he receives divine forgiveness which remits sin. Thus, he is converted to a newness of life. His spirit is healed.

From what Jesus said at the time he healed the man sick with the palsy, it would seem that remittance of sins is the therapy which heals and that the two terms are synonymous. Concerning that incident, Luke says, "The power of the Lord was present to heal" (Luke 5:17). Jesus, recognizing the faith of the palsied man and his associates, "said unto him, Man, thy sins are forgiven thee" (Luke 5:20). For this the Pharisees charged him with blasphemy, saying within themselves, "Who can forgive sins but God?" (Luke 5:21). Perceiving their thoughts, Jesus said,

Whether is easier, to say, Thy sins be forgiven thee; or to say, Rise up and walk?

[Then he added] But that ye may know that the Son of man hath power upon earth to forgive sins,

[He said to the sick of the palsy] Arise, and take up thy couch, and go into thine house (Luke 5:23-24).

This, of course, the man immediately did.

In this instance there was a physical healing. Sometimes there is also a healing of the nervous system or of the mind. But always the remittance of sins which attends divine forgiveness heals the spirit. This accounts for the fact that in the scriptures conversion and healing are repeatedly associated.

For example, in 1837 the Lord said to Thomas B. Marsh, then president of the Quorum of the Twelve,

Pray for thy brethren of the Twelve. Admonish them sharply for my name's sake, and let them be admonished for their sins, . . . And after their temptations, and much tribulation, behold, I, the Lord, will feel after them, and if they harden not their hearts, and stiffen not their necks against me, they shall be *converted,* and I will heal them (D&C 112:12, 13).

Jesus frequently spoke of his healing the converted. Citing Isaiah, he said,

This people's heart is waxed gross, and their ears are dull of hearing, and their eyes they have closed; lest at any time they should see with their eyes, and hear with their ears and should understand with their heart, and should be converted and I should heal them (Matthew 13:15).

At the opening of his mortal ministry, he told his fellow townsmen in Nazareth that he had been sent "to heal the brokenhearted" (Luke 4:18).

To the distraught Nephites, he thus spoke out of the awful darkness which attended his crucifixion:

O all ye that are spared because ye were more righteous than they, will ye not now return unto me, and repent of your sins, and be converted, that I may heal you? (3 Nephi 9:13).

Somebody recently asked how one could know when by the power of the Holy Spirit his soul is healed. When this occurs, he will recognize it by the way he feels, for he will feel as the people of Benjamin felt when they received remission of sins. The record says, "The Spirit of the Lord came upon them, and they were filled with joy, having received a remission of their sins, and having peace of conscience" (Mosiah 4:3).

When Alma was converted, he said:

I could remember my pains no more; yea, I was harrowed up by the memory of my sins no more.

And oh, what joy, and what marvelous light I did behold; yea, my soul was filled with joy as exceeding as was my pain!

Yea, I say unto you, my son, that there could be nothing so exquisite and so bitter as were my pains. Yea, and again I say unto you, my son, that on the other hand, there can be nothing so exquisite and so sweet as was my joy (Alma 36: 19-21).

As Jesus ministered among the Nephites, he told them not to administer the sacrament to the unworthy but to continue laboring with them.

For ye know not but what they will return and repent, and come unto me with full purpose of heart, and I shall heal them; and ye shall be the means of bringing salvation unto them (3 Nephi 18-32).

Getting people's spirits healed through conversion is the only way they can be healed. I know this is an unpopular doctrine and a slow way to solve the problems of men and nations. As a matter of fact, I am convinced that relatively few among the billions of earth's inhabitants will be converted. Nevertheless, I know and solemnly witness that there is no other means by which the sin-sick souls of men can be healed or for a troubled world to find peace.

In know that the unbelieving will reject this divine way. But this is nothing new. They have been rejecting it ever since the time of Cain. They have from the beginning refused to accept Christ and his gospel. They killed the ancient prophets. They burned Abinadi. They stoned Samuel the Lamanite. They crucified the Lord himself. In our own day they martyred Joseph Smith, Jr., the great prophet of the restoration.

But all that has happened in the past has not, and all that occurs in the future will not, change the truth that conversion to Jesus Christ and his gospel is the one and only way. For still it must be said that "there is none other way given under heaven by which men must be saved" (see Acts 4:12). To this I witness in solemn testimony.

Treasure these things up in your hearts, and let the solemnities of eternity rest upon your minds.

D&C 43:34

This book of the law shall not depart out of thy mouth; but thou shalt meditate therein day and night, that thou mayest observe to do according to all that is written therein: for then thou shalt make thy way prosperous and then thou shalt have good success.

Joshua 1:8

THE STANDARD WORKS OF THE CHURCH •

An article published in Relief Society Magazine
June 1969.

THE DOCTRINE AND COVENANTS AND PEARL OF GREAT PRICE

The Doctrine and Covenants is a book of modern scripture. It was first accepted by the Church as one of its standard works August 17, 1835. Forty-one years later, in the 1876 edition of the book, 26 sections were added. Four years later, in semiannual conference of October 1880, President George Q. Cannon said:

I hold in my hand the Book of Doctrine and Covenants and also the book The Pearl of Great Price, which books contain revelations of God. In Kirtland, the Doctrine and Covenants in its original form, as first printed, was submitted to the officers of the Church and the members of the Church to vote upon. As there have been additions made to it by the publishing of revelations which were not contained in the original edition, it has been deemed wise to submit these books with their contents to the Conference, to see whether the Conference will vote to accept the books and their contents as from God, and binding upon us as a people and a church (*Conference Report,* Oct. 10, 1880).

President Joseph F. Smith said,

I move that we receive and accept the revelations contained in these books, as revelations from God to the Church
of Jesus Christ of Latter-day Saints, and to all the world.

The motion was seconded and sustained by unanimous
vote of the whole Conference (Ibid.).

Ten years later, October 6, 1890, in like procedure,
the Church adopted the Manifesto.

In this manner, the Doctrine and Covenants, with
its present content, became and now is one of the
standard works of the Church

By the October 10, 1880, action, the Saints also
accepted the contents of the Pearl of Great Price as
revelation from God and binding upon them as a people
and as a Church.

During the next twenty-two years, under the direction of the presidency of the Church, the content of
the book was somewhat revised. Consequently, in October 1902, President Joseph F. Smith, said to the Saints
in conference assembled:

I hold in my hand a copy of the revised edition of the
Pearl of Great Price. The Pearl of Great Price as it originally
existed, was presented before the General Conference and accepted as one of the standard works of the Church. Since then
the book has undergone a revision; that is to say, all the revelations that it formerly contained which were also in the Book
of Doctrine and Covenants, have been eliminated from it. . . .
We now present this book in its revised form—the original
matter being preserved as it was before, only divided into
chapters and verses—for your acceptance as a standard work
of the church.

It was moved and seconded that the book be accepted as
a standard work of the church, and the motion carried unani-
mously (*Conference Report,* Oct. 6, 1902, p. 82).

The Pearl of Great Price contains:

1. Visions of Moses as revealed to Joseph Smith, the
Prophet, in June 1830.

2. The writings of Abraham while he was in Egypt, called the book of Abraham, written by his own hand upon papyrus, as translated by the Prophet Joseph Smith.

3. The following writings of the Prophet Joseph Smith:
   a. His translation of the last verse of the 23rd chapter, and the 24th chapter of Matthew (King James Version).
   b. Extracts from the history of Joseph Smith, the Prophet, which deal principally with events incident to the First Vision and the coming forth of the Book of Mormon.
   c. The Articles of Faith of The Church of Jesus Christ of Latter-day Saints.

THE BIBLE

The Bible is a book which contains that part of the word of God revealed to men in ancient and New Testament times, which has been preserved in writing. It consists of the Old and the New Testament. We believe it "to be the word of God as far as it is translated correctly" (Eighth Article of Faith). We do not, however, believe that it contains all the Lord revealed to his people in ancient times.

From what we can draw from the scriptures relative to the teachings of heaven [said the Prophet Joseph], we are induced to think that much instruction has been given to man since the beginning which we do not possess now.

We have what we have, and the Bible contains what it does contain . . . through the kind providence of our Father a portion of His word which He delivered to His ancient saints, has fallen into our hands, is presented to us with a promise of reward if obeyed, and with a penalty if disobeyed (*History of the Church* 2:18).

THE BOOK OF MORMON

The first thing revealed in this dispensation about the Book of Mormon was spoken by Moroni on his first appearance to the Prophet Joseph on the night of September 21, 1823.

He [Moroni] said there was a book deposited, written upon gold plates, giving an account of the former inhabitants of this continent, and the source from whence they sprang. He also said that the fulness of the everlasting Gospel was contained in it as delivered by the Savior to the ancient inhabitants (Joseph Smith 2:34).

After the Prophet obtained and translated the record and published the book, the Lord himself said that he, the Prophet, was given power to translate it through the mercy and power of God and that it contains ". . . a record of a fallen people, and the fulness of the gospel of Jesus Christ to the Gentiles and to the Jews also," and that "as your Lord and your God liveth it is true" (D&C 1:29; 20:9; 17:6).

In November of 1841, some twelve years after its publication, the Prophet Joseph said, "I told the brethren that the Book of Mormon was the most correct of any book on earth, and the keystone of our religion, and a man would get nearer to God by abiding by its precepts, than by any other book" (*History of the Church* 4:461).

Of all men, Joseph Smith was best qualified to make this appraisal. No other person comprehended the content of the Book of Mormon as he did. As he translated, the Holy Ghost enlightened his mind and quickened his understanding. As the glorious teachings contained in the record were revealed to him, they made an everlasting impression upon his mind and soul. The Book of Mormon was, for Joseph Smith, a handbook from which he first learned the fundamental principles of the gospel.

The King James Version of the Bible, and the Book of Mormon were both available to the Church at the time of its organization April 6, 1830. They were then, and ever since have been used, by the Church as standard works. As early as February 9, 1831, the Lord, in the revelation embracing the law of the Church, gave this instruction: "The elders, priests and teachers of this church shall teach the principles of my gospel, which are in the Bible and the Book of Mormon, in the which is the fulness of the gospel" (D&C 42:12).

As quoted above, the Prophet Joseph declared the Book of Mormon to be the keystone of our religion.

So far as I am advised, the nearest the Church has come to accepting the Bible and the Book of Mormon by formal vote was in the general conference October 6, 1902, when it accepted the Pearl of Great Price as one of the standard works of the Church. The Pearl of Great Price then contained, as it now does, the eighth Article of Faith, which reads: "We believe the Bible to be the word of God as far as it is translated correctly; we also believe the Book of Mormon to be the word of God."

Although the revelations recorded in the Bible, the Book of Mormon, the Doctrine and Covenants, and the Pearl of Great Price were given in different dispensations, yet, in the words of the Prophet Joseph Smith, "all things which God communicated to His people were calculated to teach them to rely upon God alone as the author of their salvation (*History of the Church* 2:17).

Set forth in these standard works is the law of heaven, which "guarantees to all who obey it a reward far beyond any earthly consideration" (Joseph Smith in *History of the Church* 2:7). It guarantees eternal life in the celestial kingdom of God.

A distinguished provision of this divine law, not common in the law of earthly governments, makes it "necessary for men to receive an understanding concerning the laws of the heavenly kingdom, before they are permitted to enter it" (Ibid., p. 8). It is this provision which makes the standard works of first importance. Surely all who acknowledge their divine authenticity must have a deep interest in their content.

The editor of the *Relief Society Magazine* spoke wisely when she characterized the subject of this article as "one which is vital to Latter-day Saint women in regard to their receiving instruction and inspiration for daily living" (Marianne C. Sharp, January 15, 1969).

I can think of no surer way to seek instruction and inspiration for daily living than to daily read and prayerfully contemplate a chapter or so in these sacred works which contain the law of heaven. To do so has ever been the counsel of the Lord.

In his farewell address to Israel, Moses reviewed the events and experiences of their wandering in the wilderness and exhorted them "to gratitude, obedience, and loyalty to Jehovah" (Dummelow, *One Volume Commentary*, p. 12).

Over and over again, he declared that their survival, happiness, and success depended upon their remembering the Lord and obeying the laws he had given them.

After reviewing some of these laws, including the Ten Commandments, Moses continued:

Hear, O Israel: The Lord our God is one Lord:
And thou shalt love the Lord thy God with all thine heart, and with all thy might.
And these words, which I command thee this day, shall be in thine heart:
And thou shalt teach them diligently unto thy children, and shalt talk of them when thou sittest in thine house, and

when thou walkest by the way, and when thou liest down, and when thou risest up.

And thou shalt bind them for a sign upon thine hand, and they shall be as frontlets between thine eyes.

And thou shalt write them upon the posts of thy house, and on thy gates (Deuteronomy 6:4-9).

In these instructions and many more, Moses stressed, as the strongest bulwark against apostasy and the most faith-promoting practice, constant consideration of the laws of God.

And it shall be [said he] on the day when ye shall pass over Jordan unto the land which the Lord thy God giveth thee, that thou shalt set thee up great stones . . .

And thou shalt write upon the stones all the words of this law very plainly (Deuteronomy 27:2, 8).

And . . . when Moses had made an end of writing the words of this law in a book, . . .

[He] commanded the Levites, which bare the ark of the covenant of the Lord, saying,

Take this book of the law, and put it in the side of the ark of the covenant of the Lord your God, that it may be there for a witness against thee (Deuteronomy 31:24-26).

That is to say, ancient Israel was to be judged by their compliance or noncompliance with the content of the Book of the Law. By the same token, modern Israel will be judged by their compliance or noncompliance with the law of heaven contained in our standard works.

When Joshua, succeeding Moses, was to lead Israel over Jordan into the Promised Land, the first instruction he received from the Lord included a solemn charge to give constant attention and strict obedience to the law contained in the books written by Moses—their standard works.

Be thou strong [said the Lord] and very courageous that thou mayest observe to do according to all the law, which Moses my servant commanded thee: turn not from it to the right hand or to the left, that thou mayest prosper withersoever thou goest.

This book of the law shall not depart out of thy mouth; but thou shalt meditate therein day and night that thou mayest observe to do according to all that is written therein: for then thou shalt make thy way prosperous, and then thou shalt have good success (Joshua 1:7, 8).

During his earthly ministry Jesus charged the Jews who disputed his Sonship to study the scriptures —to which they looked for eternal life—to learn of him. "Search the scriptures," he said, "for . . . they are they which testify of me" (John 5:39).

Nephi, son of Lehi, thus expressed his attitude toward the standard works available to him:

Upon these [plates] I write the things of my soul, and many of the scriptures which are engraven upon the plates of brass, For my soul delighteth in the scriptures, and my heart pondereth them, and writeth them for the learning and the profit of my children (2 Nephi 4:15).

Jacob associates the teaching of the scriptures with the establishment of peace and love among the people and their ability to recognize and resist false doctrine: "And it came to pass [he said] that peace and the love of God was restored again among the people; and they searched the scriptures, and hearkened no more to the words of this wicked man" (Jacob 7: 23).

King Benjamin emphasized to his sons the importance of sacred records and their continual use as

he . . . taught them concerning the records which were engraven on the plates of brass, saying: My sons, I would that he should remember that were it not for these plates, which contain these records and these commandments, we must have suffered in ignorance, even at this present time, not knowing the mysteries of God.

For it were not possible that our father, Lehi, could have

remembered all these things, to have taught them to his children, except it were for the help of these plates; for he having been taught in the language of the Egyptians therefore he could read these engravings, and teach them to his children, that thereby they could teach them to their children, and so fulfilling the commandments of God, even down to this present time.

I say unto you, my sons, were it not for these things, which have been kept and preserved by the hand of God, that we might read and understand of his mysteries, and have his commandments always before our eyes that even our fathers would have dwindled in unbelief, and we should have been like our brethren, the Lamanites, who know nothing concerning these things, or even do not believe them when they are taught them, because of the traditions of their fathers, which are not correct.

O my sons, I would that ye should remember that these sayings are true, and also that these records are true. And behold, also the plates of Nephi, which contain the records and the sayings of our fathers from the time they left Jerusalem until now, and they are true; and we can know of their surety because we have them before our eyes.

And now, my sons, I would that ye should remember to search them diligently, that ye may profit thereby (Mosiah 1:3-7).

The missionary prowess of the sons of Mosiah was in part due to the fact that "they had searched the scriptures diligently, that they might know the word of God" (Alma 17:2).

The Savior himself thus spoke to the Nephites concerning the writings of the Old Testament prophets:

And now, behold, I say unto you, that ye ought to search these things. Yea, a commandment I give unto you that ye search these things diligently; for great are the words of Isaiah.

For surely he spake as touching all things concerning my people which are of the house of Israel; therefore it must needs be that he must speak also to the Gentiles.

And all things that he spake have been and shall be, even according to the words which he spake.

Therefore give heed to my words; write the things which I have told you; and according to the time and the will of the Father they shall go forth unto the Gentiles.

And whosoever will hearken unto my words and repenteth and is baptized, the same shall be saved. Search the prophets, for many there be that testify of these things (3 Nephi 23:1-5).

No one of our standard works is of more importance to us than the Doctrine and Covenants. The revelations there recorded were given specifically for our guidance. The degree to which we conform to the law of heaven prescribed therein will determine our place in the heavenly kingdom. Under these circumstances, it would seem that every believing Church member would desire to follow the Lord's directions to:

Search these commandments, for they are true and faithful, and the prophecies and promises which are in them shall all be fulfilled (D&C 1:37).

Treasure these things up in your hearts, and let the solemnities of eternity rest upon your minds (D&C 43:34).

Give diligence to make your calling and election sure: for if ye do these things, ye shall never fall.

2 Peter 1:10

CALLING AND ELECTION •

An address delivered at general conference October 1, 1965.

The theme I have in mind to discuss is "Making One's Calling Election Sure." To do this one must receive a divine witness that he will inherit eternal life. The supreme objective of men who understand God, their relationship to him, and his designs for them is to gain eternal life. This is as it should be, for eternal life "is the greatest of all the gifts of God" (D&C 14:7). To bring men to eternal life is God's work and glory. To this end he conceives, brings into being, directs, and uses all his creations (Moses 1:38, 39).

Eternal life is the quality of life which God himself enjoys. The gospel plan, authored by the Father and put into operation by the atonement of Jesus Christ, brings eternal life within the reach of every man. The Lord gave this assurance when he said, "If you keep my commandments and endure to the end you shall have eternal life" (D&C 14:7).

The fulness of eternal life is not attainable in mortality, but the peace which is its harbinger and which

comes as a result of making one's calling and election
sure is attainable in this life. The Lord has promised
that "he who doeth the works of righteousness shall
receive his reward, even peace in this world and eternal
life in the world to come" (D&C 59:23).

I think the peace here referred to is implied in the
Prophet's statement, "I am going like a lamb to the
slaughter, but I am calm as a summer's morning. I
have a conscience void of offense toward all men" (*History of the Church* 6:555).

I also think it is implicit in this statement of the
late Apostle Alonzo A. Hinckley, which he wrote in a
letter to the First Presidency after he had been advised
by his physician that his illness would be fatal:

> I assure you I am not deeply disturbed over the final results. I am reconciled and I reach my hands to take what my Father has for me, be it life or death. . . .
>
> As to the future, I have no misgivings. It is inviting and glorious, and I sense rather clearly what it means to be saved by the redeeming blood of Jesus Christ and to be exalted by his power and be with him ever more (*Deseret News* Church Section, March 27, 1949, p. 24).

MAKE YOUR CALLING AND ELECTION SURE

Now I come directly to my theme.

I take my text from 2 Peter and, as he did, I direct
my remarks "to them that have obtained like precious
faith with us" (2 Peter 1:1).

Peter, having put the saints in remembrance of
gospel fundamentals, admonished them to "give diligence to make your calling and election sure: for if ye
do these things, ye shall never fall" (2 Peter 1:10).

By making their calling and election sure, the
saints were to gain entrance into the everlasting king-

dom of our Lord and Savior Jesus Christ. To this fact
Peter bore powerful witness. He reviewed his experience on the Mount of Transfiguration with James and
John where, he says, they heard the voice of God the
Father declare of Jesus, "This is my beloved Son in
whom I am well pleased." Then by way of instruction
that such an experience did not of itself make one's
calling and election sure, he added, "We have also a
more sure word of prophecy" (Ibid., 1:11, 17, 19).

THE SURE WORD OF PROPHECY

Speaking on Sunday, the 14th day of May, 1843,
the Prophet Joseph Smith took this statement of Peter
for his text. From the Prophet's sermon I quote:

Notwithstanding the apostle exhorts them to add to their
faith, virtue, knowledge, temperance, etc., yet he exhorts them
to make their calling and election sure. And though they had
heard an audible voice from heaven bearing testimony that
Jesus was the Son of God, yet he says we have a more sure
word of prophecy than to hear the voice of God saying, This
is my beloved Son, etc.

[Answering his own question, the Prophet continued]:
Though they might hear the voice of God and know that Jesus
was the Son of God, this would be no evidence that their election and calling was made sure, that they had part with Christ,
and were joint heirs with Him. They then would want that
more sure word of prophecy, that they were sealed in the
heavens and had the promise of eternal life in the kingdom of
God. Then, having this promise sealed unto them, it was an
anchor to the soul, sure and steadfast. Though the thunders
might roll and lightnings flash, and earthquakes bellow, and
war gather thick around, yet this hope and knowledge would
support the soul in every hour of trial, trouble and tribulation. . . .

[Then speaking directly to his listeners, the Prophet continued:] I would exhort you to go on and continue to call upon
God until you make your calling and election sure for yourselves, by obtaining this more sure word of prophecy (*History
of the Church* 5:388-89).

A week later, May 21, 1843, the Prophet preached another sermon on the same text, from which I quote:

We have no claim in our eternal compact, in relation to eternal things, unless our actions and contracts and all things tend to this end. But after all this, you have got to make your calling and election sure. If this injunction would lie largely on those to whom it was spoken [he said], how much more are those of the present generation!

[And then in conclusion] It is one thing to be on the mount and hear the excellent voice, etc., etc., and another to hear the voice declare to you, You have a part and lot in that kingdom (Ibid., 5:403).

These two sermons were given by the Prophet just thirteen months before his martyrdom. Four years earlier, however, he had thus instructed the Twelve:

After a person has faith in Christ, repents of his sins, and is baptized for the remission of his sins and receives the Holy Ghost (by the laying on of hands), which is the first Comforter, then let him continue to humble himself before God, hungering and thirsting after righteousness, and living by every word of God, and the Lord will soon say unto him, Son, thou shalt be exalted. When the Lord has thoroughly proved him, and finds that the man is determined to serve Him at all hazards, then the man will find his calling and his election made sure, then it will be his privilege to receive the other Comforter, which the Lord hath promised the Saints, as is recorded in the testimony of St. John, in the 14th chapter (Ibid., 3:380).

THE PROMISE OF ETERNAL LIFE

In the 88th section of the Doctrine and Covenants is recorded a revelation in which the Lord, addressing some of the early Saints in Ohio, said:

I now send upon you another Comforter, even upon you my friends, that it may abide in your hearts, even the Holy Spirit of Promise; which other Comforter is the same that I promised unto my disciples, as is recorded in the testimony of John.

This Comforter is the promise which I give unto you of eternal life, even the glory of the celestial kingdom (D&C 88:3, 4).

I should think that all faithful Latter-day Saints "would want that more sure word of prophecy, that they were sealed in the heavens and had the promise of eternal life in the kingdom of God" (*History of the Church* 5:388).

As I read the sacred records, I find recorded experiences of men in all dispensations who have had this sure anchor to their souls, this peace in their hearts.

Lehi's grandson Enos so hungered after righteousness that he cried unto the Lord until "there came a voice unto [him from heaven] saying: Enos, thy sins are forgiven thee, and thou shalt be blessed." Years later he revealed the nature of this promised blessing when he wrote:

I soon go to the place of my rest, which is with my Redeemer; for I know that in him I shall rest. And I rejoice in the day when my mortal shall put on immortality, and shall stand before him; then shall I see his face with pleasure, and he will say unto me: Come unto me, ye blessed, there is a place prepared for you in the mansions of my Father (Enos 5:27).

To Alma the Lord said, "Thou art my servant; and I covenant with thee that thou shalt have eternal life" (Mosiah 26:20).

To his twelve Nephite disciples, the Master said:

What is it that ye desire of me, after that I am gone to the Father?
And they all spake, save it were three, saying: We desire that after we have lived unto the age of man, that our ministry, wherein thou has called us, may have an end, that we may speedily come unto thee in thy kingdom.

And he said unto them: Blessed are ye because ye desired this thing of me; therefore, after that ye are seventy and two years old ye shall come unto me in my kingdom; and with me ye shall find rest (3 Nephi 28:1-3).

As Moroni labored in solitude abridging the Jaredite record, he received from the Lord this comforting assurance:

Thou hast been faithful; wherefore, thy garments shall be made clean. And because thou hast seen thy weakness thou shalt be made strong, even unto the sitting down in the place which I have prepared in the mansions of my Father (Ether 12:37).

Paul, in his second epistle to Timothy, wrote:

I am now ready to be offered, and the time of my departure is at hand.
I have fought a good fight, I have finished my course, I have kept the faith;
Henceforth there is laid up for a me a crown of righteousness, which the Lord, the righteous judge, shall give me at that day (2 Timothy 4:6-8).

In this dispensation many have received like assurances. In the spring of 1839, while the Prophet Joseph and his associates were languishing in Liberty Jail, Heber C. Kimball labored against great odds caring for the Saints and striving to free the brethren. On the 6th of April he wrote:

My family having been gone about two months, during which time I heard nothing from them; our brethren being in prison; death and destruction following us everywhere we went; I felt very sorrowful and lonely. The following words came to mind, and the Spirit said unto me, "write," which I did by taking a piece of paper and writing on my knee as follows: . . .
Verily I say unto my servant Heber, thou art my son, in whom I am well pleased; for thou art careful to hearken to my words, and not trangress my law, nor rebel against my servant Joseph Smith, for thou hast a respect to the words of mine anointed, even from the least to the greatest of them; *there-*

fore thy name is written in heaven, no more to be blotted out for ever (Orson F. Whitney, *Life of Heber C. Kimball*, 1888 ed., p. 253; italics added).

To the Prophet Joseph Smith the Lord said:

I am the Lord thy God and will be with thee even unto the end of the world, and through all eternity; for *verily I seal upon you your exaltation, and prepare a throne for you in the kingdom of my Father, with Abraham your father* (D&C 132: 49; italics added).

Now, in conclusion I give you my own witness. I know that God our Father lives; that we are, as Paul said, his offspring. I know that we dwelt in his presence in pre-earth life and that we shall continue to live beyond the grave. I know that we may return into his presence if we meet his terms. I know that while we are here in mortality there is a means of communication between him and us. I know it is possible for men to so live that they may hear his voice and know his words; that to receive the Holy Spirit of promise while here in mortality is possible. And so, in the words of the Prophet Joseph, "I . . . exhort you to go on and continue to call upon God until [by the more sure word of prophecy] you make your calling and election sure for yourselves" (*History of the Church* 5:389), in the name of Jesus Christ. Amen.

SATAN, THE GREAT DECEIVER •

Contributing to society's present desperate sickness is the widely accepted pernicious fallacy that God is dead and the equally pernicious doctrine that there is no devil. Satan himself is the author of these falsehoods. To believe them is to surrender to him. Such surrender has led, and is now leading, men to destruction.

We Latter-day Saints know that God lives. With like certainty we know that Satan lives. The reality of their existence is conclusively established by the scriptures and by human experience.

IN THE BEGINNING

Abraham's account of the earliest specific event of which the scriptures speak—the great pre-earth heavenly council—identifies God, Jesus, Satan, and the spirits of men as participators in that council. In his account Abraham says:

Now the Lord had shown unto me, Abraham, the intelligences that were organized before the world was; . . .
And God . . . stood among those that were spirits, . . . and he said unto me: Abraham, thou art one of them; . . .
And . . . God, . . . said unto those who were with him:

We will go down, for there is space there, and we will take of these materials, and we will make an earth whereon these may dwell;

And we will prove them herewith, to see if they will do all things whatsoever the Lord their God shall command them;

And they who keep their first estate shall be added upon; and they who keep not their first estate shall not have glory in the same kingdom with those who keep their first estate; and they who keep their second estate shall have glory added upon their heads for ever and ever.

And the Lord said: Whom shall I send? And one answered like unto the Son of Man: Here am I, send me. And the Lord said: I will send the first.

And the second was angry, and kept not his first estate; and, at that day, many followed after him (Abraham 3:22-28).

This scripture reveals knowledge concerning things as they were in the distant past; it speaks of God's plans for the creation of this earth to be a dwelling place whereon the spirits, among whom he then stood, could in mortality demonstrate their worth; it refers to the gospel plan and, without naming them, to Christ and Satan.

Amplifying these truths, the Lord said to Moses:

That Satan, whom thou hast commanded in the name of mine Only Begotten, is the same which was from the beginning, and he came before me, saying—Behold, here am I, send me, I will be thy son, and I will redeem all mankind, that one soul shall not be lost, and surely I will do it; wherefore give me thine honor (Moses 4:1).

In this last dispensation the Lord has confirmed what he revealed in these ancient scriptures. To the Prophet Joseph, he said:

The devil was before Adam, for he rebelled against me, saying, Give me thine honor, which is my power; and also a third part of the hosts of heaven turned he away from me because of their agency (D&C 29:36).

In 1832 Joseph Smith and Sidney Rigdon testified that they saw in vision

that an angel of God who was in authority in the presence of
God, who rebelled against the Only Begotten Son, . . . was
thrust down from the presence of God and the Son (D&C
76:25).

The Prophet succinctly summed up the great pre-
earth controversy in these words:

The contention in heaven was—[said he] Jesus said there
would be certain souls that would not be saved; and the devil
said he could save them all, and laid his plans before the grand
council, who gave their vote in favor of Jesus Christ. So the
devil rose up in rebellion against God and was cast down, with
all who put up their heads for him (*Teachings of the Prophet
Joseph Smith*, p. 357).

SATAN COMES TO EARTH

When Satan and his followers were thrust down
from the presence of God and the Son, they came to
earth.

During the vision given to Moses, the Lord said:

Because . . . Satan rebelled against me, and sought to
destroy the agency of man, which I, the Lord God, had given
him, and also, that I should give unto him mine own power;
by the power of mine Only Begotten, I caused that he should
be cast down.

And he became Satan, yea, even the devil, the father of
all lies (Moses 4:3, 4).

In the Garden of Eden, Satan

sought . . . to beguile Eve, for he knew not the mind of God,
wherefore he sought to destroy the world.

And he said unto the woman: Yea, hath God said—Ye
shall not eat of every tree of the garden? (And he spake by
the mouth of the serpent.)

And the woman said unto the serpent: We may eat of the
fruit of the trees of the garden;

But of the fruit of the tree which thou beholdest in the

midst of the garden, God hath said—Ye shall not eat of it, neither shall ye touch it, lest ye die.

And the serpent said unto the woman: Ye shall not surely die;

For God doth know that in the day ye eat thereof, then your eyes shall be opened, and ye shall be as gods, knowing good and evil (Moses 4:5-11).

Not only did Satan tempt Adam and Eve in the Garden; he continued to tempt them and their children after they had been driven from the Garden. When they received the gospel, Adam and Eve rejoiced in it. They

Blessed the name of God, and . . . made all things known unto their sons and their daughters.

And Satan came among them saying: I am also a son of God; and he commanded them, saying: Believe it not; and they believed it not, and they loved Satan more than God. And men began from that time forth to be carnal, sensual, and devilish (Moses 5:12-13).

The record says that years later, in the days of Seth, when

the children of men were numerous upon the face of the land. . . . Satan had great dominion among men, and raged in their hearts; and from thenceforth came wars and bloodshed; and a man's hand was against his brother, in administering death, because of secret works, seeking for power (Moses 6:15).

From then until now Satan has been in the earth. In Job's time

there was a day when the sons of God came to present themselves before the Lord, and Satan came also among them.

And the Lord said unto Satan, Whence comest thou? Then Satan answered the Lord, and said, From going to and fro in the earth, and from walking up and down in it (Job 1:6, 7).

In his diary for August 11, 1831, the Prophet wrote:

After we had encamped upon the bank of the river at McIlwaine's Bend, Brother Phelps, in open vision by daylight,

saw the destroyer in his most horrible power, ride upon the
face of the waters; others heard the noise, but saw not the
vision (*History of the Church* 1:203).

Satan's Purpose and Methods

Satan is evil: totally and always. He ever seeks
to defeat the gospel plan and "destroy the souls of
men" (D&C 10:27). "He persuadeth no man to do
good, no, not one; neither do his angels; neither do they
who subject themselves unto him" (Moroni 7:17).

At the Last Supper, just prior to his ordeal in
Gethsemane, Jesus thus warned Peter: "Simon, Simon,
. . . Satan hath desired to have you, that he may sift
you as wheat" (Luke 22:31).

Satan is irrevocably committed to countering and
overcoming the influence of the Spirit of Christ upon
men. He is the representative, promoter, and advocate of that "opposition in all things" referred to by
Lehi in his instruction to his son Jacob (2 Nephi 2:11,
14-18).

His methods are various, devious, and countless.

By every possible means he seeks to darken the minds of
men and then offers them falsehood and deception in the guise
of truth. Satan is a skillful imitator, and as genuine gospel
truth is given the world in ever-increasing abundance, so he
spreads the counterfeit coin of false doctrine. . . . [As] "the
father of lies" he has . . . become, through the ages of practice
in his nefarious work [such an adept] that were it possible he
would deceive the very elect (Joseph F. Smith in *Latter-day
Prophets Speak*, Daniel H. Ludlow, pp. 20-21).

The devil is an orator; he is powerful; he took our Savior
on to a pinnacle of the Temple, and kept Him in the wilderness for forty days. . . . The devil can speak in tongues; . . . he
can tempt all classes (Joseph Smith in *History of the Church*
3:392).

President John Taylor said:

It is not every revelation that is of God, for Satan has the power to transform himself into an angel of light; he can give visions and revelations as well as spiritual manifestations and table-rappings (John Taylor in *Latter-day Prophets Speak*, p. 22).

We read in the Doctrine and Covenants that he can appear "as an angel of light" (D&C 128:20; 129:8).

At the opening of every gospel dispensation, he has made a frontal attack against the advent of the truth. We have already noted how he deceived the sons and daughters of Adam and Eve in the first dispensation.

At the beginning of the Mosaic dispensation, after he had seen the great vision recorded in Moses chapter one,

the presence of God withdrew from Moses, . . . And as he was left unto himself, he fell unto the earth.

And . . . it was . . . many hours before Moses did again receive his natural strength . . .

[When he did] Satan came tempting him, saying: Moses, son of man worship me.

And . . . Moses looked upon [him] and said: Who art thou . . . that I should worship thee?

For behold, I could not look upon God, except his glory should come upon me, . . . But I can look upon thee in the natural man. . . .

And I can judge between thee and God; for God said unto me: Worship God, for him only shalt thou serve.

Get thee hence, Satan; deceive me not; . . .

And now, when Moses had said these words, Satan cried with a loud voice, and rent upon the earth, and commanded, saying: I am the Only Begotten, worship me.

And it came to pass that Moses began to fear exceedingly; and as he began to fear, he saw the bitterness of hell. Nevertheless, calling upon God, he received strength, and he commanded, saying: Depart from me, Satan, for this one God only will I worship, which is the God of glory.

And now Satan began to tremble, and the earth shook; and Moses received strength, and called upon God, saying: In the name of the Only Begotten, depart hence, Satan.

And it came to pass that Satan cried with a loud voice, with weeping, and wailing, and gnashing of teeth; and he departed . . . from the presence of Moses (Moses 1:9, 10, 12-16, 19-22).

In the days of Jesus, Satan attacked the Master himself. Luke says that

Jesus . . . was led by the Spirit into the wilderness.

Being forty days tempted of the devil. And in those days he did eat nothing: and when they were ended, he . . . hungered.

And the devil said unto him, If thou be the Son of God, command this stone that it be made bread.

And Jesus answered him saying, It is written, That man shall not live by bread alone, but by every word of God.

And the devil, taking him up into an high mountain, shewed unto him all the kingdoms of the world. . . .

And . . . said unto him, All this power will I give thee, and the glory of them, . . .

If thou . . . wilt worship me, all shall be thine.

And Jesus answered and said unto him, Get thee behind me, Satan: for it is written, Thou shalt worship the Lord thy God, and him only shalt thou serve.

And he brought him to Jerusalem, and set him on a pinnacle of the temple, and said unto him, If thou be the Son of God, cast thyself down from hence:

For it is written, He shall give his angels charge over thee, . . .

And in their hands they shall bear thee up, lest at any time thou dash thy foot against a stone.

And Jesus answering said unto him, It is said, Thou shalt not tempt the Lord thy God.

And when the devil had ended all the temptation he departed from him for a season (Luke 4:1-13).

That Satan was present and contested the opening of this last dispensation, we learn from the Prophet's statement:

I was seized upon by some power which entirely overcame me, and had such an astonishing influence over me as to bind my tongue so that I could not speak. Thick darkness gathered around me, and it seemed to me for a time as if I were doomed to sudden destruction.

. . . Not to an imaginary ruin but [by] the power of some actual being from the unseen world, who had such marvelous power as I had never before felt in any being (Joseph Smith 2:15, 16).

Satan's attack against the coming forth of the Book of Mormon is detailed in the 10th section of the Doctrine and Covenants. Speaking to the Prophet in that revelation, the Lord said:

Because you have delivered the writings [the 116 manuscript pages of the Book of Mormon] into [the] hands of [Martin Harris], wicked men have taken them from you.

And, behold, Satan hath put it into their hearts to alter the words which you have caused to be written, . . .

And, on this wise, the devil has sought to lay a cunning plan, that he may destroy this work; . . .

He has put it into their hearts to get thee to tempt the Lord thy God, in asking to translate it over again.

And then, behold, they say and think in their hearts—

. . . If God giveth him power again, . . . [to bring] forth the same words, behold, we have the same with us, and we have altered them;

Therefore they will not agree, and we will say that he has lied in his words and that he has no gift, and that he has no power;

Therefore, we will destroy him, and also the work; . . .

Verily, verily, I say unto you, that Satan has great hold upon their hearts, . . .

Satan stirreth them up, that he may lead their souls to destruction.

And thus he has laid a cunning plan, thinking to destroy the work of God; . . .

And thus he flattereth them, and leadeth them along until he draggeth their souls down to hell;

And thus he goeth up and down, to and fro in the earth, seeking to destroy the souls of men (D&C 10:5, 8, 10, 12, 15-20, 22, 23, 26, 27).

Another evidence of Satan's effort to thwart the spread of the gospel in this dispensation was his encounter with the brethren who took the gospel to England in 1837. Heber C. Kimball says that Saturday evening, July 29th, 1837,

it was agreed that I should go forward and baptize, the next morning, in the river Ribble, which runs through Preston. . . .

Sunday, July 30th, about daybreak, Elder Isaac Russell . . . who slept with Elder Richards . . . , came up to the third story, where Elder Hyde and myself were sleeping, and called out, "Brother Kimball, I want you should get up and pray for me that I may be delivered from the evil spirits that are tormenting me to such a degree that I feel I cannot live long, unless I obtain relief."

I had been sleeping on the back of the bed. I immediately arose, slipped off at the foot of the bed, and passed around to where he was. Elder Hyde threw his feet out, and sat up in the bed, and we laid hands on him, I being mouth, and prayed that the Lord would have mercy on him, and rebuked the devil.

While thus engaged, I was struck with great force by some invisible power, and fell senseless on the floor. The first thing I recollected was being supported by Elders Hyde and Richards, who were praying for me; Elder Richards having followed Russell up to my room. Elders Hyde and Richards then assisted me to get on the bed, but my agony was so great I could not endure it, and I arose, bowed my knees and prayed. I then arose and sat up on the bed, when a vision was opened to our minds, and we could distinctly see the evil spirits, who foamed and gnashed their teeth at us. We gazed upon them about an hour and a half. . . . We were not looking towards the window, but towards the wall. Space appeared before us, and we saw the devils coming in legions, with their leaders, who came within a few feet of us.

They came towards us like armies rushing to battle. They appeared to be men of full stature, possessing every form and feature of men in the flesh, who were angry and desperate; and I shall never forget the vindictive malignity depicted on their countenances as they looked me in the eye; and any attempt to paint the scene which then presented itself, or portray their malice and enmity, would be vain. I perspired exceedingly, my clothes becoming as wet as if I had been taken out of the river.

I felt excessive pain, and was in the greatest distress for some time. I cannot even look back on the scene without feeling of horror; yet by it I learned the power of the adversary, his enmity against the servants of God, and got some understanding of the invisible world. We distinctly heard those spirits talk and express their wrath and hellish designs against us. However, the Lord delivered us from them and blessed us exceedingly that day.

Elder Hyde's supplemental description of that fearful scene is as follows (taken from a letter addressed to President Kimball) :

Every circumstance that occurred at that scene of devils is just as fresh in my recollection at this moment as it was at the moment of its occurrence, and will ever remain so. After you were overcome by them and had fallen, their awful rush upon me with knives, threats, imprecations and hellish grins, amply convinced me that they were no friends of mine. While you were apparently senseless and lifeless on the floor and upon the bed (after we had laid you there), I stood between you and the devils and fought them and contended with them face to face, until they began to diminish in number and to retreat from the room. The last imp that left turned round to me as if to apologize, and appease my determined opposition to them, "I never said anything against you!" I replied to him thus: "It matters not to me whether you have or have not; you are a liar from the beginning! In the name of Jesus Christ, depart!" He immediately left, and the room was clear. That closed the scene of devils for that time.

Years later, narrating the experience of that awful morning to the Prophet Joseph, Heber asked him what it all meant and whether there was anything wrong with him that he should have such a manifestation.

"No, Brother Heber," he replied, "at that time you were nigh unto the Lord; there was only a veil between you and Him, but you could see Him. When I heard of it, it gave me great joy, for I knew that the work of God had taken root in that land. It was this that caused the devils to make a struggle to kill you" (Orson F. Whitney, *Life of Heber C. Kimball*, pp. 143-146).

SATAN'S SUCCESS

As a deceiver, Satan has had great success.

1. He succeeded in deceiving Eve (Moses 4:5-19).

2. He succeeded with Cain. When his parents, Adam and Eve, taught him the gospel, he rejected their words,

saying, Who is the Lord that I should know him? . . .
And Cain loved Satan more than God (Moses 5:16, 18).
And Cain went into the field, and Cain talked with Abel, his brother. And it came to pass that while they were in the field, Cain rose up against Abel, his brother, and slew him (Moses 5:32).

Enoch beheld in vision that

the power of Satan was upon all the face of the earth.
And he saw angels descending out of heaven; and he heard a loud voice saying: Wo, wo be unto the inhabitants of the earth.
And he beheld Satan; and he had a great chain in his hand, and it veiled the whole face of the earth with darkness; and he looked up and laughed, and his angels rejoiced (Moses 7:24-26).

On this pattern did Satan promote wickedness during antediluvian times, until the Lord had to bring in the floods and cleanse the earth by water.

In ancient America Satan led two mighty civilizations—the Jaredites and Nephites—to utter destruction by internecine war.

Following the mortal ministry of Jesus and his apostles, Satan literally drove the Church of Christ from the earth.

LIMITATIONS ON SATAN'S POWER

But notwithstanding Satan's successes, he has no power over men except as they surrender to him.

Men are free according to the flesh [said Lehi] and all things are given them which are expedient unto man. And they are free to choose liberty and eternal life, through the great mediation of all men, or to choose captivity and death, according to the captivity and power of the devil; for he seeketh that all men might be miserable like unto himself (2 Nephi 2:27).

Jacob, the son of Lehi, thus admonished his people "Cheer up your hearts, and remember that ye are free to act for yourselves—to choose the way of everlasting death or the way of eternal life" (2 Nephi 10:23).

To the saints of his day, James wrote: "Resist the devil, and he will flee from you" (James 4:7).

Earlier in these remarks we noted how Satan fled from the presence of Moses.

President George Albert Smith used to say that there is a well-defined line between the territory of the Lord and that of the devil; that when one stays on the Lord's side of the line, the devil cannot cross over. It is when we get into his territory that he takes possession of us.

The Prophet Joseph Smith declared: "The devil has no power over us, only as we permit him. The moment we revolt at anything which comes from God, the devil takes over" (*Teachings of the Prophet Joseph Smith*, p. 181).

We can all profit by heeding this admonition given by Samuel the Lamanite:

And now remember, remember my brethren, that whosoever perisheth, perisheth unto himself; and whosoever doeth iniquity, doeth it unto himself; for behold, ye are free; ye are permitted to act for yourselves; for behold, God hath given unto you a knowledge and he hath made you free.

He hath given unto you that ye might know good from evil, and he hath given unto you that ye might choose life or death; and ye can do good and be restored unto that which is good, or have that which is good restored unto you; or ye can do evil, and have that which is evil restored unto you (Helaman 14:30, 31).

IN CONCLUSION

The general acceptance of Satan's declaration "I'm no devil, for there is none" (2 Nephi 28:22) accounts in large measure for the decadence in our deteriorating society.

We must not be deceived by the sophistries of men declaring the non-existence of Satan. He does exist. He is a real person with great power, and we had better believe it. He and his countless followers, seen and unseen, are exercising a controlling influence upon men and their affairs in our world today.

An ancient American prophet, visioning our day and observing what is now going on among us, warned that if Satan is not checked he will bring this generation to destruction. Addressing himself to our present situation, Nephi said:

The kingdom of the devil must shake, and they which belong to it must needs be stirred up unto repentance, or the devil will grasp them with his everlasting chains, and they be stirred up to anger, and perish;

For behold, at that day shall he rage in the hearts of the children of men, and stir them up to anger against that which is good.

And others will he pacify, and lull them away into carnal security, that they will say: All is well in Zion; yea, Zion prospereth, all is well—and thus the devil cheateth their souls, and leadeth them away carefully down to hell.

And behold, others he flattereth away and telleth them there is no hell; and he saith unto them: I am no devil, for there is none—and thus he whispereth in their ears, until he grasps them with his awful chains, from whence there is no deliverance (2 Nephi 28:19-22).

Now I am not calling attention to these things to frighten or discourage you. I refer to them because I know they are true, and I am persuaded that if we are to "conquer Satan and . . . escape the hands of the servants of Satan who do uphold his work" (D&C 10: 5), we must understand and recognize the situation as it is. This is no time for us to bury our heads in the sand, to equivocate or panic. The difficulties of our times have not caught us unawares. A hundred and forty years ago the Lord clearly revealed the tenor of our times. We know that as the second coming of the Savior approaches, the tempo of Satan's campaign for the souls of men is being, and will continue to be, accelerated. We know that the experiences of the intervening years will try men's souls.

We are fortified for the ordeal, however, by our knowledge that God lives; and his "eternal purposes . . . shall roll on, until all his promises shall be fulfilled" (Mormon 8:22). We know that, to qualify us to prevail against Satan and his wicked hosts, the gospel of Jesus Christ has been restored in these latter days. We know that the Spirit of Christ and the power of his priesthood is an ample shield to the power of Satan. We know that there is available to each of us the gift of the Holy Ghost—the power of revelation—which embraces the gift of discernment by which we may unerringly detect the devil and the counterfeits he is so successfully foistering upon this gullible generation. Our course is clear and certain. It is to strictly

obey the commandments of the Lord as they are recorded in the scriptures and given by the living
prophets.

In conclusion, I bear my witness to the truth of
the things I have called your attention to in these remarks.

I know that God lives. Through my own experiences I have come to know of his Spirit and his power.
I know also that Satan lives. I have detected his spirit
and felt his power—not to the extent the Prophet
Joseph did, but in like manner.

I know that at the second advent of Christ, the
signs of which are mounting, "Satan shall be bound"
and "have no place in the hearts of the children of men"
(D&C 45:44).

I bear further witness to the truth of the Savior's
prediction that at the time of his coming

they that are wise and have received the truth, and have tak-
en the Holy Spirit for their guide, and have not been deceived
. . . shall . . . abide the day.

And the earth shall be given unto them for an inheritance; and they shall multiply and wax strong, . . .

For the Lord shall be in their midst, and his glory shall
be upon them, and he will be their king and their lawgiver
(D&C 45:55, 57-59).

That we may take the Holy Spirit for our guide,
recognize Satan, his representatives and their works,
and not be deceived by them, to the end that we may
be partakers of the promised blessings, I humbly pray.

Bring ye all the tithes into the storehouse, that there may be meat in mine house, and prove me now herewith, saith the LORD of hosts, if I will not open you the windows of heaven and pour you out a blessing, that there shall not be room enough to receive it.

Malachi 3:10

BLESSINGS OF AN HONEST TITHE ●

An address delivered to Brigham Young University student body November 5, 1968.

WHAT IS TITHING

A year or so ago while the president of one of our missions in Mexico was sitting in a barber chair, the barber began to talk to him about his finances. He asked the mission president for his advice. The barber was having difficulty paying his bills with his small income.

The mission president said, "Well, I can tell you what I'd tell members of my church, and what I do tell them when they ask me this question. I tell them the first thing to do is to pay their tithing."

"What is tithing?" asked the barber.

After listening to the mission president's explanation, he exploded, "Well, that's just great, isn't it! I come to you with a question as to how I can pay my bills with the little I make, and you come up with a fancy new idea of how I can spend the first ten percent of it!"

A DIVINE OBLIGATION AND A BLESSING

If he had understood and had had faith in the gospel of Jesus Christ, he would have recognized the wisdom of the mission president's counsel. He would have known that in paying tithing he would be obeying a divine law, upon compliance with which great blessings are predicated. He would have known that in paying tithing he would have been discharging an obligation which he owed to his Maker.

In 1838 the Lord revealed the law of tithing. Four years earlier he had withdrawn the commandment that the Saints live the United Order. This had left them without a revenue law, and the Church was having grave financial difficulties.

Under these circumstances an answer was given to the supplication of the Prophet Joseph Smith: "O Lord show, unto thy servants how much thou requireth of the properties of thy people for a tithing" (head note to Section 119). The Lord answered:

Verily, thus saith the Lord, I require all their surplus property to be put into the hands of the bishop of my church in Zion,

For the building of mine house, and for the laying of the foundation of Zion and for the priesthood, and for the debts of the Presidency of my Church.

And this shall be the beginning of the tithing of my people.

And after that, those who have thus been tithed shall pay one-tenth of all their interest annually; and this shall be a standing law unto them forever, for my holy priesthood, saith the Lord (D&C 119:1-4).

A LEGAL OBLIGATION TO THE LORD

From this scripture it is apparent that tithing is a debt which everyone owes to the Lord for his use of the things that the Lord has made and given to him to use. It is a debt just as literally as the grocery bill, or a light bill, or any other duly incurred obligation. As a matter of fact, the Lord, to whom one owes tithing, is in a position of a preferred creditor. If there is not enough to pay all creditors, he should be paid first. Now I am sure this sounds a little shocking, but it is the truth. Other creditors of tithe-payers, however, need not worry, for the Lord always blesses the person who has faith enough to pay his tithing so that his ability to pay his other creditors is not thereby reduced.

As an acknowledgment, and in return for his bounty, the Lord requires us to return to him as tithing ten percent of our interest annually. In the law of the gospel, tithing is, then, as has already been said, a legal obligation. It is not a mere freewill offering. And although the Lord does not enforce it as we enforce the payment of debts in our society by foreclosing the mortgage or turning off the water or the lights, a penalty for nonpayment is always exacted.

The Lord has prepared all earthly blessings for his children; he has given them the law of tithing, and he has made known the great rewards incident to its payment. In the exercise of their agency, men themselves decide whether to pay or not to pay tithing. This is their option, but there is an option they do not have —they cannot refuse to pay tithing and receive the blessings promised the tithe-payer.

Is Tithing Worthwhile?

In light of these fundamental principles, what do you think about the payment of tithing? Do you think it is worthwhile? I think it is on several counts. To begin with, I consider it as a sound financial investment. For to those who will pay their tithing, the Lord has said that he will open you the windows of heaven, and pour you out a blessing, that there shall not room enough to receive it.

And I will rebuke the devourer for your sakes, and he shall not destroy the fruits of your ground; neither shall your vine cast her fruit before the time in the field, saith the LORD.

. . . And all nations shall call you blessed: for ye shall be a delightsome land, saith the LORD of hosts (Malachi 3:10-12).

A SOUND FINANCIAL INVESTMENT

That this promise of a material reward has universal application is evidenced by the fact that it was repeated by the resurrected Savior himself to the Nephites, and by the further fact that he instructed the Nephites to write it in their records so that it might come to us in the Book of Mormon (see 3 Nephi 24:8-11).

Furthermore, when Moroni visited the Prophet Joseph Smith on the evening of September 21, 1823, he quoted to him part of the third chapter in Malachi, in which chapter this promise is made. In harmony with this scripture, I have heard President J. Reuben Clark, a modern prophet, say over and over again that the Lord would never let one of his Saints who had been faithful in the payment of tithes and offerings go without the necessities of life.

That the Lord faithfully fulfills his promise in this respect is witnessed by all people who obey the law. The record is uniform as far back as 700 B.C.

Hezekiah at that time commanded the people who dwelt in Jerusalem to pay their tithes and offerings. The children of Israel brought in abundance the tithe of all things and laid them by heaps, and when Hezekiah questioned the priests and the Levites concerning the heaps, Azariah, the chief priest, answered him and said, "Since the people began to bring the offerings into the house of the Lord, we have had enough to eat, and have left plenty: for the Lord hath blessed his people; and that which is left is this great store" (see 2 Chronicles 31:2-10).

I myself, and no doubt you also, have heard many people tell of temporal blessings resulting from the payment of tithing. I bear you my witness that payment of tithing is a sound financial investment.

WORTHWHILE FIRE INSURANCE

Second, the payment of tithing is worthwhile as fire insurance. Through his prophets the Lord has told us that incident to his second coming, which we are now anticipating, there will be a great conflagration. Malachi thus refers to it in connection with his pronouncement about tithes and offerings:

For, behold, the day cometh, that shall burn as an oven; and all the proud, yea, and all that do wickedly, shall be stubble: and the day that cometh shall burn them up, saith the LORD of hosts, that it shall leave them neither root nor branch (Malachi 4:1).

This prophecy was quoted by Jesus to the Nephites (see 3 Nephi 25:1, 2) and, with slight variation, by Moroni to Joseph Smith. In September 1831 the Lord in a revelation made this further reference to the burning which will accompany his second coming:

Behold, now it is called today until the coming of the Son of Man, and verily it is a day of sacrifice, and a day for the tithing of my people; for he that is tithed shall not be burned at his coming.

For after today cometh the burning . . . for verily I say, tomorrow all the proud and they that do wickedly shall be as stubble; and I will burn them up, for I am the Lord of Hosts; and I will not spare any that remain in Babylon.

Wherefore, if ye believe me, ye will labor while it is called today [That is, if you believe this, you will pay your tithing.] (D&C 64:23-25).

Names Not on the Records

About fourteen and a half months after this revelation was given, the Lord gave this additional warning:

It is contrary to the will and commandment of God that those who receive not their inheritance by consecration, agreeable to his law, which he has given, that he may tithe his people, to prepare them against the day of vengeance and burning, should have their names enrolled with the people of God (D&C 85:3).

How would you like to have your name stricken off the records?

Neither is their genealogy to be kept, or to be had where it may be found on any of the records or history of the church.

Their names shall not be found, neither the names of the fathers, nor the names of the children written in the book of the law of God, saith the Lord of Hosts (D&C 85:4, 5).

Consequences of Failure to Obey

Now I am, of course, aware that these quotations from sections 64 and 85 of the Doctrine and Covenants refer to the tithe prescribed in the law of consecration. However, failure to obey the law of tithe by which we are now bound is fraught with like consequences. This is evident from the fact that the Lord said, with respect to the law which is binding upon us today:

Verily I say unto you, it shall come to pass that all those who gather unto the land of Zion shall be tithed of their surplus properties, and shall observe this law, or they shall not be found worthy to abide among you.

And I say unto you, if my people observe not this law, to keep it holy and by this law sanctify the land of Zion unto me, . . . behold, . . . it shall not be a land of Zion unto you.

And this shall be an ensample unto all the stakes of Zion. . . . (D&C 119:5-7).

It is because the Saints in Jackson County were

not able to live the law by which they were to be tithed that the Lord permitted them to be expelled.

OBEDIENCE TO CELESTIAL LAW

Tithing is a part of the celestial law referred to in this revelation. Obedience to it is a prerequisite to being quickened in the resurrection by the fulness of the celestial glory. Without such fulness one coming into the presence of the Lord would be consumed, for God dwells in "eternal burnings."

So you see, my young brethren and sisters, tithing, is in a very real sense, a form of fire insurance—insurance against burning both in this life and in the life to come.

PREREQUISITE TO HIGHER ORDINANCES

A third reason for paying tithing is that to do so helps to qualify one to receive the higher ordinances of the priesthood. Just over three months after the martyrdom of the Prophet Joseph, in an epistle of the Twelve to the Church, President Brigham Young said:

Yes, brethren, we verily know and bear testimony, that a cloud of blessing and endowment, and of the keys of the fulness of the priesthood, and of things pertaining to eternal life, is hanging over us, and ready to burst upon us; or upon as many as live worthy of it, so soon as there is a place found on earth to receive it. [At this time they were building the Nauvoo temple in which they were looking forward to obtaining their endowments.] Therefore [President Young continued], let . . . no man or set of men . . . draw your minds away from this all important work. But enter steadily and regularly upon a strict observance of the law of tithing, and of freewill offerings [you see, he distinguishes between tithing and freewill offerings—tithing is a law], till Jehovah shall say it is enough; your offerings are accepted: then come up to the House of the Lord, and be taught in his ways, and walk in his paths (*History of the Church* 7:281-82).

In a conference seven days later President John Taylor, then a member of the Council of the Twelve, said:

One of the clerks had asked whether any should be baptized [for the dead] who had not paid their tithing; [and his answer was] it is our duty to pay our tithing, one-tenth of all we possess, and then one-tenth of the increase, and a man who has not paid his tithing is unfit to be baptized for his dead. . . . It is our duty to pay our tithing. If a man has not faith enough to attend to these little things, he has not faith enough to save himself and his friends (Ibid., 7:292-93).

At that time, and ever since, the payment of tithing has been one of the evidences that a person is worthy of temple endowments. And well it might be, for as President Stephen L Richards once said, speaking of tithing:

I feel certain that it is not only the test, the acid test, of true loyalty and devotion, but that it is likewise the greatest of the developers of true spiritual allegiance. It has been said that you can tell what a man thinks of a cause by the way he puts his money into it. Talk is cheap. It has never caused any particular wear and tear upon the jaw and they say that the tongue is the only organ of the body that never gives out, so that all our protestations by word of mouth are easily given, but when a man puts his hand down in his pocket and takes out the hard-earned money that comes from his labor, and devotes that to the establishment of a cause, you know without further evidence that he is sincere (BYU Leadership Week, 1939).

THE LORD'S REVENUE SYSTEM

Although, as Dr. Talmage has said:

Tithing is the Lord's revenue system [which might be cited as a fourth reason for paying it], and He requires it of the people, not because He is lacking in gold or silver, but because they [we] need to pay it . . . the prime or great purpose behind the establishment of the law of the tithe is the development of the soul of the tithe-payer, rather than the providing of revenue. The latter is an all-important purpose, for so far as money is needed for the carrying on of the work of the Church the Lord requires money that is sanctified by the faith of the giver; but blessings beyond estimate, as gaged by the coin of the realm, are assured unto him who strictly conforms to the law of the tithe *because the Lord so commanded* (*Articles of Faith,* p. 526-28).

As is true with respect to all of God's commandments, the payment of tithing brings a peace and happiness unknown to the defaulter.

PAY AN HONEST TITHING

My plea this day to all members of the Church is: Pay an honest tithing and be blessed, and don't quibble over the amount you should pay. In the words attributed to President Young: "We do not ask anybody to pay tithing unless they are disposed to do so, but if you pretend to pay tithing, pay it like honest men" (*Journal of Discourses* 8:202).

PRESIDENT BRIGHAM YOUNG

Evidently Brother Brigham had heard a lot of quibbling, for he said in the October conference in 1844:

There has been so much inquiry it becomes irksome: the law is for a man to pay one-tenth of all he possesses for the erecting of the House of God, the spread of the gospel, and the support of the priesthood. When a man comes into the church he wants to know if he must reckon his clothing, bad debts, lands, etc. It is the law to give one-tenth of what he has got, and then one-tenth of his increase or one-tenth of his time (*History of the Church* 7:301).

Three months later he said, in a letter from the Twelve to the Church:

It is the duty of all saints to tithe themselves one-tenth of all they possess when they enter into the new and everlasting covenant; and then one-tenth of their interest, or income yearly afterwards (Ibid., p. 358).

Brother Young said on another occasion (I struck it out of my speech, but I think I will say it anyhow), "They say we cut people off the Church for not paying tithing; we never have yet, but they ought to be. God does not fellowship them" (*Discourses of Brigham Young*, 1951 edition, p. 177).

President Heber J. Grant

Before you quibble about how much tithing you owe, think about this statement of President Grant's:

I have found a great many people who do not know what their tithing is. I have never met people of that kind but what I believe if I were in partnership with them and they had a tenth interest in that partnership, they would know pretty well what that tenth was. I do not think they would have any difficulty whatever in finding how much I owed them. So I am inclined to think that if we wanted to, we would have no difficulty in finding out what is one-tenth of our income, and that is what we owe to the Lord (*Improvement Era*, Jan. 1941).

Now I am thoroughly persuaded that we could all profit by developing within ourselves the spirit which President Grant always evidenced toward this divine law of tithing. For a glimpse of that spirit, I call attention to the remarks he made in the 1899 October conference.

President Lorenzo Snow

In that conference President Snow, after telling of the increase of tithing paid by the Saints in 1899 over what they had paid in 1898 (you remember that it was at this time that President Snow had the revelation down in St. George as to how the Church should get out of debt by paying tithing), continued:

God bless the Latter-day Saints. I want to have this principle so fixed [he was referring to the principle of tithing] upon our hearts that we shall never forget it. As I have said more than once, I know that the Lord will forgive the Latter-day Saints for their past negligence in paying tithing, if they will now repent and pay a conscientious tithing from this time on.

PRESIDENT GRANT IN 1899

President Grant at that time was a young apostle, and in his conference talk he said:

I wish to bear my testimony to the Latter-day Saints that all of us who will obey the commandments of God will be prospered in the land. Sacrifice doth bring forth the blessings of heaven. I bear testimony to the truth of what Brother Lund has said today, that if the people will pay their tithes and offerings, they will not only be blessed in their material affairs, but they will be abundantly blessed with increased outpouring of the Spirit of the Lord. . . .

I bear witness to you, as an Apostle of the Lord Jesus Christ, that material and spiritual prosperity is predicated upon the fulfillment of the duties and responsibilities that rest upon us as Latter-day Saints. [Then this.] *I have rejoiced exceedingly that the debts which the people owe to the Lord in tithing have been forgiven by the Prophet of God. But I want to say to those who are able to pay those debts, it will be a great deal better for them if they will do so, notwithstanding, they have been forgiven* (*Conference Report*, Oct. 1899; italics added).

Great courage that man had and a great spirit!

TRUTH IN THE LORD'S PROMISES

Now I bear you my testimony, brothers and sisters, that I know this matter of tithing is a great principle and that blessings come from it. My parents taught me to pay tithing, and in the words of Enos I say to their honor, "Blessed be the name of my God for it" (Enos 1).

President Wilkinson mentioned as he was introducing me this morning that we were refugees from Mexico. During the years that followed, Father had a real time—a difficult time getting enough food to feed his family. I remember about two years after we came out of Mexico (that would be about 1914) Father got a job in Oakley, Idaho, teaching in the Cassia Academy for eighty dollars a month.

When Father and his brother came out of Mexico, they both had large families. Knowing that they would have a difficult time making a living (they brought nothing out of Mexico except what they could bring in one trunk), they joined together and pooled their earnings. After a short stay in El Paso, Texas, they went together to Los Angeles, California, where they worked as carpenters. Later they moved to Oakley, Idaho, where they could raise their families in a Latter-day Saint environment.

When one of them was out of work, they divided the income of the other and thus eked out an existence for both families. My uncle got out of work one winter in Idaho. That left them the eighty dollars that my father received for teaching with which to support about seventeen people. They had to pay rent; they had to buy everything they ate and they had to buy fuel, except that I went out on the side hill and dug the sagebrush from under the snow for fuel. I kept warm digging and Mother kept warm poking it into the stove. The rest of them nearly froze.

The question came up in the family council—did Father pay tithing on that eighty dollars? If he didn't, he would have forty dollars a month to care for the family; if he did, it would be cut down by four dollars and he would have thirty-six a month. I remember that council. I remember that they decided they would pay their tithing, and I remember that they sent me with the tithing to the bishop. It was cold, and I didn't have warm clothes and I wondered what really had gone wrong with Father. I learned from that—the training of my parents—that there is truth in the Lord's promises.

A Personal Experience

I know that you have a great feeling if you live that law. As I say, I give credit to my parents. I remember that after we were married—my wife and I— I was working my way through school, working at the post office eight hours a day, and carrying a full course of law. We had lost a baby and had a large hospital bill. I decided to quit the post office and start the practice of law. I quit in September and failed to pay tithing in September because I had built up a retirement benefit with the government that was to be paid to me in November with which I felt I could pay my tithing. But it didn't come in November and it didn't come in December. I had to report that year to my bishop that I had not paid a full tithe. But I did not feel good about it, so I kept a record and paid it in installments at eight percent interest until I had paid the deficit in full. I had a good feeling after I got it paid. I knew the Lord had understood and accepted my performance.

I tell you now that I know from my own experience, and I bear you my witness as an apostle of the Lord Jesus Christ—a special witness which I am happy to bear to all the world under any circumstance—that there is a peace and a comfort and assurance which come to one who will pay an honest tithing, a liberal tithing. If you ever come to a time when you do not know how much you owe, pay a little more. It is better to pay too much than too little.

A BLESSING

Now the Lord bless you. I have heard about your faithfulness in this matter. Continue faithful; don't ever fail. We are living for *eternal life*. We are not here at this university just to learn how to make a living in this life; we are here to learn how to prepare for eternal lives. When you get where I am now, on the sunset side of the slope, and the days are drawing near when you won't be here and need the things of this world any longer, it will be a wonderful thing to have a record that you can rely upon to give you a place in the presence of our Father in heaven with the righteous of all ages. This you can obtain by observing faithfully day by day and year by year the law of tithing and the other simple practices of the gospel of Jesus Christ.

I leave my blessing with you and pray that God our Father will give you the ability to live so that you may fulfill the purposes of this life and come back into his presence. In the name of Jesus Christ. Amen.

To obey is better than sacrifice, and to hearken than the fat of rams.

For rebellion is as the sin of witchcraft, and stubbornness is as iniquity and idolatry.

1 Samuel 15:22, 23

OBEDIENCE •

An address delivered at general conference October 1946.

THE PRINCIPLE OF OBEDIENCE

I want to say a word about the principle of obedience, and I pray that the Lord will bring the thoughts to my mind in organized fashion. We who are here have great hopes for peace in this world and exaltation in the presence of God in the world to come. That is our objective. We hope for something more than the rest of the world hopes for in this respect. We are no better than the rest of the world, let me say, except to the degree to which we accept the commandments of the Lord and obey them. But we have great hopes that we can gain an exaltation in the presence of our Heavenly Father.

It is my firm conviction, however, that the only saving hope we have in this matter is that hope which is based upon a faith strong enough to impel obedience to the things which we know are right. I don't have very much respect for a man who testifies that he has faith in the principle of tithing unless he lives it. Neither do I think his faith will do him any good unless he does pay his tithing. And I almost have contempt for the men who say they have faith in the leadership of this Church who do not follow in their living the things which the leaders of the Church teach them. I refer, of course, to the men whom we sustain as prophets, seers, and revelators.

The principle of obedience to the laws of the gospel is fundamental. It lies at the base. The Prophet Joseph Smith learned it very early in his ministry. He learned it when he went that first morning, after the visits of Moroni, to the Hill Cumorah. He had gone there under the direction of the angel, who had told him that he should have no thought in mind other than to bring to pass the righteousness of God and the accomplishment of his purposes in the earth. Joseph's family was very poor, and as he walked toward the hill, he thought about the intrinsic value of the things that the angel had told him were buried there. He wondered if the plates, or something else to be found with them, could not be used to relieve the poverty of his parents and their family. When he uncovered the box and saw the gold plates, he reached to take them out and received a shock that set him back. He reached again and received a more severe shock. Then the third time, thinking all he needed was physical strength, he reached with all his might to take the plates and received still another shock which sapped his strength, and he cried out, "Why can I not obtain this book?" And unexpectedly to him, the angel said, "Because you have not kept the commandments of the Lord." And then Joseph received a great manifestation that I have not time here to tell you about, but it kept him reminded all the days of his life that he had to obey in order to receive the promised blessings. The angel told him that he could not get the plates then and that he would not be able to get them until he was not only willing to obey the laws of God but also was able to do so.

OBEDIENCE BRINGS BLESSINGS

That is a lesson we all must learn. The Prophet later, through the inspiration of the Lord, stated this principle thus:

There is a law, irrevocably decreed in heaven before the foundations of this world, upon which all blessings are predicated—

And when we obtain any blessing from God, it is by obedience to that law upon which it is predicated (D&C 130:20, 21).

Our obedience, brothers and sisters, must be self-impelled. We should not render obedience because we are forced to do it, or because the bishop is looking, or because the General Authorities are present. We must render obedience because we love righteousness and have a testimony of the truth in our hearts and because we want to go back to our Father in heaven and help take all his children with us.

Furthermore, we ought to obey his commandments as they are given. We ought not to twist and turn and bend them to our will; we ought to obey them as they come from the mouths of these men who sit here on this stand, because they speak for God. If we do not, our faith is vain.

SAUL AND THE AMALEKITES

Now I want to take an example from the Old Testament scripture to illustrate what I have in mind and to help drive this principle home. There was a very wicked clan of people, a nation, who lived in the days of Saul, known as the Amalekites. They had been wicked for a long time. Even back in the days of Father Abraham they had persecuted the people of

God, and he had said, through his prophets, on numerous occasions that when they became ripened in iniquity, they should be destroyed.

That time came in the days of Saul. Through the Prophet Samuel, the Lord told Saul to go and destroy the Amalekites, every one of them and all their livestock. Saul went with his army and destroyed all the people except their king, Agag, whom he spared in violation of the commandment of the Lord. He likewise destroyed all the ordinary livestock, but when he came to the choice sheep and the cattle and the fatlings and the lambs, the pressure of the people who desired to possess them was so great on Saul that he yielded and took them with him as he returned.

The Lord told Samuel what had happened, and Samuel went out to meet Saul, who greeted him with the salutation:

> Blessed be thou of the Lord: I have performed the commandment of the Lord.
> And Samuel said, What meaneth then this bleating of the sheep in mine ears, and the lowing of the oxen which I hear? (1 Samuel 15:13, 14).

Then Saul began to justify himself. He argued that his partial performance was a complete performance and that he had done what the Lord had asked him to do. Samuel called to his attention when he was humble. "When thou wast little in thine own sight," he said, "the Lord took you out of obscurity, and raised you up, and magnified you, and made you king of Israel, and now you have chosen to disobey the commandment of the Lord" (see 1 Samuel 15:17-19). Saul hit on the best excuse he could find when he said that they had brought the cattle and sheep and lambs and fatlings back to offer as sacrifices unto the Lord. He thus claimed to be relying on the commandment to offer sacrifices.

And Samuel said, Hath the Lord as great delight in burnt offerings and sacrifices, as in obeying the voice of the Lord? Behold, to obey is better than sacrifice, and to hearken than the fat of rams.

For rebellion is as the sin of witchcraft, and stubbornness is as iniquity and idolatry. Because thou hast rejected the word of the Lord he hath also rejected thee from being king (1 Samuel 15:22, 23).

That brought something home to Saul. He was being told by the prophet who had anointed him king that he had been rejected because he had not obeyed the Lord. He then showed some regrets. But he did not exhibit that godly sorrow which worketh repentance, but rather the sorrow of the world which worketh death. He asked Samuel to pray with him that he might again prevail with the Lord. Samuel said he could not do that, but at Saul's persistent urging he did so without success, for the Lord did not again accept Saul. You know the sequel. Saul lost his kingdom, and David was chosen to take his place.

FULL OBEDIENCE REQUIRED

Now there are a number of things in this incident which can be applied in our lives today. First, Saul received his directions through the prophet living in his day. We come to conference to receive directions from the living prophets in our day. Second, Saul used his own judgment as to whether he would perform the commandment given to him and decided that he would not do it exactly as he was commanded. And third, when he was called to account, he prevaricated about it. He said, "I have done it."

There is another very interesting thing about this incident. When Samuel confronted Saul with what he had done, Saul said, "Because I feared the people, . . . [I] obeyed their voice." That reminded me of the statement of the Lord in the third section of the Doctrine and Covenants, where he told the Prophet Joseph that he should not have yielded to the persuasions of men. This revelation was given, you will remember, after Martin Harris had lost the one hundred and sixteen manuscript pages of the Book of Mormon translation. With Saul it was the fear of the people, and with the Prophet it was the persuasions of men. The Prophet learned never to yield again.

That is where our temptations come from, my brothers and sisters. The people around us do not believe what the prophets say, and we yield to their arguments. I know, of course, that there is great faith in Israel, and I suppose you do not need this talk, but there are many people who do need it.

The other day I was at a conference not far from here, and a man stood up to talk—a humble middle-aged man who had a house full of children to rear with only a limited amount of means with which to do it. He said, "I want to tell you about a letter I received from my mother." And this is about what she had written in that letter: "My son, for many years I have been looking forward to the time when I would reach my present age in order that I might receive an old-age pension so that I would not need to call upon you for support out of your limited income. And now, just as I reach it, the Church says don't take it. I don't know that I understand all the reasons why the Church says don't take it, but I do know that the Church has always been right. Therefore, please continue to remit each month." And the man said, "I am glad to remit."

ADAM'S IMPLICIT OBEDIENCE

I liked that. I like that spirit and that action. It reminded me of the obedience evidenced by our great progenitor Adam, the first man. He was commanded by the Lord, you remember, after he and Eve had left the Garden to build an altar and offer sacrifice, and he did it. He built an altar and offered sacrifices, and after many days an angel of the Lord stood by Adam and said, "Why dost thou offer sacrifice unto the Lord? And Adam said unto him: I know not, save the Lord commanded me" (Moses 5:6).

What a lesson! Here was a man, a great man. In our understanding, he stands next to the Redeemer of the world. He built an altar and killed the offering and offered it on the altar without knowing why he did it. How men have changed! Had Adam been a modern, he would not have offered that sacrifice until someone had presented to him a human argument which to his mind justified sacrificing the animal rather than putting it in his cold-storage locker.

But, thank goodness, Adam was not a modern. He had faith, a faith which impelled him to obey the commandment of the Lord, and after he had obeyed he learned why the commandment was given. The angel told him that the sacrifice was in the similitude of the sacrifice of the Only Begotten of the Father, and he taught him the principles of the gospel, which Adam accepted and obeyed, thereby receiving all the blessings thereof which he never could have received without that obedience.

As Adam had to obey, so must we. God help us to listen to his living prophets and get their messages and obey them as they are given so that we may gain the great rewards which the Lord holds out to us, I humbly pray in the name of Jesus Christ. Amen.

CHURCH WELFARE — A LIGHT TO THE WORLD •

An address delivered at general conference April 1947, commemorating the entry of the Saints into the Salt Lake Valley 100 years ago.

This entire centennial year we are appropriately dedicating to the honor and memory of our pioneer fathers who a century ago arrived in these mountain valleys after a long and tedious journey. Truly, they played well their important role in the great pioneering drama of this last dispensation.

But that drama did not begin nor did it end with the taming of the wilderness and the subjugation of the desert. The Church is commissioned to hold up a light to the world and a standard for its members in all things pertaining to righteous living and the eternal welfare of men. The Lord made this abundantly clear in March 1831 when he said:

I have sent mine everlasting covenant into the world, to be a light to the world, and to be a standard for my people, and for the Gentiles to seek to it, and to be a messenger before my face to prepare the way before me (D&C 45:9).

The everlasting covenant spoken of in this revelation is the gospel of Jesus Christ, and the keys of the gospel have been committed to the Church. Continuous pioneering—going before and preparing the way for others to follow—is therefore the inescapable responsibility of the Church. Its over-all pioneering assignment, as the revelation states, is to prepare the way for the second advent of the Redeemer.

PIONEERING CONTINUOUS

Much pioneering was done before the Saints crossed the plains; and a beginning was made even before the Church was organized, for a flood of new light and knowledge burst upon the world in the Prophet's first vision. Surely the Prophet Joseph Smith was a mighty pioneer in obtaining a knowledge of God and of religious truth. The Church has been a pioneer in many other fields, particularly in health and education.

To some extent the pioneering movements of the Church have followed a common pattern. Usually a present need has been felt, to meet which divine guidance has been sought and received, and always the solution has struck at the fundamental issues of the problem involved so that in the process not only has the immediate need been met, but the building of the kingdom of God has also been advanced.

Since pioneering is a continuous responsibility of the Church, we Latter-day Saints of today, if we are true to our heritage and professions, must also be pioneers. I believe that we are. We heard here Friday, in the welfare section of the annual report, something of what has been accomplished during the last ten years and of what is now being done in Church welfare. After thinking of these activities in connection with the pioneer movements of the Church, I am persuaded that the Church today is meeting its pioneering responsibility through its welfare program, and I believe that if we carry it forward to its full possibilities, we shall accomplish a pioneer task in our day and time equal to the one accomplished by the pioneers of 1847.

MEANING OF THE WELFARE PROGRAM

I believe that through the welfare program the Church is attempting to abide by the second commandment, "Thou shalt love thy neighbour as thyself" (Matthew 22:39). I believe that it was for want of such love that the United Order experiment was terminated; that the records will show that the reason was the selfishness and greed of the people; that had the people lived the United Order, we could have had a millennium then, a hundred years ago; that if we do not go forward with the welfare program and live it now, it will be because of our selfishness and greed, and the Lord will take the program away from us; and that in such case the members of the Church a hundred years from now will look back upon our day with the realization of the fact that we could have brought in a millennium if we had but lived this law. When we live it, then only will swords be beat into plowshares and that day of peace arrive.

President Grant characterized it as "one of the greatest and most important things the Church has ever undertaken to put over."

The development of the welfare program has followed the usual pattern. In the first place, it emerged under its present name out of a pressing current need. There has been some criticism of it on this point, as if the function of the Church was not to deal with problems of the day. But how can it be a light to the world if it does not deal with the problems which plague the world?

The Church was dealing with an immediate problem when it undertook the great western trek a century ago. The Prophet Joseph was dealing with a current question when he received his first vision, for others in the community in which he lived, as well as he, wondered which of the contending sects had the truth. It was not the nature of the problem but what was done about it which set the Prophet apart from his fellows and marked him as a pioneer.

In the second place, the welfare plan was inspired by the Lord and is divinely led. President Grant, the prophet through whom the Lord established it under its present name, so considered it. President George Albert Smith has referred to it as the "Lord's great welfare program." President Clark, President McKay, and Elder Harold B. Lee of the Council of the Twelve, all men who stood close to President Grant in the early days of this program, have testified that it was inspired of the Lord, as have others of these men whom we sustain as prophets, seers, and revelators. Of course, acceptance of it as being of divine origin has not been universal. No truth was ever so accepted when first revealed.

APPRECIATION EXPRESSED FOR WELFARE WORKERS

I call to mind a visit from a venerable brother who came to my office some three years ago to protest what some of the brethren had said about Church welfare. In the course of the conversation he said he had emigrated to Utah during the administration of President Wilford Woodruff because that prophet of the Lord had advised it. He thought President Woodruff spoke by the inspiration of God. He also thought that President Snow and President Joseph F. Smith so spoke. I asked him if he thought President Grant, who was, at

the time of our conversation, the president of the
Church, spoke by the inspiration of the Lord, and he
said, "I think he ought to keep his mouth shut about
welfare questions."

It is not so difficult to profess acceptance of the
dead prophets. The real test comes on the acceptance
of what the living ones say, for that requires absolute
sincerity and the courage of one's convictions.

And right here, lest I forget it, let me parentheti-
cally pass along to you, my brethren and sisters who by
the tens of thousands have heard the voice of the Lord
in the welfare program and have accepted it and are
carrying on as true pioneers, my tribute. I express to
you my sincere appreciation.

In this connection, I have record of 3,088 people
who deserve special mention. On the strength of their
belief that the welfare program is the Lord's plan,
1,729 of them have discontinued and 1,359 of them
have refrained from accepting public relief, all against
a tremendous public and private pressure to take it.
From a bishop's letter to me of January 28, 1947, I
quote the following:

A check of the ward record shows me that there have been
thirty-five people who have either stopped taking the old age
pension or have refused it since the plan's inception. There
are also six other families who have accepted the Church
program, each of them being eligible for more than a hundred
dollars a month of government money. Of the forty-one
mentioned who have refused government aid or dole, we are
helping only ten. Only one receives all her sustenance; all
are working except one, who is our present problem. All
forty-one have received some help. I sincerely believe that
the support received by these people which has meant the
most, is moral support. These fine people have accepted the
Church guarantee of help and, while leaning on that promise,
have gone ahead on their own resources very largely, and are
living happy, useful lives.

Financially, we have had to ask for approximately three hundred dollars from the stake and the Presiding Bishopric during the past year, but since we have had three funerals from among the group and severe sickness, we still feel good about it. If our people were to pay an honest fast offering, we should have had hundreds to spare.

The import of the figures given in this letter is tremendous. Of forty-one persons who were receiving public relief, thirty-one of them are now self-sustaining. Only one of the remaining ten needs to be wholly supported. From the resources of this one ward in fast offerings and welfare contributions and through the welfare storehouse, plus just three hundred dollars from some other wards' fast offerings, the public welfare funds are being saved $2,175 a month, or $26,100 a year. You yourself may compute what it would mean by way of a saving from public welfare funds if every ward and stake in the Church made the welfare program function fully. Here indeed is a practical demonstration of the inspiration of the plan.

I doubt not but that thousands of you who are within the sound of my voice can bear truthful witness from your own experiences that the program is divinely led, and I testify that all the rest of you can have that witness for yourselves if you will follow the admonition given by Moroni with respect to the Book of Mormon (see Moroni 10:4, 5).

And although it neither adds to nor detracts from the divine origin of the plan, it is a common experience, while showing visitors through Welfare Square, to hear them express surprise, if not actual amazement, at the program and its accomplishments and to hear them express their conclusions that nothing short of a religious motive and a great spiritual faith could induce people to carry on such an endeavor.

As it does in other things, the Church through its welfare program strikes at the fundamental issues underlying the problems to be solved, for the Church is never an opportunist. It does not deal in half measures. To solve the liquor and tobacco evils, it teaches Church members to abstain from the use of liquor and tobacco. The solution of the Church to social disease is chastity and virtue. To eliminate war, the Church would substitute for hate in the hearts of men and for force, love and meekness.

The Church does likewise in its welfare program. It affords an opportunity for its members, while receiving the help they need, to preserve and develop within themselves through self-effort those pioneer virtues of industry and thrift which are the priceless possessions of every self-respecting person and which are indispensable to man's eternal progression. In this way the Church would conquer idleness and indolence and exalt the poor, saving them from the awful degradation of the temporal political and spiritual bondage into which the panaceas of the world inevitably lead because they neglect the development of these fundamental virtues.

To finance its welfare plan, the Church accepts the freewill offerings and consecrations in cash and services of God-fearing people who are voluntarily seeking to subscribe to the Master's admonition to love one's neighbor as oneself.

FAITH NECESSARY TO CARRY FORWARD THE WORK OF THE CHURCH

Thus the Church, through its welfare program, is not only meeting the immediate problem of supplying the necessities of life for its members, administering to them according to their need, but also at the same time it is building the kingdom of God by pioneering a way in which all men, rich and poor alike, may be brought together as one in love and unity. Certainly the Church in this work is going before and preparing a way for others to follow. It is holding up a light to the world, a standard for its members and for the Gentiles to seek to attain.

And there are among the Gentiles those who are seeking such a light, and some have caught a glimpse of it. Recently an industrialist who had come to Utah to establish a manufacturing industry told me that the thing which first attracted him to Utah was the statement of President Grant in the middle thirties calling upon Church members to avoid the curse of idleness, eschew the dole, give a full day's work for a day's pay, and preserve in their living the pioneer virtues of industry, thrift, and self-respect. He said that those statements sounded to him like a rallying call of a great leader in a disintegrating civilization. Such was his reaction to the battle cry of God's living prophet.

Now, my brothers and sisters, how far shall we go in this modern pioneering work? Shall we succeed? The answer to these questions depends upon how much faith and courage you and I have. You will recall that at the time President Grant characterized it as "one of the greatest and most important things the Church has ever undertaken to put over," he added: "And it will be put over because we have the ability and the power to do it."

For my single self, I am persuaded from all I see and hear in the world of today, and such inspiration as I enjoy bears to me the same witness, that a continuation of our way of life is contingent upon a triumph in the lives of men of the principles of thought and action implemented by the welfare plan. I feel no doubt about the ultimate outcome. To me the unknowns in the

equation are the time it will take and how much suffering will be required to bring us to obedience. For the
Lord has said his "people must needs be chastened until
they learn obedience [to these principles], if it must
needs be, by the things which they suffer" (D&C
105:6).

He also makes it clear that this obedience must
come as a prerequisite to the redemption of Zion (see
D&C 105:1-6). And none of us doubts that Zion will
be redeemed. It is therefore abundantly clear that the
Church, through its welfare plan, is pursuing its over-
all pioneering assignment of being a messenger before
the face of the Lord, preparing the way for his glorious
coming. God grant that we shall not falter. I pray in
the name of Jesus Christ. Amen.

Remember in all things the poor and the needy, the sick and the afflicted, for he that doeth not these things, the same is not my disciple.

D&C 52:40

CARING FOR THE POOR •

Responding to the question "Master, which is the great commandment in the law?" Jesus answered:

Thou shalt love the Lord thy God with all thy heart, and with all thy soul, and with all thy mind.

This is the first and great commandment.

And the second is like unto it, Thou shalt love thy neighbour as thyself.

On these two commandments hang all the law and the prophets (Matthew 22:36-40).

James considered this second commandment, to "love thy neighbour as thyself," to be a "royal law." in his general epistle to the twelve tribes, he wrote: "If ye fulfill the royal law according to the scripture, Thou shalt love thy neighbour as thyself, ye do well" (James 2:8).

While caring for the poor is by no means all that is involved in loving one's neighbor as oneself, it is nevertheless a major obligation inherent in the "royal law." The statement of the law and the obligation to care for the poor are repeatedly associated in the scriptures. The law is first stated in the 19th chapter of Leviticus. In the same chapter, the Lord gave ancient Israel these instructions concerning the care of their poor:

And when ye reap the harvest of your land, thou shalt
not wholly reap the corners of thy fields, neither shalt thou
gather the gleanings of thy harvest.

And thou shalt not glean thy vineyard, neither shalt thou
gather every grape of thy vineyard; thou shalt leave them
for the poor and stranger: I am the Lord your God (Leviticus
19:9, 10).

During the last few weeks it has been my pleasure
to meet with stake and ward welfare workers in many
stakes. Your performance gives me great joy and inspires in me a hope for an early redemption of Zion.
With all my heart, I salute you.

As evidence of your love for your neighbors, you
faithfully carry on your numerous welfare activities.
At the coal mine, in the mills and factories, and in can-
neries you toil. In orchards, fields, and on the ranches
you endure the heat and the cold. On construction jobs
and in sewing rooms you labor. You battle floods and
disease. You sit in council late into the nights, wres-
tling with problems of policy and procedure incident to
your divine service. You find work for the unem-
ployed. In times of distress you administer to the suffering and give comfort to the bereaved.

Freely do you contribute of your means, not alone
in acquiring welfare facilities, but also as a continuing
practice you contribute the cash value of two meals
each month so that your bishops may have not only
commodities with which to warm and feed the cold
and hungry and clothe the naked, but money also with
which to provide their other needs. Your accomplishments during the last twenty years in doing all this
voluntarily and without expectation or hope of personal gain is a modern miracle. It has brought you to
a state of perfection in gospel living unmatched since
the golden Nephite era (4 Nephi 1-3).

As you thus labor for your brethren and sisters, you merit the assurance that you are in very deed ministering to your Redeemer. Such assurance you have in King Benjamin's words: "When ye are in the service of your fellow beings, ye are only in the service of your God" (Mosiah 2:17).

You have it from the Lord himself in this dispensation, for "Inasmuch," said he, "as ye impart of your substance upon the poor, ye will do it unto me" (D&C 42:31).

You also have the satisfaction of knowing that you are discharging an obligation which has always been laid upon the members of Christ's Church.

The method of implementation at a given time has varied with the degree of perfection in gospel living attained by the saints. But the obligation to care for the poor has persisted. It is as much a part of the requirements of the gospel of Jesus Christ, and the discharge thereof is certainly a prerequisite to exaltation in the celestial kingdom, as are baptism and the laying on of hands. It has been taught and practiced in some form in every gospel dispensation.

We have already noted what the Lord required of the children of Israel with respect thereto, even as they emerged from four hundred years of slavery. Simple as were the instructions, they contained the two basic principles of every God-given plan for implementing this phase of the "royal law"—first, those who had were to give and, second, those who received were to labor for what they received. It was pursuant to this program that Ruth gleaned in the field of Boaz.

Away back before the flood Enoch, to a generation vexed with wars and bloodshed, taught the gospel of Jesus Christ in mighty power, including the procedure

required by the celestial law in loving one's neighbor
as one's self. Those who believed it, lived it, with the
result that "the Lord came and dwelt with [them] and
they dwelt in righteousness . . . And the Lord called
his people ZION, because they were of one heart and
one mind, and dwelt in righteousness; and there was
no poor among them" (Moses 7:16-18).

Now, my brethren and sisters, they did not remove
the poor from among them by turning them over to be
cared for through some dole system sponsored by the
warring nations. They provided for their own in the
prescribed manner. By full observance of the law of
Enoch, they became equal in all things, temporal and
spiritual, thereby obtaining that "union required by
the law of the celestial kingdom."

When Jesus told the lawyer that in order to inherit
eternal life he must love his neighbor as himself, the
lawyer "said unto Jesus, And who is my neighbour?"
Then Jesus, with consummate teaching skill, responded
with his Good Samaritan parable.

A certain man went down from Jerusalem to Jericho,
[he said] and fell among thieves, which stripped him of his
raiment, and wounded him, and departed, leaving him half
dead.

And by chance there came down a certain priest that way:
and when he saw him, he passed by on the other side.

And likewise a Levite, when he was at the place, came
and looked on him, and passed by on the other side.

But a certain Samaritan, as he journeyed, came where he
was: and when he saw him, he had compassion on him,

And went to him, and bound up his wounds, pouring in
oil and wine, and set him on his own beast, and brought him
to an inn, and took care of him.

And on the morrow when he departed, he took out two
pence, and gave them to the host, and said unto him, Take
care of him; and whatsoever thou spendest more, when I
come again, I will repay thee.

Which now of these three, thinkest thou, was neighbour unto him that fell among the thieves?

And he said, He that shewed mercy on him. Then said Jesus unto him, Go, and do thou likewise (Luke 10:30-37).

How difficult it is for some people to observe this aspect of the "royal law" is illustrated in the encounter Jesus had with the rich young man who asked, "Master, what good thing shall I do, that I may have eternal life?" When Jesus specified a number of things, including "thou shalt love thy neighbour as thyself,"

The young man saith unto him, All these things have I kept from my youth up: what lack I yet?

Jesus said unto him, If thou wilt be perfect, go and sell that thou hast, and give to the poor, and thou shalt have treasure in heaven: and come and follow me.

But when the young man heard that saying, he went away sorrowful: for he had great possessions (Matthew 19:16-22).

Notwithstanding the required sacrifices, the saints of the apostolic church tried to live the law. Being of one heart and one soul, they disposed of their lands and houses and laid the proceeds "at the apostles' feet: and distribution was made unto every man according as he had need" (Acts 4:32-37).

The obligation to care for the poor is taught in the Book of Mormon as impressively as it is in the Bible.

Alma commanded the members of the church in his day that they

should impart of their substance, every one according to that which he had; if he have more abundantly he should impart more abundantly; and of him that had but little, but little should be required; and to him that had not should be given.

And thus they should impart of their substance of *their own free will and good desires towards God*, ...

And this he said unto them, *having been commanded of God* (Mosiah 18:27-29; italics added).

Similar teachings and performances are repeatedly recorded throughout the book.

King Benjamin taught that caring for the poor is essential to retention of remission of one's sins.

And now, . . . for the sake of retaining a remission of your sins from day to day [he said], . . . I would that ye should impart of your substance to the poor, every man according to that which he hath, such as feeding the hungry, clothing the naked, visiting the sick and administering to their relief, both spiritually and temporally, according to their wants (Mosiah 4:26).

Amulek, that great missionary companion of Alma, taught that the efficacy of prayer depended upon one's caring for the needy. After explaining how, by reason of Christ's atonement, mercy satisfied justice for all those who exercise "faith unto repentance," he continued:

Therefore may God grant unto you, my brethren, that ye may begin to exercise your faith unto repentance, that ye begin to call upon his holy name, that he would have mercy upon you;

Yea, cry unto him for mercy; for he is mighty to save.

Yea, humble yourselves, and continue in prayer unto him.

Cry unto him when ye are in your fields, yea, over all your flocks.

Cry unto him in your houses, yea, over all your household, both morning, mid-day, and evening.

Yea, cry unto him against the power of your enemies.

Yea, cry unto him against the devil, who is an enemy to all righteousness.

Cry unto him over the crops of your fields, that ye may prosper in them.

Cry over the flocks of your fields, that they may increase.

But this is not all; ye must pour out your souls in your closets, and your secret places, and in your wilderness.

Yea, and when you do not cry unto the Lord, let your hearts be full, drawn out in prayer unto him continually for your welfare, and also for the welfare of those who are around you.

Now, one would think if a man so prayed he would be a pretty good man, wouldn't he? But Amulek did not think that was enough. He added:

And now behold, my beloved brethren, I say unto you, do not suppose that this is all; for after ye have done all these things, if ye turn away the needy, and the naked, and visit not the sick and afflicted, and impart of your substance, if ye have, to those who stand in need—I say unto you, if ye do not any of these things, behold, your prayer is vain, and availeth you nothing, and ye are as hypocrites who deny the faith.

Therefore, if ye do not remember to be charitable, ye are as dross, which the refiners do cast out, (it being of no worth) and is trodden under foot of men (Alma 34:17-29).

Following Christ's ministry among the Nephites, they lived the "royal law" in its fulness. "Every man did deal justly one with another, and they had all things common among them" (4 Nephi 2, 3).

As is true with respect to all other aspects of the gospel, the Lord has revealed the aforesaid principles anew in this last dispensation.

We learn from and are edified by ancient scriptures. We are bound and will be judged by the modern scriptures. It is therefore imperative that we know what the scriptures of this dispensation teach.

In the first modern revelation concerning the obligation of the Church to care for the poor, the Lord said:

Let every man esteem his brother as himself, and practice virtue and holiness before me.

And again I say unto you, let every man esteem his brother as himself.

For what man among you having twelve sons, and is no respecter of them, and they serve him obediently, and he saith unto the one: Be thou clothed in robes and sit thou here; and to the other: Be thou clothed in rags and sit thou there—and looketh upon his sons and saith I am just?

Behold, this I have given unto you as a parable, and it is even as I am. I say unto you, be one: and if ye are not one ye are not mine (D&C 38:24-27).

To make it plain that he was speaking of temporal needs, the Lord continued:

And now, I give unto the church in these parts a commandment, that certain men among them shall be appointed, . . .
And they shall look to the poor and the needy, and administer to their relief that they shall not suffer (D&C 38:34, 35).

A few weeks later he said:

If thou lovest me . . . thou wilt remember the poor, and consecrate of thy properties for their support. . . .
And inasmuch as ye impart of your substance unto the poor, ye will do it unto me (D&C 42:29-31).

The importance of caring for the poor and needy is dramatically emphasized in the revelation received by the Prophet in Kirtland June 7, 1831, in which the Lord paired off the brethren he was sending to Missouri. These brethren, all but destitute, were to make their way as best they could across four states. The Prophet himself walked almost the whole distance from St. Louis to Independence, a distance of about 300 miles. Nevertheless, and notwithstanding the fact that they were facing these hardships, the Lord thus concluded his instructions to them: "And remember in all things the poor and the needy, the sick and the afflicted, for he that doeth not these things, the same is not my disciple" (D&C 52:40).

Since these brethren in their extremity could not qualify as his disciples without remembering "the poor and the needy, the sick and the afflicted," what will be our plight if we fail to remember them?

In the early 1830's the Lord directed the Saints

to implement the "royal law" by living the United Order. In this they failed.

You will recall that the Lord, explaining to the brethren of Zion's Camp why they could not redeem their brethren who had been evicted from their homes in Jackson County, Missouri, said (I am reading from the 105th section of the Doctrine and Covenants, which was given to the brethren of Zion's Camp after they had been turned back from redeeming Zion):

> Verily I say unto you who have assembled yourselves together that you may learn my will concerning the redemption of mine afflicted people—
>
> Behold, I say unto you, were it not for the transgressions of my people, speaking concerning the church and not individuals, they might have been redeemed even now.
>
> But behold, they have not learned to be obedient to the things which I required at their hands, but are full of all manner of evil, and do not impart of their substance, as becometh saints, to the poor and afflicted among them;
>
> And are not united according to the union required by the law of the celestial kingdom;
>
> And Zion cannot be built up unless it is by the principles of the law of the celestial kingdom; otherwise I cannot receive her unto myself.
>
> [And then this statement] And my people must needs be chastened until they learn obedience, if it must needs be, by the things which they suffer (D&C 105:1-6).

Thus, because they did not learn to impart of their substance as becometh saints to the poor and afflicted among them, the Lord permitted them to be driven from Missouri, and the requirement that they live the United Order was withdrawn. But the "royal law" was not withdrawn. It remained in full force. At least partially to fulfill it, the Saints since then have been bound by the law of tithing and the "fast."

In the 1930's, just a century following the United Order experiment, the Lord inspired the inauguration of the present Church welfare plan. In it we are being given another opportunity to show our metal, to stand up and be counted, to prove ourselves worthy—or unworthy, as the case may be—of rising toward a fuller compliance with the "royal law."

The Lord has given us specific instruction as to how we must provide for the poor in this, our day, and he has left no doubt about the dire consequences if we fail to so provide. Here is what he said:

I, the Lord stretched out the heavens, and built the earth, my very handiwork; and all things therein are mine.

And it is my purpose to provide for my saints, for all things are mine.

But it must needs be done in mine own way; and behold this is the way that I, the Lord, have decreed to provide for my saints, that the poor shall be exalted, in that the rich are made low.

For the earth is full, and there is enough and to spare; yea, I prepared all things, and have given unto the children of men to be agents unto themselves.

Therefore, if any man shall take of the abundance which I have made, and impart not his portion, according to the law of my gospel, unto the poor and the needy, he shall, with the wicked, lift up his eyes in hell, being in torment (D&C 104:14-18).

According to my understanding, the law of the gospel by which we may today determine the portion of our abundance we should impart unto the poor includes tithing, fast offerings, and welfare contributions.

Again I say that in this divine service we have the satisfaction of knowing that we are discharging an obligation which has from the beginning been laid upon the saints of God, and which obligation rests now in full force upon us, the Saints of the latter days.

Personally, I am very pleased with the progress

we are making. I believe the Lord is pleased also, for he is blessing our efforts remarkably.

Let us continue to merit his approval. We should not be discouraged if some Church members are not enthusiastic about the present established Church program for caring for the poor. Their apathy is due to a lack of appreciation of what the Lord designs to accomplish by it. Sometimes when I get a little low in spirits about this matter, I am revived by reading the following quotation from President Brigham Young:

> The Lord revealed to Joseph, that the people would gather out from Babylon, and establish the Kingdom of God upon the principles of heaven. They went up to Jackson Co., Mo., with this in their faith and with the express understanding that when they got there, everything was to be laid at the feet of the Bishop . . . who was to distribute it among the people, according to the Revelation. . . . But they could not bear this; consequently, they were driven from Jackson County, and finally they were driven from the State. . . . While we were in Winter Quarters, the Lord gave to me a Revelation, just as much as He ever gave one to anybody. He opened his mind, and showed me the organization of the Kingdom of God in family capacity. I talked it to my brethren; I would throw out a few words here, and a few words there, to my first counselor, to my second counselor, and the Twelve Apostles, but with the exception of one or two of the Twelve, it would not touch a man. They believed it would come, O yes, but it would be by and by (*Journal of Discourses* 18:242-244).

Now we've come a long way since President Young said this. Today many of the Saints are catching a glimpse of the import of the "royal law."

Let us go forward, never slackening our efforts. And let us not be discouraged by the charge that some welfarees are unworthy of the help they receive. If such there be, they shall in due time be weeded out, for the Lord has said, "He that is idle shall not eat the

bread nor wear the garments of the laborer" (D&C
42:42). "And the idler shall not have place in the
church, except he repent and mend his ways" (D&C
75:29).

The building of Zion and the escape of the Saints
from the tribulations yet to be poured out upon the
nations turn upon a full compliance with the "royal
law." We can with profit let our minds dwell upon
these things. For Zion, the New Jerusalem, is yet to
be built, and it is to be "a land of peace, a city of refuge,
a place of safety for the saints of the most high God;
. . . And there shall be gathered unto it out of every
nation under heaven; and it shall be the only people
that shall not be at war one with another. . . . And
every man that will not take his sword against his
neighbor must needs flee unto Zion for safety" (D&C
45:66, 69, 68).

When shall we build it? you ask. Well, according
to the scriptures, not until we can fully and ungrudg-
ingly yield obedience to the "royal law." For the Lord
has made it plain that Zion cannot be built up until
the Saints become united according to the "union required by the laws of the celestial kingdom," which
laws, he explains, require us to impart of our substance
"as becometh saints, to the poor and afflicted" among
us (D&C 105:1-6).

Surely, my brethren and sisters, we should take
courage and great joy in our labors as we contemplate
the many issues which turn upon keeping the "royal
law." In fact, Jesus taught that the final judgment
will turn upon it.

As he sat upon the Mount of Olives just two days
before the final Passover, his anxious disciples plied
him with many questions. Concerning his second
coming, he said:

When the Son of man shall come in his glory, and all the holy angels with him, then shall he sit upon the throne of his glory:

And before him shall be gathered all nations; and he shall separate them one from another, as a shepherd divideth his sheep from the goats:

And he shall set the sheep on his right hand, but the goats on the left.

Then shall the King say unto them on his right hand, Come, ye blessed of my Father, inherit the kingdom prepared for you from the foundation of the world:

For I was an hungred, and ye gave me meat: I was thirsty, and ye gave me drink: I was a stranger, and ye took me in:

Naked, and ye clothed me: I was sick, and ye visited me: I was in prison, and ye came unto me.

Then shall the righteous answer him, saying, Lord, when saw we thee an hungred, and fed thee? or thirsty, and gave thee drink?

When saw we thee a stranger, and took thee in? or naked, and clothed thee?

Or when saw we thee sick, or in prison, and came unto thee?

And the King shall answer and say unto them, Verily I say unto you, Inasmuch as ye have done it unto one of the least of these my brethren, ye have done it unto me.

I know President Grant understood this scripture. I remember when we were gathering clothes to ship to Europe for our people in distress. I remember the packages he sent. In one were two suits of clothes direct from the cleaners. I doubt if President Grant had ever worn them. In another came shirts from the laundry wrapped in cellophane paper, and ready to be worn.

In other packages we received were thousands of pounds of clothing—much of it ragged, dirty, and unfit to wear. I contemplated at that time, as I do now, how the donors of those goods would feel when they realized the truth of this statement of the Master that

"Inasmuch as ye have done it unto one of the least of these my brethren, ye have done it unto me."

Then shall he say also unto them on the left hand, Depart from me, ye cursed, into everlasting fire, prepared for the devil and his angels:

For I was an hungred, and ye gave me no meat: I was thirsty, and ye gave me no drink:

I was a stranger, and ye took me not in: naked, and ye clothed me not: sick, and in prison, and ye visited me not.

Then shall they also answer him, saying, Lord, when saw we thee an hungred, or athirst, or a stranger, or naked, or sick, or in prison, and did not minister unto thee?

Then shall he answer them, saying, Verily I say unto you, Inasmuch as ye did it not to one of the least of these, ye did it not to me.

And these shall go away into everlasting punishment: but the righteous into life eternal (Matthew 25:31-46).

Surely, my brothers and sisters, we have great reason to be encouraged and a great motive to go forward in this work. That each of us may, through full compliance with the "royal law according to the scriptures," be qualified on that great day for a place among the righteous, I humbly pray in the name of Jesus Christ. Amen.

Men are free according to the flesh; and all things are given them which are expedient unto man. And they are free to choose liberty and eternal life, . . . or to choose captivity and death.

2 Nephi 2:27

DECISIONS AND FREE AGENCY •

An address delivered at general conference October 5, 1968.

I purpose to make a few remarks about the foundation principle upon which the gospel of Jesus Christ is built—the principle of agency.

In this year of decisions we shall have opportunity to exercise our voting franchise. There seems to be no end to the advice available as to how we should do this. Out of the din of confusion comes the contention that the way to exercise it and really demonstrate that we have it is to help make Utah a wide-open state by voting for liquor by the drink. With all right-minded people we reject this fallacious contention. By the same token, we join with all fair-minded men in defense of every man's right to make his own choice.

Against the background of current events, I have thought it not inappropriate to make a few remarks concerning the making of decisions and the effect of one's decisions upon his own agency.

Our political institutions have been structured upon the premise that man is a free agent by divine endowment. Upon this premise the Magna Charta was wrung from King John in 1215. Contending for this principle, the Pilgrim Fathers were harried out of their native land by King James. After taking temporary refuge in Holland, they came to America where they founded a new state in which they could implement their ideals of freedom. A century and a half later, the colonists wrote the principle of free agency into the Declaration of Independence. Following the revolution, the founding fathers perpetuated it in the Constitution.

Our national strength has always been in our devotion to freedom. When asked, "What constitutes the bulwark of our liberty and independence?" Abraham Lincoln replied: "It is not in our frowning battlements, or bristling seacoasts, our army and navy. . . . Our reliance is in the law of liberty which God has planted in us."

We Latter-day Saints know that the right of men to make their own decisions is God-given. To Moses the Lord said: "I gave unto [men] their knowledge, in the day I created them; and in the Garden of Eden, gave I unto man his agency (Moses 7:32).

This the Lord confirmed to Joseph Smith when he said: "I gave unto [Adam] that he should be an agent unto himself" (D&C 29:35).

Through an ancient American prophet, the Lord said, "Remember, my brethren . . . ye are free; ye are permitted to act for yourselves; for behold, God hath given unto you a knowledge and he hath made you free" (Helaman 14:30).

Latter-day Saints not only believe that freedom to make one's own choices is an inalienable divine right, but they know that the exercise of it is essential to man's growth and development. Deprived of it, men would be but puppets in the hands of fate.

The preservation of free agency is more important than the preservation of life itself. As a matter of fact, without it there would be no existence.

All truth [says the Lord] is independent in that sphere in which God has placed it, to act for itself, as all intelligence also; otherwise there is no existence.

Behold, here is the agency of man (D&C 93:30, 31).

The foregoing are but samples of the scriptures which set forth the principle of free agency accepted and implemented by The Church of Jesus Christ of Latter-day Saints. Neither the Church, its officers, nor any of its responsible representatives ever seek to abridge one's freedom to make his own decisions—be it in the voting booth or elsewhere. Representations to the contrary are either ignorantly or maliciously made. Usually such representations are calculated to influence people in the exercise of their agency—the very objective they impute to and so condemn in others. Only Satan and wicked men seek to abridge men's agency. The Lord never does. Neither do his servants.

The divine gift of free agency, however, is not a self-perpetuating endowment. Men themselves have and most of them do abridge their own agency by the decisions they themselves voluntarily make.

Every choice one makes either expands or contracts the area in which he can make and implement future decisions. When one makes a choice he irrevocably binds himself to accept the consequences of that choice.

Jesus, in his Prodigal Son parable, gives a classic illustration of this truth. You will remember that in it he has a young man exercising his inherent right of

choice who makes a decision to take his portion of his
father's estate and go and see the world. This he does,
whereupon nature follows its uniform course. When
the prodigal's substance is squandered, he makes
another choice, which takes him back home where he
meets "the ring, and the robe, and the fatted calf."
His felicitous father gives him a welcome, but the
consequence of his earlier decision "is following him
up, for the farm is gone. The 'father' himself cannot
undo the effect of the foregone choice" (*Such Is Life*,
Collins, pp. 85-88).

From the very beginning God has, through his
prophets, made it clear that expanded freedom follows
wise choices and that freedom is restricted by unwise
decisions.

> Behold, I set before you this day a blessing and a curse,
> [said Moses to the children of Israel], a blessing, if ye obey
> the commandments of the Lord your God, . . . and a curse,
> if ye will not obey [them] (Deuteronomy 11:26-28).

Lehi said that

> men are free according to the flesh; and all things are given
> them which are expedient unto man. And they are free to
> choose liberty and eternal life . . . or to choose captivity and
> death (2 Nephi 2:27).

There is a great lesson on this point, as it affected
a whole nation, in Israel's rejecting judges which were
recommended by the Lord and choosing to be ruled by
kings. Near the end of his administration as judge of
Israel, the people said to Samuel: "Behold, thou art old,
and thy sons walk not in thy ways: now make us a king
to judge us like all the nations."

Samuel, being grieved by this desire of the people,
sought the Lord and was directed by the Lord to say
to Israel:

This will be the manner of the king that shall reign over you: He will take your sons, and appoint them for himself, for his chariots, and to be his horsemen; and some shall run before his chariots.

And he will appoint him captains over thousands, and captains over fifties; and will set them to ear his ground, and to reap his harvest, and to make his instruments of war, and instruments of his chariots.

And he will take your daughters to be confectionaries, and to be cooks, and to be bakers.

And he will take your fields, and your vineyards, and your oliveyards, even the best of them, and give them to his servants.

And he will take the tenth of your seed, and of your vineyards, and give to his officers, and to his servants.

And he will take your menservants, and your maidservants, and your goodliest young men, and your asses, and put them to his work.

He will take the tenth of your sheep: and ye shall be his servants.

And ye shall cry out in that day because of your king which ye shall have chosen you; and the Lord will not hear you in that day [This message Samuel delivered.].

Nevertheless the people refused to obey the voice of Samuel; and they said, Nay; but we will have a king over us;

That we also may be like all the nations. . . .

And the Lord said unto Samuel, Hearken unto the voice of the people . . . for they have not rejected thee, but they have rejected me, that I should not reign over them (1 Samuel 8:11-22).

The Lord here followed his uniform course. He refused to interfere with Israel's right of choice, even though their choice was to reject him. Israel, having been warned by both their God and his prophet Samuel, exercised their agency contrary to the advice of both. They got their king and they suffered the consequences. In due time their kingdom was divided; they were taken captive and ultimately became slaves.

Realizing that liberty depends upon the decisions we make ought to inspire in us a desire to make such

choices as will preserve and expand our freedom; and
I believe it does so inspire us. What people lack and
desperately need today, as they have always needed,
is a sure guide for making right decisions. How wonderful it would be if all could enjoy the blessing recently pronounced upon the head of a young man, to
whom a patriarch said:

You have the power of discernment, to look forward into
the future and discern and understand the results which come
from righteous living. . . . You can recognize the effect of
evil tendencies even in their beginning. . . . You are, as it
were, a watchman upon the tower of Zion, because of this
power which the Lord has blessed you with and this understanding which you have and which will grow with you through
your years to see and understand the results, which are small
in their beginning.

This is indeed a wonderful blessing. And what is
equally wonderful is that it is available to us all if we
will but qualify for it. All we need to do is follow the
pattern prescribed by Mormon as he sought, even as I
am now seeking, to emphasize the importance of making right decisions. Brother Lee read it this morning,
and I am going to read it again because of its great
importance. To his people, Mormon said:

Take heed, my beloved brethren, that ye do not judge
that which is evil to be of God, or that which is good and of
God to be of the devil.

For behold my brethren, it is given unto you to judge
[You bearers of the priesthood, this is directly to you.] that
ye may know good from evil; and the way to judge is as plain,
that ye may know with a perfect knowledge, as the daylight
is from the dark night.

For behold, the Spirit of Christ is given to every man,
that he may know good from evil; wherefore, I show unto
you the way to judge; for every thing which inviteth to do
good, and to persuade to believe in Christ, is sent forth by
the power and gift of Christ; wherefore ye may know with a
perfect knowledge it is of God.

But whatsoever thing persuadeth men to do evil, and believe not in Christ, and deny him, and serve not God, then ye may know with a perfect knowledge it is of the devil; for after this manner doth the devil work, for he persuadeth no man to do good, no, not one; neither do his angels; neither do they who subject themselves unto him.

And now, my brethren, seeing that ye know the light by which ye may judge, which light is the light of Christ, see that ye do not judge wrongfully; for with that same judgment which ye judge ye shall also be judged.

Wherefore, I beseech of you, brethren, that ye should search diligently in the light of Christ that ye may know good from evil (Moroni 7:14-19).

Let us be ever conscious of the fact that our characters are fashioned by the decisions we make. Free agency does not guarantee freedom and liberty. Freedom and liberty and peace are the products of right decisions made in the exercise of free agency.

By the making of proper decisions, Jesus Christ became the Son of God and our Redeemer. By making wrong decisions, Lucifer, son of the morning, became Satan.

Inherently, they were both endowed with free agency.

> One ship drives east
>   And another drives west
> With the selfsame winds that blow.
>   'Tis the set of the sail
> And not the gale
>   Which tells us the way to go.
> —Ella Wheeler Wilcox

James Russell Lowell suggests the consequences and the importance of decisions, in these lines:

> To every man and nation
>   comes the moment to decide,
> In the strife of Truth with Falsehood,
>   for the good or evil side;

Some great cause, God's new Messiah,
    offering each the bloom or blight,
Parts the goats upon the left hand
    and the sheep upon the right,—
And the choice goes by forever 'twixt
    that darkness and that light!

I bear you my solemn witness that these principles are true and that they are ever operating in our lives. I bear further witness to what you and I both know— that if we would benefit from these principles and be on the way to eternal life, we must put them into practice now in our daily lives. We must be guided by them in our temporal as well as our spiritual affairs, in the voting booth as well as in our churches. On election day a month hence, we shall have opportunity to test our commitment to these principles of the gospel. This is so because at least one of the issues there to be decided, the one raised by Liquor Initiative Petition No. A, is of a vital moral nature. No amount of sophistry can make it otherwise. The Lord himself and his living mouthpiece have so declared it. Let no man fault his God or his state by failing to vote upon that issue.

If on that day in the privacy of the voting booth we so exercise our franchise as to satisfy ourselves and please our God, we shall have made a decision calculated to preserve our free agency and expand the area in which we can exercise it in the future.

And finally when the issues are determined, whether we stand with the winners or the losers, of this we may be sure: To make the proper choice on any issue is of far more importance to us personally than is the immediate outcome of the issue upon which we make a decision. The choices we make will affect the scope of our agency in the future. As of now we have the right of decision. What we will have tomorrow depends upon how we decide today. In conclusion, I put

to you the question and the admonition given by Elijah
to Israel: "How long halt ye between two opinions?
if the Lord be God, follow him: but if Baal, then follow
him (1 Kings 18:21).

God grant us discernment and the courage to make
right decisions, I humbly pray in the name of Jesus
Christ. Amen.

Pray always, that you may come off conquerer; yea, that you may conquer Satan, and that you may escape the hands of the servants of Satan that do uphold his work.

D&C 10:5

PRAY ALWAYS •

An address delivered at general conference October 7, 1944.

I have been pondering that marvelous appeal for prayer made by President Grant yesterday in his message. I have been considering it in connection with a passage of scripture, a commandment which the Lord gave to the Prophet Joseph Smith. Perhaps I was impressed because I had been thinking, as I am sure you have been, of the great hold which Satan has upon the inhabitants of the earth today. The commandment was:

Pray always, that you may come off conqueror; yea, that you may conquer Satan, and that you may escape the hands of the servants of Satan that do uphold his work (D&C 10:5).

The subject of prayer deserves the consideration not only of Latter-day Saints, but of all people.

One of our greatest needs today is to turn to God in true prayer so that we may conquer Satan and escape the hands of the servants of Satan that uphold his work. I should like to call your attention to some of the essentials of effective prayer. One of them is belief in God, the Eternal Father, as taught by Joseph Smith.

There is a world of difference in the attitude in which one prays understandingly to "our Father which art in heaven" and that of one whose prayer is addressed to some unknown god thought of as "cosmic energy," "universal consciousness," or as "the first great cause." No man prays to a theoretical god with the faith and expectation that his petition will receive sympathetic personal consideration. But one can understandingly pray to the true and living God with the assurance that his prayers will be heard and answered. When God is believed in as our Eternal Father, we can to a degree understand our relationship to him —that he is the Father of our spirits, a loving parent who is interested in his children individually and whom they can love with all their hearts, might, mind, and strength.

Such a belief is essential to true prayer because intelligent beings will not pray fervently to a God they do not know. Such praying will be done only by people who believe their prayers can be heard and answered by an understanding, sympathetic parent.

Associated with belief in God, the Eternal Father, is belief in his Son Jesus Christ and an acceptance of his divine mission as the Redeemer of the world. This belief is as basic to true prayer as is belief in God, the Eternal Father. It is because Jesus is our Redeemer, and therefore our advocate with the Father, that we must always pray unto the Father in his name. While yet in mortality, he said to his disciples: "I am the way, the truth, and the life: no man cometh unto the Father but by me" (John 14:6). He promised them that if they prayed *in his name*, they should receive whatsoever they should ask (John 14:13, 14, 15, 16; 16:23, 24, 26). To the Nephite multitude, whom he taught after his resurrection, he said, "Ye must always pray unto the Father in my name" (3 Nephi 18: 19), and to this generation, "Thou shalt continue in calling upon God *in my name*" (D&C 24:5).

I call attention to this matter of praying to God in the name of his Son Jesus Christ because on a number of occasions recently I have heard prayers in religious services which were not offered *in his name*. Latter-day Saints ought not to be ignorant of these commandments nor hesitant about obeying them.

Our hearts are filled with gratitude beyond expression for what the Savior has done for us. We sing with feeling, "Oh, it is wonderful that he should care for me, enough to die for me!" Every time we partake of the sacrament we witness unto the Father that we are willing to take upon us the name of his Son. A prayer not offered in his name suggests insincerity or lack of understanding.

When we pray unto the Father in the name of Jesus for specific personal things, we should feel in the very depths of our souls that we are willing to subject our petitions to the will of our Father in heaven. "Thy will, O God, thy will be done" should never be lip service only. "Thy will be done on earth as it is in heaven" (3 Nephi 13:10) is the pattern given by Jesus in the Lord's prayer and emphasized in Gethsemane when in blood-sweat and agony he prayed, "Not my will, but thine, be done" (Luke 22:42).

This principle we learned in our home through a rather impressive experience. During the early years of our married life, my wife and I intensely desired what we considered to be a particular blessing. We set about through fasting and prayer to obtain it. We considered many of the scriptures which seemed to make a blanket promise that "whatsoever ye shall ask in prayer, believing, ye shall receive" (Matthew

21:22). We asked, we believed, we thought we had
faith, but though we fasted often and prayed fervently,
the years rolled by without bringing us the desired
answer to our prayers. Finally we concluded that we
had not fully understood; that we were not giving
proper consideration to the will of the Lord. Rather, we
were concentrating our faith and prayers upon receiving the particular thing which by predetermination we
had set our hearts upon. We had to reconsider the conditions of the promise. We found that Jesus had stated
them in full to the Nephites as follows: "whatsoever
ye shall ask the Father in my name, *which is right*, believing that ye shall receive, behold it shall be given
unto you" (3 Nephi 18:20), and to this generation thus,
"Whatsoever ye ask the Father in my name it shall be
given to you, *that is expedient for you*" (D&C 88:64).
We had to learn to be as earnest in praying "if it be
thy will" as we were when presenting our personal
appeals.

We need have no fear that our well-being will not
be served by such an approach. It is God's work and
glory "to bring to pass the immortality and eternal
life of man" (Moses 1:39). I think I am within the
mark when I say that the obtaining of eternal life by
each individual person, including specifically you and
me, is part of the work of God and adds to his glory.
His will concerning us and our affairs cannot be other
than for our advancement toward immortality and
eternal life. Submitting to his will will in every instance
be for our own good. And this we must do in faith if
we would have peace and happiness in our present state
of imperfect living.

The time will come when we shall know the will
of God before we ask. Then everything for which we
pray will be "expedient." Everything for which we

ask will be "right." That will be when, as a result of righteous living, we shall so enjoy the companionship of the Spirit that he will dictate what we ask. On this point the Lord has said, "He that asketh in the Spirit asketh according to the will of God; wherefore it is done even as he asketh" (D&C 46:30), and again, "And if ye are purified and cleansed from all sin, ye shall ask whatsoever you will in the name of Jesus and it shall be done. But know this, it shall be given you what you shall ask" (D&C 50:29, 30). Nephi, the son of Helaman, so lived. He with unweariness declared the word of God. He sought not his own life but the will of God and to keep his commandments continually, and to him the Lord said, "All things shall be done unto thee according to thy word, for thou shalt not ask that which is contrary to my will" (Helaman 10:5).

Now in submitting our requests to the will of our Eternal Father and asking in the name of Jesus, when, where, and for what shall we pray?

The psalmist sang, "Evening, and morning, and at noon, will I pray" (Psalm 55:17). During his earthly mission, the Savior taught by parable that "men ought always to pray, and not to faint" (Luke 18:1). In this dispensation, He has said in many revelations, "Pray always." He said this to the Prophet Joseph Smith (D&C 10:5), to Martin Harris (D&C 19:38), to Thomas B. Marsh (D&C 31:12), and to many other individuals; he said it to the Church (D&C 20:22), and finally he said, "What I say unto one I say unto all; pray always lest that wicked one have power in you, and remove you out of your place" (D&C 93:49).

As there is no limitation as to when we should pray, so there seems to be no limitation as to where we should pray or about what we should pray.

In every thing by prayer and supplication with thanksgiving let your requests be made known unto God (Philemon 4:6).

Cry unto him for mercy; for he is mighty to save. . . .
Cry unto him when ye are in your fields, yea, over all your flocks.

Cry unto him in your houses, yea, over all your household, both morning, mid-day, and evening.

Yea, cry unto him, against the power of your enemies.

Yea, cry unto him against the devil, who is an enemy to all righteousness.

Cry unto him over the crops of your fields, that ye may prosper in them. . . .

But this is not all; ye must pour out your souls in your closets, and your secret places, and in your wilderness.

Yea, and when you do not cry unto the Lord, let your hearts be full, drawn out in prayer unto him continually for your welfare and also for the welfare of those who are around you (Alma 34:18-27).

Pray in your families unto the Father, always in my name [said the Savior], that your wives and your children may be blessed (3 Nephi 18:21).

Pray vocally as well as in thy heart; yea, before the world as well as in secret, in public as well as in private (D&C 19:28).

Call upon the Lord, that his kingdom may go forth upon the earth, that the inhabitants thereof may receive it, and be prepared for the days to come, in the which the Son of Man shall come down in heaven, clothed in the brightness of his glory, to meet the kingdom of God which is set up on the earth.

Wherefore, may the kingdom of God go forth, that the kingdom of heaven may come, that thou, O God, mayest be glorified in heaven so on earth, that thine enemies may be subdued; for thine is the honor, power and glory, forever and ever. Amen (D&C 65:5, 6).

Most all of you who are within the sound of my voice are witnesses that no person in true prayer ever called upon God in vain. There is hardly one of you who cannot personally testify, out of your own experience, of the power of prayer.

In the spring of 1820 Joseph Smith, Jun., one of God's mightiest spirit sons (but then a little known fourteen-year-old boy in the backwoods of New York state), while reading the Bible in search of light on a vital problem, was moved upon by the Spirit to ask God in faith for the wisdom he lacked. Retiring to a secluded spot in a wooded grove, he kneeled down and began to offer up the desires of his heart to God in vocal prayer. It was while this boy was so engaged in humble prayer, and in answer to that prayer, that the great vision of the Father and the Son was given, which opened this last dispensation of the gospel.

A great deal more could be said upon this vital subject of prayer, but this is not the time nor place for me to say it. In conclusion, I plead with all men everywhere to turn to God in true prayer. This is the number one requisite for peace in the world. It is the only way that we can conquer Satan and escape the hands of the servants of Satan that uphold this work. We Latter-day Saints know that God is our Eternal Father, that Jesus Christ is his Son and our Redeemer, and that we must bring our desires and our lives in harmony with his divine will, praying to him always about all things in the name of Jesus. Let us see to it that from henceforth no day shall pass in which we do not fervently, in family and in private prayers, express our gratitude to our Heavenly Father and seek his guidance and protecting care, I humbly pray in the name of Jesus Christ. Amen.

Ye fearful saints, fresh courage take;
The clouds ye so much dread
Are big with mercy, and shall break
In blessings on your head.

William Cowper

COURAGE ●

An address delivered at general conference April 1951.

If I can enjoy the Spirit of the Lord, for which I earnestly pray, I desire to give you a message of hope and courage. I am prompted to this desire by the fact that in my recent travels among the people, I have sensed a growing spirit of uneasiness and foreboding.

SPIRIT OF UNEASINESS

Following a welfare meeting held a few months ago on the Pacific coast in which we had counseled the people to obtain permanent welfare production projects that they might produce the necessities to carry on our welfare work without calling upon the Saints year after year for cash contributions, a sister told me she was comforted by our advice, that she felt it would not have been given if the people were not to stay there permanently. She had been disturbed and worried by talk that bombs might be dropped in that area, necessitating their moving inland.

This brought to my mind an experience from the days of my youth when in the colonies of Old Mexico we were agitated over whether the troubles incident to the Madero Revolution would necessitate our leaving the country. At the peak of the disturbances, our stake president (who was my uncle, Junius Romney) planted an orchard of young apple trees. I well remember how my mind was relieved by hearing people say that if we were facing expulsion, the stake president would not be planting trees which would take years to mature. Notwithstanding the comfort I got out of that assurance, we did have to leave.

Need for Hope and Courage

I was, of course, unable to advise the good sister whether bombs would be dropped, nor did I know whether the city would have to be evacuated, but I did have a great desire to give her some comfort and courage which would ease her mind.

I remembered that President Joseph F. Smith had said that leaders in the Church "should be men not easily discouraged, not without hope, and not be given to foreboding of all sorts of evils to come"; that if they "sometimes feel the weight and anxiety of momentous times, they should be all the firmer and all the more resolute in those convictions which come from a God-fearing conscience and pure lives. It is a matter of the greatest importance," he concluded, "that the people be educated to appreciate and cultivate the bright side of life rather than to permit its darkness and shadows to hover over them" (*Gospel Doctrine*, p. 193).

Calamities Ahead

I could not give her, nor can I extend to you, much hope and courage based upon an expectation that we are about to enter upon a period of world peace and security. I do not expect any such happy circumstances to prevail in the immediate future. As I read the signs of the times, in light of the revealed word of God, we are in line for something quite different.

A long time ago the Lord raised the curtain on the scene of destruction awaiting the inhabitants of the earth if they followed to the end the course they were then pursuing. More that a hundred years ago he said that a desolating scourge should go forth among the inhabitants of the earth and if they repented not, it should continue from time to time until the earth was empty and the inhabitants thereof utterly destroyed.

For all flesh is corrupted before me; and the powers of darkness prevail upon the earth, among the children of men. . . .

All eternity is pained, and the angels are waiting the great command to reap down the earth, to gather the tares that they may be burned (D&C 38:11, 12).

I am convinced that the overwhelming majority of men have chosen to continue down the path they were then following. I can discern no change in their course sufficient to justify in me a hope that the calamities which the Lord said he knew would come upon the inhabitants of the earth because the people would not accept him will be turned aside.

Courage of Faith

But we Latter-day Saints must not let ourselves be so engulfed with forebodings that we fail to obtain and enjoy such hope and courage as is within our reach —the hope and courage born of faith in the power of righteousness to ultimately triumph. I have boundless confidence in that power. I am persuaded beyond all doubt that the destiny of men and nations is in the hands of the Almighty, who has respect for righteousness, and not in the hands of conniving politicians

whose wisdom has perished, whose understanding has
come to naught, and who have no respect for righteousness. If it were not so, I should be in utter despair.
I believe that the record and the word of God justify
us in so placing our hope.

CHARGE TO JOSHUA

I cite your attention to the calling of Joshua, the
successor to Moses whose mission it was to lead Israel
over Jordan and divide among them the Promised
Land which was then inhabited by an armed and hostile
people. It was a difficult and arduous assignment. To
strengthen him for it, the Lord gave Joshua a great
promise and a great charge. This is the promise:

> There shall not any man be able to stand before thee all
> the days of thy life: as I was with Moses, so I will be with thee:
> I will not fail thee, nor forsake thee.

And this is the charge:

> Be strong and of a good courage: for unto this people shalt
> thou divide for an inheritance the land, which I sware unto
> their fathers to give them. Only be thou strong and very
> courageous. . . .

Now note with care how Joshua was directed to show
his strength and courage, and also that prosperity was
to follow his performance.

> That thou mayest observe to do according to all the law,
> which Moses my servant commanded thee: turn not from
> the right hand or to the left, that thou mayest prosper whither-
> soever thou goest.

Moses had been the living prophet during the days of
Joshua.

> This book of the law shall not depart out of thy mouth;
> but thou shalt meditate therein day and night, that thou mayest
> observe to do according to all that is written therein: for then

thou shalt make thy way prosperous and then thou shalt have good success.

The book of the law was the standard church work of that day.

Have not I commanded thee? Be strong and of a good courage; be not afraid, neither be thou dismayed: for the Lord thy God is with thee whithersoever thou goest (Joshua 1:5-9).

As I read the scripture, I feel that Joshua's obedience to the teachings of Moses and to the contents of the book of the law was the test of his strength and courage. The extent to which he was to prosper, be unafraid and undismayed, and have the Lord with him depended upon his rating in that test.

We can demonstrate our strength and courage in the same way, and be unafraid and undismayed and have the Lord with us whithersoever we go, by observing the teachings of the living prophets and observing to do according to all that is written in the standard works of the Church.

Teachings of Wilford Woodruff

During the last years of President Woodruff's life, his mind dwelt much upon the calamities which were coming upon the earth, and he gave many warnings of them. But he did not leave his hearers in despair. Always he held out to them hope and courage conditioned on their righteousness. Here is a sample of his teachings:

Over the millions of people on this earth, there hangs a cloud of darkness almost entirely upon their shoulders. Can you tell me where the people are who will be shielded and protected from these great calamities and judgments which are even now at our doors? I'll tell you. The priesthood of God who honor their priesthood, and who are worthy of their blessings, are the only ones who shall have their safety and protection. They are the only mortal beings. No other people have

a right to be shielded from these judgments. They are at our
very doors; not even this people will escape them entirely. They
will come down like the judgments of Sodom and Gomorrah.
And none but the priesthood will be safe from their fury.

But he concluded with this note of assurance:

If you do your duty, and I do my duty, we shall have protection, and shall pass through the afflictions in peace and
safety (*Improvement Era,* 17:1164-65).

On another occasion he had this to say:

I will say to the Latter-day Saints, if they will be faithful,
and do what they should do, and listen to the counsel given to
them, they need not have any fears about anything, for the
whole work is in the hands of God, the destinies of nations lie
there. It is better for a people to be wise, to get righteousness,
to be the friends of God, than to occupy any other positions
in life (*Journal of Discourses* 2:199; *Discourses of Wilford
Woodruff,* p. 6).

PROTECTION OF RIGHTEOUS

Nephi, speaking of our day, which by the power
of God he had seen in vision, said the Lord would not
suffer the wicked to destroy the righteous, but that
he would "preserve the righteous by his power, even if
it so be that the fulness of his wrath must come, and
the righteous be preserved, even unto the destruction
of their enemies by fire. Wherefore, the righteous need
not fear" (1 Nephi 22:16, 17).

The Lord renewed this same promise of protection
to the righteous in 1831 when he said he was angry
with the wicked, that he was withholding his Spirit
from the inhabitants of the earth, that he had decreed
wars upon the face of the earth, and that the wicked
should destroy the wicked.

And the saints also shall hardly escape; nevertheless, I,
the Lord, am with them, and will come down in heaven from

the presence of my Father and consume the wicked with un-
quenchable fire (D&C 6:33, 34).

Two or three months later he continued:

The hour is not yet but is nigh at hand, when peace shall
be taken from the earth, and the devil shall have power over
his own dominion.

And also the Lord shall have power over his saints, and
shall reign in their midst (Ibid., 1:35, 36).

I am persuaded that a complete surrender to the
principles of righteousness would lift God's people
out of the turmoil of this present world. Such has been
the record in the past, as witness the experiences of
Enoch and his people and the record of the Nephites
following their visit from the risen Redeemer.

ZION, A PLACE OF SAFETY

I believe a similar performance by us in our day
would bring the same results. I not only believe, but
I know it would and that it will yet be done. I don't
know just how soon, but I am looking forward with
certainty to the fulfilment of the words spoken by the
Lord to the Church in its infancy, when he directed
the Saints to gather together their riches to purchase
an inheritance in Zion, which he said was to be a land
of peace, a city of refuge, a place of safety for the
Saints of the most high God. There the glory of the
Lord is to be a terror to the wicked and a comfort to
the righteous. Zion's inhabitants are to be the only
people that shall not be at war one with another, and
every man that will not take up his sword against his
neighbor must flee unto it for safety.

And it shall come to pass that the righteous shall be
gathered out from among all nations, and shall come to Zion,
singing with songs of everlasting joy (Ibid., 45:71).

HOPE IN THE FUTURE

Now I know, my brothers and sisters, that we will have our souls tested before we reach these glories of the future, but if we have them in view and live righteously, we shall thereby be sustained for the trials we must endure. Paul said it was the glory set before Jesus for which he endured the cross, and President Young said it was the vision of Zion as it shall be which sustained the Saints as they pulled their covered wagons from ruts and mudholes and trudged across the plains. Therefore, with hope in the future, let us lift up our hearts and rejoice, and with strength and courage let us gird up our loins and take upon us the whole armor of righteousness so that we may be able to withstand these evil days and that, having done all, we may be able to stand.

And as we journey through these anxious times,

The Lord bless thee, and keep thee:

The Lord make his face to shine upon thee and be gracious unto thee:

The Lord lift his countenance upon thee, and give thee peace (Numbers 6:24-26).

This I humbly pray in the name of Jesus Christ. Amen.

SOCIALISM
AND THE UNITED ORDER COMPARED •

An address delivered to Brigham Young University student body March 1, 1966.

I have been asked to direct these remarks to the question: Is socialism the United Order?

SOCIALISM DEFINED

Perhaps an appropriate first step in comparing socialism and the United Order would be to define the terms.

Webster defines socialism as:

A political and economic theory of social organization based on collective or governmental ownership and democratic management of the essential means for the production and distribution of goods; also, a policy or practice based on this theory (*Webster's New International Dictionary,* 2d ed., unabridged, 1951).

George Bernard Shaw, the noted Fabian Socialist, says that

socialism, reduced to its simplest legal and practical expression, means the complete discarding of the institution of private **property** by transforming it into public property

and the division of the resultant income equally and indis-
criminately among the entire population (*Encyclopedia Britannica*, 1943 ed., p. 295).

George Douglas Howard Cole, M.A., noted author
and university reader in economics at Oxford, who
treats socialism for the *Encyclopedia Britannica*, says
that because of the shifting sense in which the word
has been used,

a short and comprehensive definition is . . . impossible.
We can only say [he concludes] that Socialism is essentially
a doctrine and a movement aiming at the collective organization of the community in the interest of the mass of people
by means of the common ownership and collective control of
the means of production and exchange (*Encyclopedia Britannica*, vol. 20).

Socialism arose "out of the economic division in
society." During the nineteenth century its growth
was accelerated as a protest against "the appalling
conditions prevailing in the workshops and factories
and the unchristian spirit of the spreading industrial
system."

The "communist manifesto" drafted by Karl Marx and
Friedrich Engels, for the Communist League . . . in . . .
1848 is generally regarded as the starting point of modern
socialism (Ibid.).

Distinction Between Socialism and Communism

The distinction between Socialism, as represented by the
various Socialist and Labour Parties of Europe and the new
world, and Communism, as represented by the Russians, is
one of tactics and strategy rather than of objective.   Communism is indeed only Socialism pursued by revolutionary
means and making its revolutionary method a canon of faith.
Communists, like other Socialists, (1) believe in the collective
control and ownership of the vital means of production, and
(2) seek to achieve, through state action the co-ordinated
control of the economic forces of society.   They differ from
other Socialists in believing that this control can be secured,

and its use in the interests of the workers ensured, only by revolutionary action leading to the dictatorship of the proletariat and the creation of a new proletarian state as the instrument of change (Ibid.).

Major Forms of Socialism

A major rift between so-called orthodox socialism and communist socialism occurred in 1875 when the German Social Democratic Party set forth its objective of winning power by taking over control of the bourgeois state, rather than by overthrowing it. In effect, the German Social Democratic Party became a parliamentary party, aiming at the assumption of political power by constitutional means.

In the 1880's a small group of intellectuals set up in England the Fabian Society, which has had a major influence on the development of modern orthodox socialism. Fabianism stands "for the evolutionary conception of socialism . . . endeavoring by progressive reforms and the nationalization of industries, to turn the existing state into a 'welfare state.'" Somewhat on the order of the German Social Democrats, Fabians aim "at permeating the existing parties with socialistic ideas [rather] than at creating a definitely socialistic party." They appeal "to the electorate not as revolutionaries, but as constitutional reformers seeking a peaceful transformation of the system" (Ibid.).

The differences in forms and policies of socialism occur principally in the manner in which they seek to implement their theories.

They all advocate:

1. That private ownership of the vital means of production be abolished and that all such property "pass under some form of co-ordinated public control."

2. That the power of the state be used to achieve their aims.

3. That with a change in the control of industry will go a change in the motives which operate in the industrial system.

So much now for the definition of socialism.

UNITED ORDER DEFINED

The United Order, the Lord's program for eliminating the inequalities among men, is based upon the underlying concept that the earth and all things therein belong to the Lord and that men hold earthly possessions as stewards accountable to God.

On January 2, 1831, the Lord revealed to the Prophet Joseph Smith that the Church was under obligation to care for the poor (see D&C 38). Later he said,

I, the Lord, stretched out the heavens, and built the earth, . . . and all things therein are mine.
And it is my purpose to provide for my saints, for all things are mine.
But it must needs be done in mine own way (D&C 104:14-16).

THE LORD'S WAY

On February 9, 1831, the Lord revealed to the Prophet what His way was (see D&C 42). In his way there were two cardinal principles: (1) consecration and (2) stewardship.

To enter the United Order, one consecrated all his possessions to the Church by a "covenant and deed which" could "not be broken." That is, he completely divested himself of all of his property by conveying it to the Church.

Having thus voluntarily divested himself of title to all his property, the consecrator received from the Church a stewardship by a like conveyance. This stewardship could be more or less than his original consecration, the object being to make "every man equal according to his family, according to his circumstances and his wants and needs" (D&C 51:3).

Right to Private Ownership Preserved

This procedure preserved in every man the right to private ownership and management of his property. At his own option he could alienate it or keep and operate it and pass it on to his heirs.

The intent was, however, for him to so operate his property as to produce a living for himself and his dependents. So long as he remained in the order he consecrated to the Church the surplus he produced above the needs and wants of his family. This surplus went into a storehouse, from which stewardships were given to others and from which the needs of the poor were supplied.

The United Order and Socialism Compared

These divine principles are very simple and easily understood. A comparison of them with the underlying hallmarks of socialism reveal similarities and basic differences.

The following are similarities: Both (1) deal with production and distribution of goods, (2) aim to promote the well-being of men by eliminating their economic inequalities, and (3) envision the elimination of the selfish motives in our private capitalistic industrial system.

Now the differences:

1. The cornerstone of the United Order is belief in God and acceptance of him as Lord of the earth and the author of the United Order.

Socialism, wholly materialistic, is founded in the wisdom of men, and not of God. Although all socialists may not be atheists, none of them in theory or practice seek the Lord to establish his righteousness.

2. The United Order is implemented by the voluntary free-will actions of men, evidenced by a consecration of all their property to the Church of God.

Socialism is implemented by external force, the power of the state.

3. As to property, the Church believes "that no government can exist in peace, except such laws are framed and held inviolate as will secure to each individual the free exercise of conscience, the right and control of property, and the protection of life" (D&C 134:2).

In harmony with this doctrine, the United Order preserves the rights of private ownership and individual management of property.

Thus in both implementation and ownership and management of property, the United Order preserves to men their God-given agency, while socialism deprives them of it.

4. The United Order is non-political.

Socialism is political, both in theory and in practice. It is thus exposed to, and riddled by, the corruption which plagues and finally destroys all political governments which undertake to abridge man's agency.

5. A righteous people is a prerequisite to the United Order.

Socialism argues that it, as a system, will eliminate the evils of the profit motive.

SOCIALISM IS NOT THE UNITED ORDER

The United Order exalts the poor and humbles the rich. In the process both are sanctified. The poor, released from the bondage and humiliating limitations of poverty, are enabled as free men to rise to their full potential both temporally and spiritually. The rich, by consecration and by imparting of their surplus for the benefit of the poor, not by constraint, but willingly as an act of free will, evidence that charity for their fellowmen characterized by Mormon as "the pure love of Christ" (Moroni 7:47).

No, socialism is not the United Order. Distinguishing between these two systems need be no more difficult than solving the problem of the farmer who could not tell one of his horses from the other. They weighed the same, pulled the same load, ran at the same speed; from the looks of their teeth they were the same age. Finally, as a last resort, he measured them, and, sure enough, the white horse was six hands higher than the black one.

SOCIALISM WAVE OF THE PRESENT AND FUTURE

Notwithstanding my abhorrence of it, I am persuaded that socialism is the wave of the present and of the foreseeable future. It has already taken over or is contending for control in most nations.

At the end of the year [1965] parties affiliated with the [Socialist] International were in control of the governments of Great Britain, Denmark, Norway, Sweden, Israel, and the Malagasy Republic. They had representatives in coalition cabinets in Austria, Belgium, Iceland, Italy, Luxemborg, and Switzerland; constituted the chief opposition in France, India, Japan, the Netherlands, New Zealand and West Germany;

and were significant political forces in numerous other coun-
tries. Many parties dominant in governments in Africa, Asia,
and Latin America announced that their aim was a socialist
society (*Encyclopedia Britannica,* 1965 Book of the Year, p.
736).

THE UNITED STATES CONVERTING TO
SOCIAL WELFARE STATE

We here in the United States, in converting our
government into a social welfare state, have ourselves
adopted much of socialism. Specifically, we have to
an alarming degree adopted the use of the power of
the state in the control and distribution of the fruits
of industry. We are on notice, according to the words
of the president, that we are going much farther, for
he is quoted as saying:

We're going to take all the money we think is unneces-
sarily being spent and take it from the "haves" and give it to
the "have nots" (*Congressional Record,* March 24, 1964).

That is the spirit of socialism: "We're going *to take.*"
It isn't the spirit of "We're going *to give.*"

AMERICAN FREE AGENCY ABRIDGED

We have also gone a long way on the road to public
ownership and management of the vital means of production. In both of these areas the free agency of
Americans has been greatly abridged. Some argue that
we have voluntarily surrendered this power to government. Be this as it may, the fact remains that the loss
of freedom with the consent of the enslaved, or even
at their request, is nonetheless slavery.

THE FRUITS OF SOCIALISM

As to the fruits of socialism, we all have our own
opinions. I myself have watched its growth in our own
country and observed it in operation in many other

lands. But I have yet to see or hear of its freeing the
hearts of men of selfishness and greed or of its bringing peace, plenty, or freedom. These things it will
never bring, nor will it do away with idleness and
promote "industry, thrift, and self-respect," for it is
founded in theory and in practice on the principles of
the evil one.

The Fruits of the United Order

As to the fruits of the United Order, I suggest
you read Moses 7:16-18 and 4 Nephi 2, 3, 15, 16. If we
had time, we could review the history (what little we
know) of Zion in the days of Enoch and about what
happened among the Nephites under those principles
of the United Order in the first two centuries following
the time of the Savior.

What Can We Do About It?

Now what can we do about it?

As I recently reminded my wife of the moratorium
on the United Order—that socialism is taking over in
the nations and that its expressed aims will surely fail
—she spiritedly put to me the question: "Well, then,
what would you suggest? That we just sit on our hands
in despair and do nothing?" Perhaps similar questions
have occurred to you. The answer is, "No. By no
means!" We have much to do, and the Lord has definitely prescribed the course we should follow with
respect to socialism and the United Order.

The Lord's Prescribed Course

He has told us that in preparation for the restoration of the gospel, he himself established the Constitution of the United States that there might be a
government which "according to just and holy prin-

ciples" would preserve to men their God-given agency. This he did because the whole gospel of Jesus Christ presupposes man's untrammeled exercise of free agency. Man is on the earth to be tested. The issue as to whether he succeeds or fails will be determined by how he uses this agency. His whole future, through all eternity, is at stake. Abridge man's agency, and the whole purpose of his mortality is thwarted. Without it, the Lord says, there is no existence (see D&C 93:30). The Lord so valued our agency that he designed and dictated "the laws and constitution" required to guarantee it. This he explained in the revelation in which he instructed the Prophet Joseph Smith to appeal for help:

According to the laws and constitution of the people, which I have suffered to be established, and should be maintained for the rights and protection of all flesh, according to just and holy principles;

That every man may act in doctrine and principle pertaining to futurity, according to the moral agency which I have given unto him, that every man may be accountable for his own sins in the day of judgment. . . .

And for this purpose have I established the Constitution of this land, by the hands of wise men whom I raised up unto this very purpose (D&C 101:77, 78, 80).

Previously he had said:

And now, verily I say unto you concerning the laws of the land, it is my will that my people should observe to do all things whatsoever I command them.

And that law of the land which is constitutional, supporting that principle of freedom in maintaining rights and privileges, belongs to all mankind, and is justifiable before me.

Therefore, I, the Lord justify you, and your brethren of my Church, in befriending that law which is the constitutional law of the land;

And as pertaining to law of man, whatsoever is more or less than this, cometh of evil.

I, the Lord God, make you free, therefore ye are free

indeed; and the law [that is, constitutional law] also maketh you free.

Nevertheless, when the wicked rule the people mourn.

Wherefore, honest men and wise men should be sought for diligently, and good men and wise men ye should observe to uphold; otherwise whatsoever is less than these cometh of evil (D&C 98:4-10).

THE CONSTITUTION—A DIVINE DOCUMENT

These scriptures reveal the fact that the Constitution is a divine document. They tell us that "according to just and holy principles" the Constitution and "the law of the land which supports the principle of freedom in maintaining rights and privileges, belongs to all mankind, and is justifiable before" God; that, "as pertaining to the law of man, whatsoever is more or less than this, cometh of evil." They remind us that the Lord has made us free, and that laws which are constitutional will also make us free.

A WARNING

Right at this point, almost as if he were warning us against what is happening today, the Lord said: "Nevertheless, when the wicked rule, the people mourn." Then, that we might know with certainty what we should do about it, he concluded: "Wherefore, honest men and wise men should be sought for diligently, and good men and wise men ye should observe to uphold."

SEEK TO SUPPORT WISE MEN IN GOVERNMENT

In its context, this instruction can only mean that we should seek diligently for and support men to represent us in government who are "wise" enough to understand freedom—as provided for in the Constitution and as implemented in the United Order—and who are honest enough and good enough to fight to preserve it.

"Under no other government in the world could the Church have been established," said President J. Reuben Clark, Jr., and he continued:

If we are to live as a Church, and progress, and have the right to worship as we are worshiping here today, we must have the great guarantees that are set up by our Constitution. There is no other way in which we can secure these guarantees (*Conference Report*, October 1942, p. 59).

WHAT WE SHOULD DO ABOUT THE UNITED ORDER

Now, not forgetting our duty to eschew socialism and support the just and holy principles of the Constitution, as directed by the Lord, I shall conclude these remarks with a few comments concerning what we should do about the United Order.

The final words of the Lord in suspending the order were: "And let those commandments which I have given concerning Zion and her law be executed and fulfilled, after her redemption" (D&C 105:34).

Further implementation of the order must therefore await the redemption of Zion. Here Zion means Jackson County, Missouri. When Zion is redeemed, as it most certainly shall be, it will be redeemed under a government and by a people strictly observing those "just and holy principles" of the Constitution which accord to men their God-given moral agency, including the right to private property. If, in the meantime, socialism takes over in America, it will have to be displaced, if need be, by the power of God, because the United Order can never function under socialism or "the welfare state" for the good and sufficient reason that the principles upon which socialism and the United Order are conceived and operated are in opposition.

Fast Offering, Tithing, Welfare Activities

In the meantime, while we await the redemption of Zion and the earth and the establishment of the United Order, we as Latter-day Saints should live strictly by the principles of the United Order insofar as they are embodied in present Church practices, such as fast offering, tithing, and welfare activities. Through these practices we could as individuals, if we were of a mind to, implement in our own lives all the basic principles of the United Order.

Let me give you some examples. You remember the principles underlying the United Order are consecration and stewardships and then the contribution of surpluses into the bishop's storehouse. When the law of tithing was instituted four years after the United Order experiment was suspended, the Lord required the people to put "all their surplus property . . . into the hands of the bishop" (D&C 119:1) ; thereafter they were to "pay one-tenth of their interest annually" (D&C 119:4). This law, still in force, implements to a degree at least the United Order principle of stewardships, for it leaves in the hands of each person the ownership and management of the property from which he produces the needs of himself and family. Furthermore, to use again the words of President Clark:

In lieu of residues and surpluses which were accumulated and built up under the United Order, we, today, have our fast offerings, our welfare donations, and our tithing, all of which may be devoted to care of the poor, as well as the carrying on of the activities and business of the Church.

Furthermore, we had under the United Order a bishop's storehouse in which were collected the materials from which to supply the needs and the wants of the poor. We have a bishop's storehouse under the welfare plan, used for the same purpose.

We have now under the welfare plan all over the Church,
. . . land projects . . . farmed for the benefit of the poor.

Thus . . . in many of its great essentials, we have [in]
the welfare plan . . . the broad essentials of the United Order.
Furthermore, having in mind the assistance which is being
given from time to time . . . to help set people up in business
or in farming, we have a plan which is not essentially unlike
that which was in the United Order when the poor were given
portions from the common fund (*Conference Report,* October
1942, pp. 57-58).

It is thus apparent that when the principles of
tithing and the fast are properly observed and the
welfare plan gets fully developed and wholly into operation, we shall not be so very far from carrying out the
great fundamentals of the United Order. The only
limitation on you and me is within ourselves.

And now in line with these remarks, for three
things I pray:

1. That the Lord will somehow quicken our understanding of the differences between socialism and the United Order and give us a vivid
   awareness of the awful portent of those differences.

2. That we will develop the understanding, the
   desire, and the courage, born of the Spirit, to
   eschew socialism and support and sustain, in
   the manner revealed and as interpreted by the
   Lord, those just and holy principles embodied
   in the Constitution of the United States for
   the protection of all flesh in the exercise of
   their God-given agency.

3. That through faithful observance of the principles of tithing, the fast, and the welfare program, we will prepare ourselves to redeem
   Zion and ultimately live the United Order.

In the name of Jesus Christ. Amen.

What was the object of gathering the Jews, or the people of God in any age of the world? . . .

The main object was to build unto the Lord a house whereby He could reveal unto His people the ordinances of His house and the glories of His kingdom, and teach the people the way of salvation; for there are certain ordinances and principles that, when they are taught and practiced, must be done in a place or house built for that purpose.

Joseph Smith, Jr., *History of the Church* 5:423

TEMPLES — THE GATES TO HEAVEN •

An address delivered to Priesthood Genealogical Seminar August 5, 1970, at Brigham Young University.

Of all the marvelous things revealed during the restoration of the gospel, one of the most significant was a knowledge of temples and their purposes. This included, of course, genealogical and other work now being accomplished under the direction of the Priesthood Genealogical Committee.

As the Prophet translated the ancient record, he learned of temples among Book of Mormon peoples. Nephi, telling of what he was doing about 570 B.C., wrote:

And I did teach my people to build buildings, and to work in all manner of wood, and of iron, and of copper, and of brass, and of steel, and of gold, and of silver, and of precious ores, which were in great abundance.

And I Nephi, did build a temple; and I did construct it after the manner of the temple of Solomon save it were not built of so many precious things; for they were not to be found upon the land, wherefore, it could not be built like unto Solomon's temple. But the manner of the construction was like unto the temple of Solomon; and the workmanship thereof was exceeding fine (2 Nephi 5:15, 16).

Later Jacob referred to teaching the people of Nephi in the temple (Jacob 1:15, 17; 2:2, 11).

About 121 B.C. "king Limhi sent a proclamation among all his people, that thereby they might gather themselves together to the temple to hear the words which he should speak unto them" (Mosiah 7:17).

Presumably this was the temple which the profligate King Noah so elegantly adorned (Mosiah 11:10, 11). It could be that all of the foregoing references are to the temple built by Nephi.

About 124 B.C. the people gathered about another temple in the land of Zarahemla to hear King Benjamin's great farewell address (Mosiah 1:18; 2:1, 5-7).

The Book of Mormon identifies a third temple located in the land Bountiful, "round about" which the people of Nephi were gathered when they first heard and saw the resurrected Savior (3 Nephi 11:1-11).

The Nephites may have had other temples also (see Alma 16:13; 23:2; 26:29; Helaman 3:9, 14).

From the Old Testament we learn that the people of Israel were temple builders. Dr. Talmage points out that they "were distinguished among nations as builders of sanctuaries to the name of the Living God" (James E. Talmage, *The House of the Lord*, p. 2.) Idolatrous peoples also built temples which were consecrated to the worship of their respective idols.

Temples have never been regarded as places of ordinary public assembly. Whether idolatrous or divine, they have always been for the most sacred ceremonies and religious practices of the people who built them.

Soon after Israel "escaped from the environment of Egyptian idolatry," Jehovah required them "to prepare a sanctuary, wherein [he] would manifest his

presence and make known his will as their accepted
Lord and King" (*The House of the Lord*, p. 2). Pursuant to detailed specifications received from Jehovah,
they built, with the finest material available to them,
the Tabernacle which housed the Ark of the Covenant.

When Israel, after forty years of wandering in
the wilderness, finally possessed a land of their own,
the tabernacle which they had carried with them "was
given a resting place in Shiloh; and thither came the
tribes to learn the will and word of God" (*The House
of the Lord*, p. 5).

"David, the second king of Israel, desired and
planned to build a house unto the Lord, declaring that
it was unfit that he, the king, should dwell in a palace
of cedar, while the sanctuary of God was but a tent"
(*The House of the Lord*, p. 6). But the Lord said unto
him: "Thou shalt not build an house for my name,
because thou hast been a man of war, and hast shed
blood" (1 Chronicles 28:3). David did, however, gather
the material and his son Solomon built the temple. Of
this structure, Brother Talmage has written:

> The temple workmen numbered scores of thousands, and
> every department was in charge of master craftsmen. To
> serve on the great structure in any capacity was an honor; and
> labor acquired a dignity never before recognized. Masonry
> became a profession, and the graded orders therein estab-
> lished have endured until this day. The erection of the Temple
> of Solomon was an epoch-making event, not alone in the
> history of Israel, but in that of the world.

> According to commonly accepted chronology, the Tem-
> ple was finished about 1005 B.C. In architecture and construc-
> tion, in design and costliness, it is known as one of the most
> remarkable buildings in history. The dedicatory services
> lasted seven days—a week of holy rejoicing in Israel. With
> fitting ceremony, the Tabernacle of the Congregation and
> the sacred Ark of the Covenant were brought into the Temple;
> and the Ark was deposited in the inner sanctuary, the Most
> Holy Place. The Lord's gracious acceptance was manifest

in the cloud that filled the sacred chambers as the priests withdrew: "So that the priests could not stand to minister by reason of the cloud: for the glory of the Lord had filled the house of God." Thus did the Temple supersede and include the Tabernacle, of which, indeed, it was the gorgeous successor.

A comparison of the plan of Solomon's Temple with that of the earlier Tabernacle shows that in all essentials of arrangement and proportion the two were so nearly alike as to be practically identical. True, the Tabernacle had but one enclosure, while the Temple was surrounded by courts, but the inner structure itself, the Temple proper, closely followed the earlier design. The dimension of the Holy of Holies, the Holy Place, and the Porch, were in the Temple exactly double those of the corresponding parts in the Tabernacle (*The House of the Lord,* pp. 6-8).

This magnificent temple was preserved in its splendor but thirty-four years. Then, because of Solomon's iniquity and Israel's apostasy, "Jehovah withdrew his protecting presence" (*The House of the Lord,* p. 8). The Egyptians despoiled it; Ahaz, king of Judah, robbed it; and Nebuchadnezzar, about 600 B.C., finally burned it.

Israel had become wicked. The tribes were divided. "The Kingdom of Israel, comprising approximately ten of the twelve tribes, had been made subject to Assyria about 721 B.C." (*The House of the Lord,* p. 9). The remaining two tribes—the kingdom of Judah—remained in subjection to Babylon for seventy years.

Then, under the friendly rule of Cyrus and Darius they were permitted to return to Jerusalem, and once more to rear a Temple in accordance with their faith. . . . The restored Temple is known in history as the Temple of Zerubbabel. [It was finished in 515 B.C.]

While this Temple was greatly inferior in richness of finish and furniture as compared with the splendid Temple of Solomon, it was nevertheless the best the people could build, and the Lord accepted it [as he had accepted the tabernacle and Solomon's temple].

About sixteen years before the birth of Christ, Herod I, king of Judea, commenced the reconstruction of the then decayed and generally ruinous Temple of Zerubbabel. For five centuries that structure had stood, and doubtless it had become largely a wreck of time. Many incidents in the earthly life of the Savior are associated with the Temple of Herod. It is evident from scripture that while opposed to the degraded and commercial uses to which the Temple had been betrayed, Christ recognized and acknowledged the sanctity of the temple precincts. The Temple of Herod was a sacred structure; by whatsoever name it might have been known, it was to Him the House of the Lord. And then, when the sable curtain descended upon the great tragedy of Calvary, when at last the agonizing cry, 'It is finished,' ascended from the cross, the veil of the Temple was rent, and the one-time Holy of Holies was bared. The absolute destruction of the Temple had been foretold by our Lord, while yet He lived in the flesh. In the year 70 A.D. the Temple was utterly destroyed by fire in connection with the capture of Jerusalem by the Roman under Titus (*The House of the Lord,* pp. 10-11).

Notwithstanding the fact that temples had always been a hallmark of true followers of the living God, so far as the records reveal, no professing Christians built a temple between the destruction of the Temple of Herod and the organization of The Church of Jesus Christ of Latter-day Saints in 1830—a period of 1,750 years. Since a knowledge concerning temples, their purpose, and the work to be performed in them was not to be found among men on earth during all this time, the question arises: Whence came a knowledge of temples to the Prophet Joseph? Certain it is that he did not obtain such knowledge from men, because they did not have it. The answer is, of course, he received it from heaven through direct revelation.

The building of temples today is, therefore, distinctively an activity of the Church of Jesus Christ, just as much so as is the doctrine expressed in these lines of Eliza R. Snow:

O my Father, thou that dwellest
In the high and glorious place!
When shall I regain thy presence,
And again behold thy face?

In the heavens are parents single?
No, the thought makes reason stare!
Truth is reason, truth eternal
Tells me I've a mother there.

Just as this great hymn could have been written by none other than a member of The Church of Jesus Christ of Latter-day Saints, so today temples can be built by no people other than Latter-day Saints. They can be conceived by no people other than members of the Church possessing an understanding of the gospel of Jesus Christ. The great eternal principles of pre-existence, eternal marriage, resurrection, exaltation, the nature of God and our relationship to him—all of these and the other great principles of the gospel—focus upon temple work. From the temples they are reflected back into the hearts of understanding Latter-day Saints.

Of all the evidences of the prophetic calling of Joseph Smith, Jr., there is hardly one which is more conclusive than the fact that within a year from the time the Church was organized he began to receive instructions from the Lord concerning the building of temples (D&C 36:8).

As early as July 1831 the Lord told him that Independence, Missouri, was the "place for the city of Zion. . . . And a spot for the temple is lying westward, upon a lot which is not far from the court-house" (D&C 57:2, 3).

The interest of the Saints in the building of temples and the city of Zion was great in those early days. Incident to the interest in temples was the spirit of gathering which then fell upon the Saints. The relationship between the spirit of gathering and the interest in temples, was thus explained by the Prophet. Taking for his text the words of the Savior,

O Jerusalem, Jerusalem, thou that killest the prophets, and stonest them which are sent unto thee, how often would I have gathered thy children together, even as a hen gathereth her chickens under her wings, and ye would not! (Matthew 23:37),

he put the question, What was the object of gathering the Jews, or the people of God in any age of the world? To which he responded:

The main object was to build unto the Lord a house whereby He would reveal unto His people the ordinances of His house and the glories of His kingdom, and teach the people the way of salvation; for there are certain ordinances and principles that, when they are taught and practiced, must be done in a place or house built for that purpose.

It was the design of the councils of heaven before the world was, that the principles and laws of the priesthood should be predicated upon the gathering of the people in every age of the world. . . . Ordinances instituted in the heavens before the foundation of the world, in the priesthood, for the salvation of men, are not to be altered or changed. All must be saved on the same principles.

It is for the same purpose that God gathers together His people in the last days, to build unto the Lord a house to prepare them for the ordinances and endowments, washings and anointings. . . . If a man gets a fulness of the priesthood of God, he has to get it in the same way that Jesus Christ obtained it, and that was by keeping all the commandments and obeying all the ordinances of the house of the Lord. . . . All men who become heirs of God and joint-heirs with Jesus Christ will have to receive the fulness of the ordinances of his kingdom; and those who will not receive all the ordinances will come short of the fullness of that glory, if they do not lose the whole (*History of the Church* 5:423-24).

Temples are necessary to a complete organization of the Church. "The church," said the Prophet, "is not fully organized, in its proper order, and cannot be, until the temple is completed, where places will be provided for the administration of the ordinances of the priesthood" (*History of the Church* 4:603). On April 8, 1844, speaking at the Church conference in Nauvoo, the Prophet told the Saints that he had

received instructions from the Lord that from henceforth wherever the Elders of Israel shall build up churches and branches unto the Lord throughout the States, there shall be a stake of Zion. In the great cities, as Boston, New York, etc., there shall be stakes. It is a glorious proclamation, and I reserved it to the last, and designed it to be understood that this work shall commence after the washings, anointings and endowments have been performed here (*History of the Church* 6:319).

Temples are great fortresses for righteousness in the world. The devil opposes them. He so stirred the enemies of our people after the first temples were built that the Saints were required to move away from Kirtland and Nauvoo. Without the great outpouring of Spirit and power given in those temples, it is doubtful whether the Church could have survived. President Stephen L Richards, at the dedication of the Los Angeles Temple, spoke about the power of the sealing ordinance reaching beyond our understanding. It is my belief that the power emanating from temples is far greater than we realize.

In addition to being a place for the Lord to "reveal unto his people the ordinances of his house and the glories of his kingdom, and teach the people the way of salvation" (*History of the Church* 5:423), a temple is a place where the living Saints receive the higher ordinances of the priesthood necessary to their exaltation.

We all know what the necessary ordinances of the gospel are: first, baptism; second, the laying on of hands for the gift of the Holy Ghost. These ordinances are administered to the living in places other than a temple, as is also the third ordinance, the laying on of hands for the bestowal of the priesthood. The higher ordinances of the gospel, however, those pertaining to the endowment and the sealing ordinance, can only be performed in temples.

The Prophet Joseph made it clear that men could not be saved—meaning exalted—unless they had these ordinances performed for themselves.

I would advise all the Saints to go to with their might and gather together all their living relatives to this place, that they may be sealed and saved, that they may be prepared against the day that the destroying angel goes forth. . . .

The question is frequently asked, "Can we not be saved without going through with all those ordinances, etc.?" I would answer, No, not the fullness of salvation. Jesus said, "There are many mansions in my Father's [kingdom] and I will go and prepare a place for you." . . . And any person who is exalted to the highest mansion has to abide a celestial law, and the whole law too (*History of the Church* 6:184).

In temples we are sealed for eternity to our wives, our husbands, our children, and our ancestors. Our leaders repeatedly speak of the home as the center of a Latter-day Saint life. Without the sealing of husbands and wives, children and parents, there would be no family relationships in the world to come; there would be no eternal homes. How terrible this would be. Without the home, heaven would be devoid of its happiness. Wherever my beloved wife and children are is heaven to me. I therefore consider the Salt Lake Temple, in which the sweetheart of my youth and I were sealed together for time and eternity, as the gate to heaven for me.

Temples are also the gates to heaven to our ancestors who were not privileged to live at a time and in a place where they could receive the sealing ordinances.

In his interview with Nicodemus, Jesus told him: "Except a man be born of water and of the Spirit," he can neither see nor "enter into the kingdom of God" (John 3:5-7).

This scripture has put apostate Christianity on the horns of a dilemma. Those who pretend to hold to the teachings of Jesus deny a place in the kingdom to the countless people who have died without baptism. Others, rebelling against the apparent unfairness of such a situation, say that the Savior must not have meant what he said. They therefore reject it and deny the necessity for baptism, as also the other saving ordinances of the gospel.

In reality there is no such dilemma, because the Lord has provided that in temples all of the indispensable ordinances of the gospel may be vicariously performed for the dead. Oh, what rejoicing there must now be in the world of spirits among our Father's faithful children as they see our modern temples being built and behold the great impetus being given to genealogical work under the able leadership of the Priesthood Genealogical Committee, assisted by thousands of intelligent, earnest workers like you who are attending this seminar.

Pondering upon the subject of temples, and the means therein provided to enable us to ascend into heaven, brings to mind the lesson of Jacob's dream. You will recall that in the 28th chapter of Genesis there is an account of his return to the land of his father's to seek a wife from among his own people. The record says that

Jacob went out from Beersheba, and went toward Haran [the place from which Abraham, his grandfather, had come].

And he lighted upon a certain place, and tarried there all night, because the sun was set; and he took of the stones of that place, and put them for his pillows, and lay down in that place to sleep.

And he dreamed, and beheld a ladder set up on the earth, and the top of it reached to heaven: and beheld the angels of God ascending and descending on it.

And, behold, the Lord stood above it [and said], I am the Lord God of Abraham thy father, and the God of Isaac: the land whereon thou liest, to thee will I give it, and to thy seed;

And thy seed shall be as the dust of the earth, and thou shalt spread abroad to the west, and to the east, and to the north, and to the south: and in thee and in thy seed shall all the families of the earth be blessed.

And, behold [the Lord continued], I am with thee, and will keep thee in all places whither thou goest, and will bring thee again into this land; for I will not leave thee, until I have done that which I have spoken to thee of.

And Jacob awaked out of his sleep, and he said, Surely the Lord is in this place; and I knew it not.

And he was afraid, and said, How dreadful is this place! this is none other but the house of God, and this is the gate of heaven.

And Jacob rose up early in the morning, and took the stone that he had put for his pillows, and set it up for a pillar, and poured oil upon the top of it.

And he called the name of that place Bethel: but the name of that city was called Luz at the first.

And Jacob vowed a vow, saying, If God will be with me, and will keep me in this way that I go, and will give me bread to eat, and raiment to put on,

So that I come again to my father's house in peace; then shall the Lord be my God:

And this stone, which I have set for a pillar, shall be God's house: and of all that thou shalt give me I will surely give the tenth unto thee (Genesis 28:10-22; italics added).

Bethel, a contraction of the word *Beth-Elohim,* means literally "the house of the Lord."

As, in his dream, Jacob saw himself on the earth at the foot of the ladder which reached to heaven where the Lord stood above it, and also beheld the angels ascending and descending thereon, he realized that the covenants he there made with the Lord were the rungs on the ladder which he himself would have to climb in order to obtain the promised blessings—blessings that would entitle him to enter heaven and associate with the Lord.

It was because he had met the Lord there and entered into covenants with him there that Jacob considered the site so sacred that he named the place Bethel (the house of the Lord) and said of it: "This is none other but the house of God, and this is the gate of heaven" (Genesis 28:17).

Jacob not only passed through the gate of heaven. By living up to every covenant he went all the way in. Of him and his forebears Abraham and Isaac, the Lord has said:

Because they did not other things than that which they were commanded, they have entered into their exaltation, according to the promises, and sit upon thrones, and are not angels but are gods (D&C 132:37).

Temples are to us all what Bethel was to Jacob, and more. They are also the gates to heaven for all our kindred dead. That we will do our duty in bringing our loved ones through them, I humbly pray.

He that is faithful in tribulation, the reward of the same is greater in the kingdom of heaven.

D&C 58:2

THE CRUCIBLE
OF ADVERSITY AND AFFLICTION •

An address delivered at general conference
October 4, 1969

I have selected as the subject of my remarks today "The Crucible of Adversity and Affliction"—something with which we are all well acquainted. My purpose is to give comfort and courage to the weary and heavy-laden, among whom we all at times find place.

Latter-day Saints know that much pain and suffering could be avoided if people would accept and follow the Savior. Our mission as a church is to bring people to a knowledge of Christ and thus avoid all unnecessary suffering. We are aware, however, that should all men accept and live his teachings, adversity and affliction would still abound, because, in the words of the Prophet Joseph Smith, "Men have to suffer that they may come upon Mount Zion and be exalted above the heavens" (*History of the Church* 5:556).

This does not mean that we crave suffering. We avoid all we can. However, we now know, and we all knew when we elected to come into mortality, that we would here be proved in the "crucible" of adversity and affliction.

As our Heavenly Father, in that great pre-earth council, stood in the midst of us, his spirit children, and announced his plan for bringing to pass our "immortality and eternal life" (Moses 1:30), he said,

> We will go down, . . . and . . . make an earth whereon these may dwell;
> And we will prove them . . . to see if they will do all things whatsoever the Lord their God shall command them (Abraham 3:24, 25).

The Prophet Joseph Smith said that "the organization of the spiritual and heavenly worlds, and of spiritual and heavenly beings . . . were . . . voluntarily subscribed to in their heavenly estate by themselves" (*History of the Church* 6:51).

The Father's plan for proving his children did not exempt the Savior himself. The suffering he undertook to endure, and which he did endure, equaled the combined suffering of all men. Eighteen hundred years after he had endured it, he spoke of it as being so intense that it

> caused myself, even God, the greatest of all, to tremble because of pain, and to bleed at every pore, and to suffer both body and spirit—and would that I might not drink the bitter cup, and shrink—
> Nevertheless, [he concluded] glory be to the Father, and I partook and finished my preparations unto the children of men (D&C 19:18, 19).

President Brigham Young pointed out that the intensity of Christ's suffering was induced by the withdrawal from him of the Father's Spirit:

> At the very moment when the crisis came . . . the Father withdrew His spirit, and cast a vail over him. That is what made him sweat blood . . . He then plead with the Father not

to forsake him. "No," says the Father, "you must have your trials, as well as others" (*Journal of Discourses* 3:205-206).

The severity of the suffering incident to the withdrawal of the Father's Spirit, is intimated in the Lord's statement, through the Prophet, to Martin Harris, in which he said:

Repent . . . lest you suffer these punishments of which I have spoken, of which in the smallest, yea, even in the least degree you have tasted at the time I withdrew my Spirit (D&C 19:20).

Fortunately, we need not endure such suffering because Jesus endured it for us, providing, of course, that we bring ourselves, through righteous living, within the reach of his atoning sacrifice.

However, just as Jesus had to endure affliction to prove himself, so must all men endure affliction to prove themselves.

Abel was slain for his righteousness, . . . Abraham . . . was laid upon the iron bedstead for slaughter; and . . . cast into the fire . . . Moses . . . was driven from his country and kindred. Elijah had to flee his country, . . . Daniel was cast into a den of lions; Micah was fed on the bread of affliction; and Jeremiah was cast into the filthy hole under the Temple. . . .

All the Saints . . . prophets and apostles, have had to come up through great tribulation (*Teachings of the Prophet Joseph Smith*, pp. 260-261).

From his own experiences, the Prophet Joseph was eminently qualified to talk about affliction, and this he most eloquently did. Writing from Liberty Jail in March 1839, he revealed something concerning the tribulations then being endured by him and his associates:

We have been taken prisoners [he said] charged falsely with every kind of evil, and thrown into prison, enclosed with strong walls, surrounded with a strong guard, who continually

watch day and night as indefatigable as the devil . . . we are
compelled to hear nothing but blasphemous oaths, and witness
a scene of blasphemy, and drunkenness and hypocrisy, and
debaucheries of every description (*History of the Church*
3:290).

But even as he protested these atrocities, his soul
expanded as he endured them. To the Saints, who themselves (at that time some 12,000 to 15,000 of them)
were being ravished and plundered, robbed and driven
from their homes, in the dead of winter, he said:

Our circumstances are calculated to awaken our spirits
to a sacred remembrance of everything, and we think that
yours are also, and that nothing . . . can separate us from the
love of God and fellowship one with another; and that every
species of wickedness and cruelty practiced upon us will only
tend to bind our hearts together and seal them together in
love (Ibid., p. 290).

A little later on in his letter he added this:

And now, beloved brethren, we say unto you, that inasmuch as God hath said that He would have a tried people,
that He would purge them as gold, now we think that this time
he has chosen his own crucible, wherein we have been tried;
and we think if we get through with any degree of safety,
and shall have kept the faith, that it will be a sign to this
generation, altogether sufficient to leave them without excuse;
and we think also, it will be a trial of our faith equal to that
of Abraham, and that the ancients will not have whereof to
boast over us in the day of judgment, as being called to pass
through heavier afflictions (Ibid., p. 294).

And then, speaking for himself and his fellow
prisoners, he said, "In His Almighty name we are determined to endure tribulation as good soldiers unto
the end" (Ibid., p. 297).

And counseling the Saints to do likewise, he said,
"Let thy bowels . . . be full of charity towards all
men" (Ibid., p. 300).

This admonition, considered in light of the circumstances under which it was given, seems to me to almost equal the Master's statement from the cross: "Father, forgive them; for they know not what they do" (Luke 23:34).

The Prophet's soul never could have reached these heights without enduring well the tribulations and afflictions heaped upon him.

President Brigham Young is quoted as observing that the Prophet was more perfect in thirty-eight years, with the severe tribulation through which he passed, than he would have been in a thousands years without it. (Truman G. Madsen, *Eternal Man*, p. 61).

The Prophet's appreciation and gratitude for the kindness of a friend, the "pure love of Christ" which filled his soul, and the assurance given him by the Lord, he expressed in the following passage (note how it reveals the purity of his heart, the tenderness of his spirit, and the nobility of his soul):

Those who have not been enclosed in the walls of prison without cause or provocation can have but little idea how sweet the voice of a friend is; one token of friendship from any source whatever awakens and calls into action every sympathetic feeling; it brings up in an instant everything that is passed; it seizes the present with the avidity of lightning; it grasps after the future with the fierceness of a tiger; it moves the mind backward and forward, from one thing to another, until finally all enmity, malice and hatred, and past differences, misunderstandings and mismanagements are slain victorious at the feet of hope; and when the heart is sufficiently contrite, then the voice of inspiration steals along and whispers, My son, peace be unto thy soul; thine adversity and thine afflictions shall be but a small moment; and then if thou endure it well, God shall exalt thee on high (*History of the Church* 3:293).

No wonder the Lord could say to him, as he did:

I seal upon you your exaltation, and prepare a throne for you in the kingdom of my Father, with Abraham your father.

Behold, I have seen your sacrifices, and will forgive all your sins; I have seen your sacrifices in obedience to that which I have told you (D&C 132:49, 50).

Now, as I noted in the beginning, my desire is to comfort and encourage and inspire all you faithful, humble people who are enduring with patience and loneliness, pain, sorrow, and at times almost despair; you who languish in hospitals and nursing homes, and all you other shut-ins; you who mourn the loss of loved ones by death or transgression; you who are experiencing diminution of strength in mind and body. In sympathy and love I say to you and all the rest of us who are being tried in the crucible of adversity and affliction: Take courage; revive your spirits and strengthen your faith. In these lessons so impressively taught in precept and example by our Great Exemplar, Jesus Christ, and his Prophet of the Restoration, Joseph Smith, we have ample inspiration for comfort and for hope.

If we can bear our afflictions with the understanding, faith and courage, and in the spirit in which they bore theirs, we shall be strengthened and comforted in many ways. We shall be spared the torment which accompanies the mistaken idea that all suffering comes as chastisement for transgression. We shall be comforted by the knowledge that we are not enduring, nor will be required to endure, the suffering of the wicked who are to "be cast out into outer darkness; [where] there shall be weeping, and wailing, and gnashing of teeth" (Alma 40:13).

We can draw assurance from the Lord's promise that

he that is faithful in tribulation, the reward of the same is greater in the kingdom of heaven.

Ye cannot behold with your natural eyes, for the present time [he said], the design of your God concerning those things which shall come hereafter, and the glory which shall follow after much tribulation.

For after much tribulation come the blessings (D&C 58:2-4).

We can experience what Paul was expressing in his epistles to the Romans when he said:

Therefore being justified by faith, we have peace with God through our Lord Jesus Christ:

By whom also we have access by faith into this grace wherein we stand, and rejoice in hope of the glory of God.

And not only so, but we glory in tribulations also: knowing that tribulation worketh patience;

And patience, experience; and experience, hope:

And hope maketh not ashamed; because the love of God is shed abroad in our hearts by the Holy Ghost which is given unto us (Romans 5:1-5).

In conclusion, I testify to the truthfulness of these things. They are part and parcel of the restored gospel of Jesus Christ. I know they are true. I have read and been impressed by the testimony of others. Paul, for example, who having thrice sought the Lord to remove "a thorn in the flesh," was answered: "My grace is sufficient for thee: for my strength is made perfect in weakness."

Then Paul answered:

Most gladly therefore will I rather glory in my infirmities, that the power of Christ may rest upon me.

Therefore I take pleasure in infirmities, in reproaches, in necessities, in persecutions, in distresses for Christ's sake: for when I am weak, then am I strong (2 Corinthians 12:9, 10).

Not only have I been impressed by the testimonies of others; I have been eyewitness to the operation of these principles in the lives of my own acquaintances. I have seen the remorse and despair in the lives of men who, in the hour of trial, have cursed God and died spiritually. And I have seen people rise to great heights from what seemed to be unbearable burdens.

Finally, I have sought the Lord in my own extremities and learned for myself that my soul has made its greatest growth as I have been driven to my knees by adversity and affliction.

To these things I bear solemn witness in the name of Jesus Christ, our beloved Savior, and in his name I invoke a comforting and sustaining blessing upon each of you, in the name of Jesus Christ. Amen.

Adam fell that men might be.
2 Nephi 2:25

THE FALL OF ADAM •

*An address delivered at general conference April
1953.*

I would like to say just a word about my testimony
of the mission of Jesus Christ. I would like to go a
little farther back for a moment, if I can be given
guidance by the Spirit of the Lord to speak the truth
accurately, and mention the great condition precedent
to the efficacy of the mission of Jesus Christ. That
condition precedent is the mission of father Adam, because without the mission of Adam there would have
been no need for the mission—the atonement—of
Jesus Christ.

I have an assignment from the First Presidency
to serve on the Church Publications Committee. This
committee is expected to read and pass upon the literature proposed for use in the study courses of our
auxiliary organizations. It would please me immensely
if, in the preparation of this literature, we could get
away from using the language of those who do not
believe in the mission of Adam. I have reference to
words and phrases such as "primitive man," "prehistoric man," "before men learned to write," and the
like. We sometimes use these terms in a way that of-

fends my feelings; in a way which indicates to me that we get mixed up in our understanding of the mission of Adam. The connotation of these terms, as used by unbelievers, is out of harmony with our understanding of the mission of Adam.

"Adam fell that men might be" (2 Nephi 2:25). There were no pre-Adamic men in the line of Adam. The Lord said that Adam was the first man (Moses 1:34, 3:7; D&C 84:16). It is hard for men to get the idea of a man ahead of Adam, before the first man. The Lord also said that Adam was the first flesh (Moses 3:7), which, as I understand it, means the first mortal on the earth. I understand from a statement in the book of Moses, which was made by Enoch, that there was no death in the world before Adam (Moses 6:48; see also 2 Nephi 2:22). Enoch said:

Death hath come upon our fathers; nevertheless we know them, and cannot deny, and even the first of all we know, even Adam.

For a book of remembrance we have written among us, according to the pattern given by the finger of God; and it is given in our own language (Moses 5:45, 46).

I understand from this that Enoch could read about Adam in a book which had been written under the tutelage of Almighty God. Thus there were no prehistoric men who could not write, because men living in the days of Adam, who was the first man, wrote.

I am not a scientist. I do not profess to know anything but Jesus Christ and him crucified and the principles of his gospel. If, however, there are some things in the strata of the earth indicating that there were men before Adam, they were not the ancestors of Adam.

Adam was the son of God. He was our elder brother, not older than Jesus, but he was our brother in the same sense that Jesus was our brother, and he "fell" to earth life. He did not come up through an unbroken line of organic evolution. There had to be a fall. "Adam fell that men might be" (2 Nephi 2:25).

I will now go on and read this scripture:

For a book of remembrance we have written among us, according to the pattern given by the finger of God; and it is given in our own language.

And as Enoch spake forth the words of God, the people trembled, and could not stand in his presence (Moses 6:46, 47).

Some men speak of the ancients as being savages, as if they had no intelligence. I tell you this man Enoch had intelligence, and Adam had intelligence, as much as any man that ever lived since or that lives now. They were mighty sons of God.

And he said unto them: Because that Adam fell, we are; and by his fall came death; and we are made partakers of misery and woe (Moses 6:48).

If Adam and Eve had not partaken of the forbidden fruit, they would have had no children, and we would not have been (2 Nephi 2:23-25; Moses 5:11).

I do not look upon Adam's action as a sin. I think it was a deliberate act of free agency. He chose to do that which had to be done to further the purposes of God. The consequences of his act made necessary the atonement of the Redeemer.

I must not go into a longer discussion, but I say again that I would be very pleased if, in our teaching of the gospel, we could keep revealed truth straight in our minds and not get it confused with the ideas and theories of men who do not believe what the Lord has revealed with respect to the fall of Adam.

Now, I believe with Enoch, "Because that Adam fell, we are; and by his fall came death" (Moses 6:48) that every man must die. I believe that to meet the de-

mands of justice, it took the atonement of Jesus Christ
to redeem men from that death, that they may be
raised again and have their spirits and their bodies,
which are separated through death, reunited. I believe
that through the atonement of Jesus Christ whatever
"trangression" Adam committed was paid for, and that
as in Adam all die, even so in Christ shall all be made
alive, every living creature (1 Corinthians 15:22; D&C
29:24, 77). I believe, too, that through the atonement of Jesus Christ my individual sins, your individual sins, and the individual sins of every human
being that ever lived or ever will live upon the earth
were atoned for, upon condition that we accept the
gospel and live it to the end of our lives.

I know that my Redeemer lives. I shall not know
it better when I stand before the bar of God to be
judged. I bear that witness to you, not from what
people have told me; I bear it out of a knowledge revealed to me by the Holy Spirit. As to this knowledge,
the Lord, after commanding the early apostles of this
dispensation to testify that the words he had spoken
to them were of him, said:

> For it is my voice that speaketh them unto you; for they
> are given by my Spirit unto you, and by my power you can
> read them one to another; and save it were by my power you
> could not have them;
> Wherefore, you can testify that you have heard my voice,
> and know my words (D&C 18:35, 36).

I am willing to bear witness to all the Saints and
to all men and women everywhere, saints and sinners,
in all the world, for it is the eternal truth.

I know that the Prophet Joseph Smith was a
prophet of God. I know he saw God, the Eternal Father,
and his Son, Jesus Christ, as he says he did. I was not
there, but I have read his account many, many, many

times. From his account I get in my mind a mental picture, but I did not get my knowledge that he had the vision from that source. I received it from the whisperings of the Holy Spirit, and I have had those whisperings in my mind the same as Enos had when he said, "The voice of the Lord came into my mind" (Enos 10).

I know that God revealed every principle of salvation necessary to the exaltation of men to the Prophet Joseph Smith. I know that his successor who sits here today, David O. McKay, holds every power and every authority and all the priesthood that the Prophet Joseph had—unless it be the keys of this last dispensation. But every power that is necessary to the salvation of men, he holds. Nobody has a testimony of the gospel that will save him unless he knows it, too.

Today being the twentieth aniversary of Brother Clark's call to the First Presidency, I want to pay him a tribute. I love him. Although the Lord had to go all the way to Mexico City to find him, I am grateful that he brought him back to give us this twenty years of service. I want to read a statement from the message he gave twenty years ago. In it he spoke of his great humility and of the apprehension he felt as to whether he could meet the requirements of his new position. In telling of the joys he anticipated, he said:

We shall have the joy of work, too, for man also is that he might work, he went forth from the innocence of Eden to the God-like knowledge of good and evil, with the Divine blessing—not curse—as it seems to me: "In the sweat of thy face shalt thou eat bread." And save in extremity, no man may rightfully violate that law by living by the sweat from the brow of his brother. It is the eternal, inescapable law that growth comes only from work and preparation, whether the growth be material, mental, or spiritual. Work has no substitute. Idleness brings neither profit, nor advantage, nor good —only a withering decay and death. The world is near to forgetting all this; I hope that we as a people shall keep it ever in remembrance, for in proportion as it is forgotten, evil will rule (*Conference Report*, April 1933, p. 103).

I have watched him work through these years, as have the other brethren. We greatly appreciate the example he has set for us.

In conclusion, let me say this by way of general statement. Work, brothers and sisters, work in the kingdom. Get the testimony of the gospel. I think it is a disgrace for men and women to stand on the same ground day after day in their testimony, their knowledge of the gospel, and their work in the Church. We should go forward. We ought to be on our mettle all the time, reaching, perfecting our lives, doing more work, going forward, preparing to meet the Redeemer. We live in the day just before his coming. We must speed the day, speed the work in preparation for that great day, that we may rest our souls in the kingdom of God, which I hope we may all do, and so pray in the name of Jesus Christ. Amen.

He that receiveth my servants receiveth me;

And he that receiveth me receiveth my Father;

And he that receiveth my Father receiveth my Father's kingdom; therefore all that my Father hath shall be given unto him.

D&C 84:36-38

LOYALTY TO TRUTH AND THE LORD'S REPRESENTATIVES •

An address delivered at general conference April 1942.

I desire to call your attention to the principle of loyalty—loyalty to the truth and loyalty to the men whom God has chosen to lead the cause of truth. I speak of "the truth" and these "men" jointly, because it is impossible fully to accept the one and partly reject the other.

I raise my voice on this matter to warn and counsel you to be on your guard against criticism. I have heard some myself and have been told about more. It comes, in part, from those who hold, or have held, prominent positions. Ostensibly, they are in good standing in the Church. In expressing their feelings, they frequently say, "We are members of the Church, too, you know, and our feelings should be considered."

They assume that one can be in full harmony with the spirit of the gospel, enjoy full fellowship in the Church, and at the same time be out of harmony with the leaders of the Church and the counsel and directions they give. Such a position is wholly untenable, because the guidance of this Church comes, not alone from the written word, but also from continuous revelation, and the Lord gives that revelation. It follows, therefore, that those who profess to accept the gospel and who at the same time criticize and refuse to follow the counsel of the leaders are assuming an indefensible position.

Such a spirit leads to apostasy. It is not new. It was prevalent in the days of Jesus. Some who boasted of being Abraham's children said of the Son of God: "Behold a man gluttonous, and a winebibber, a friend of publicans and sinners" (Matthew 11:19). But those who stood by him, enjoying the spirit of truth, knew him, as did Peter, who said "Thou art the Christ, the Son of the living God" (Matthew 16:19).

In the days of the Prophet Joseph, there was criticism against him and the counsel he gave. Some of the leading brethren of the Church charged him with being a fallen prophet. They did not deny the gospel, but they contended that the Prophet had fallen.

These were critical times for the Church. They have now long since passed into history, but the records remain. The issues are now clear. Joseph Smith was the Lord's prophet, and so continued, notwithstanding all the abuse directed at him. He now sits enthroned in yonder heavens. Those who criticized him apostatized and left the Church. Thomas B. Marsh, who left the Church in 1839 because he became jealous of the Prophet, found his way in 1857 to Salt Lake City, and in addressing the Saints, said:

If there are any among this people who should ever apostatize and do as I have done, prepare your backs for a good whipping if you are such as the Lord loves. *But if you will take my advice, you will stand by the authorities.*

As we look back upon these important events, it

seems that the issues were always so clearly drawn that anyone could have seen the truth. And yet there seems always to have been great intellects on the side of error. This is one of life's tragedies. Surely there can be nothing of more importance than to be always and everlastingly on the side of truth as we meet the complex problems of our lives. It is comforting to know that that is where we may be if we will but hearken to the Spirit of truth. For the Lord has said that "the Spirit giveth light to every man that cometh into the world; and the Spirit enlighteneth every man through the world, *that hearkens to the voice of the Spirit*" (D&C 84:46). That this is no idle promise is shown by the fact that on nearly all occasions there have stood with God's spokesmen those who were loyal to the truth and to the men whom God had chosen to lead the cause of truth. At the time of the attack on the Prophet in Kirtland, Brigham Young was present, and when the criticism was expressed, he arose and in plain and forceful language said that Joseph was a prophet and he knew it "and that they might rail and slander him as much as they pleased, they could but destroy their own authority and cut the thread that bound them to the prophet of God and sink themselves to hell." Later he said:

Some of the leading men at Kirtland were much opposed to the Prophet meddling with temporal affairs, thinking that his duty embraced spiritual things alone and that the people should be left to attend to their temporal affairs without interference whatever from prophets and apostles. In a public meeting, I said: "Ye elders of Israel: Now, will some of you draw the line of demarcation between the spiritual and temporal within the Kingdom of God, so that I may understand it!" Not one of them could do it. When I saw a man standing in the path before the Prophet, I felt like hurling him out of the way and branding him as a fool.

Here was loyalty—loyalty both to the truth and to the man whom God had called to represent it.

Why was it that the vision of Brigham Young was clear and that of Thomas B. Marsh was clouded— that Brigham Young remained true to the Prophet and that Thomas B. Marsh criticized him? It was because Brigham Young always hearkened to the Spirit of truth and Thomas B. Marsh did not.

Last October I attended a conference in an outlying stake. A number of the speakers had just attended for the first time a general conference. Their reports were soul stirring. One bishop wished that every member of his ward might attend just one conference in the Tabernacle. Another, when he stood with the vast congregation for the first time, was so moved that tears ran down his cheeks, and his voice so choked that he could not join in the singing. A third was impressed with President Grant's closing remarks. He said as he finished his talk: "Three times the President said 'I bless you, I bless you, I bless you.'"

In another outlying stake, an ex-bishop said to me that the conference was nothing but a political convention. In another a man said that whether he would follow the counsel of the leaders depended upon what subject they discussed.

How are these different responses accounted for? I will tell you. The members of the one group were observing and keeping the commandments of God, and the others were not; one group was walking in the light of truth, and the other was in the dark; one group enjoyed the *Spirit of the Lord*, and the others did not.

If we are to be on the side of truth, we must have the Spirit of the Lord. To the obtaining of that Spirit, prayer is an indispensable prerequisite. Praying will keep one's vision clear on this question of loyalty as on all other questions. By praying I do not mean,

however, just saying prayers. Prayers may be said in a
perfunctory manner. Access to the Spirit of God,
which is a directing power, cannot be so obtained. The
divine injunction to pray is not to be satisfied in a
casual manner nor by an effort to obtain divine approval of a predetermined course. A firm resolve to
comply with the will of God must accompany the
petition for knowledge as to what his will is. When
one brings himself to the position that he will pursue
the truth wherever it may lead, even though it may
require a reversal of his former position, he can, without hypocrisy, go before the Lord in prayer. Then,
when he prays with all the energy of his soul, he is
entitled to and he will receive guidance. The mind and
will of the Lord as to the course he should take will be
made known unto him.

I assure you, however, that the Spirit of the Lord
will never direct a person to take a position in opposition to the counsel of the presidency of His Church.
Such could not be, and I will tell you why. The Spirit
of the Lord is "truth." The Prophet Joseph Smith says
that "The glory of God is intelligence, or, in other
words, *light and truth.*"

The presidency, in directing the Church and its
affairs and in counseling the people, do so under the
directing power of this *"light and truth."* When a
man and the presidency are both directed on the same
subject by "light and truth," there can be no conflict.
And so, all who are out of harmony in any degree with
the presidency have need to repent and to seek the
Lord for forgiveness and to put themselves in full
harmony.

In response to a contention that to follow such a
course is tantamount to surrendering one's "moral
agency," suppose a person were in a forest with his

vision limited by the denseness of the growth about him. Would he be surrendering his agency in following the directions of one who stands on a lookout tower, commanding an unobstructed view? To me, our leaders are true watchmen on the towers of Zion, and those who follow their counsel are exercising their agency just as freely as would be the man in the forest. For I accept as a fact, without any reservation, that this Church is headed by the Lord Jesus Christ and that he, through the men whom he chooses and appoints to lead his people, gives it active direction. I believe that he communicates to them his will and that they, enjoying his Spirit, counsel us.

The Savior himself gave us the great example on this point. As he labored and suffered under the weight of the sins of this world in the accomplishment of the great atonement, he cried out in the agony of his soul, "O my Father, if it be possible, let this cup pass from me: Nevertheless not as I will, but as thou wilt" (Matthew 26:39). And so saying, he subjected himself to the will of his Father in the consummation of his supreme mission. Who will say that in so doing he surrendered his free agency?

That we may all have the vision and the courage to be loyal to the truth and loyal to the men whom God has chosen to lead in the cause of truth, I humbly pray in the name of Jesus Christ. Amen.

Can ye look up to God at that day with a pure heart and clean hands?

Alma 5:19

"A PURE HEART AND CLEAN HANDS" •

An address delivered at Logan Institute of Religion May 11, 1967.

My text, "A Pure Heart and Clean Hands," is lifted from an impassioned interrogation addressed by Alma, in the year 83 B.C., to backsliding members of the church in the city of Zarahemla. To put it in context I quote the following:

And now . . . I ask . . . you, my brethren . . . have ye spiritually been born of God? . . . Have ye experienced this mighty change in your hearts?

Do ye exercise faith in the redemption of him who created you? Do you look forward with an eye of faith, and view this mortal body raised in immortality, . . . to stand before God to be judged according to the deeds which have been done in the mortal body?

I say unto you, can you imagine to yourselves that ye hear the voice of the Lord, saying unto you, in that day: Come unto me ye blessed, for behold, your works have been the works of righteousness upon the face of the earth?

Or . . . can ye imagine yourselves brought before the tribunal of God with your souls filled with guilt and remorse, having . . . a remembrance that ye have set at defiance the commandments of God? I say unto you, can ye look up to God at that day with a pure heart and clean hands? (Alma 5:14-16, 18, 19).

Alma is here implying that the "exercise of faith in the redemption" of Christ, sufficient to bring about the mighty change in one's heart, to which he refers, is prerequisite to obtaining "a pure heart and clean hands." He is also implying that if on the great judgment day one can look up to God with a "pure heart and clean hands," he will hear the voice of the Lord saying unto him, "come unto me ye blessed," and that if he cannot do so, his soul will be filled with guilt and remorse.

He uses the phrase "a pure heart and clean hands" to indicate a state of purity—the condition one attains unto, when, through faith in the Lord Jesus Christ, repentance, baptism by immersion, and baptism by fire and the Holy Ghost, he receives forgiveness of sins which works in him a spiritual rebirth, a birth through which he comes back into harmony with, and is sensitive and alive to, the things of the Spirit. *Healed* is the term frequently used in the scriptures to denote the state of such an one.

On that great day, according to Alma, those who have "a pure heart and clean hands" will receive "an inheritance at the right hand" of God. While those who do not will wail and mourn, for they at long last will recognize that they cannot be saved but must await "an everlasting destruction."

We may well ponder Alma's question: "Can ye look up to God at that day with a pure heart and clean hands?" for there can scarcely be another question upon the answer to which so much depends. To me it suggests the same consideration as does the following statement found in the 21st section of the Doctrine and Covenants: "Let virtue garnish thy thoughts unceasingly; then shall thy confidence wax strong in the presence of God" (v. 45).

Realizing that it will not be long now until I shall be summoned to appear before the judgment bar, these scriptures are becoming more and more meaningful to me. Adding to my concern is the fact that if I appear there without "a pure heart and clean hands," I will have no justifiable excuse, because by the power of the Holy Spirit I have been given a knowledge of that "law, irrevocably decreed in heaven" upon which the possession of such a pure heart and clean hands is predicated (D&C 130:20). This law is, of course, of the celestial and not of this world, but its provisions are as fixed and certain as are the laws of the physical universe. If we cannot obey them, we cannot obtain the blessings which obedience to them brings, for the Lord himself has said that "he who is not able to abide the law of a celestial kingdom cannot abide a celestial glory" (D&C 88:22).

The provisions of this celestial law, as already indicated, are "faith in the Lord Jesus Christ, repentance, baptism by immersion and baptism by fire and the Holy Ghost." Because to abide by these principles and ordinances is prerequisite to obtaining, and a guarantee that one will obtain "a pure heart and clean hands," let us take a little closer look at them.

Faith in the Lord Jesus Christ requires belief in him. That is, acceptance as truth of all that has been revealed concerning him and his mission. For example: That he is the firstborn spirit son of God; that he was chosen and ordained in the great heavenly council to be our Redeemer; that he came to earth in the meridian of time as the Only Begotten of God in the flesh, lived a sinless life, taught the gospel, suffered in Gethsemane, died on the cross, was buried, rose again the third day, and ascended into heaven; that through his victory over death he brought about universal

resurrection; and that through his atonement he implemented the merciful plan of salvation whereby men
may be forgiven of their sins, which forgiveness creates
in them pure hearts and clean hands.

This belief must, however, be more than mental
assent. James emphasized this when he said, "Thou
believest that there is one God; thou doest well: the
devils also believe, and tremble" (James 2:19).

It must also be more than the knowledge referred
to by Mark in his account of a man with an unclean
spirit who, when he saw Jesus, cried out: "What have
we to do with thee, thou Jesus of Nazareth? . . . I know
thee who thou art, the Holy One of God" (Mark
1:23, 24).

A saving belief or faith in the Lord Jesus Christ
is accompanied by some of its fruits. "The ancients
quenched the violence of fire, escaped the edge of the
sword, women received their dead, etc. By faith the
worlds were made. A man who has none of the gifts
has no faith" (*History of the Church* 5:218). Paul says
that by faith

the elders obtained a good report.
By faith Abel offered unto God a more excellent sacrifice than Cain, by which he obtained a witness that he was
righteous, . . .
By faith Enoch was translated that he should not see
death; . . .
He that cometh to God must believe that he is, and that
he is a rewarder of them that diligently seek him (Hebrews
11:2, 4-6).

The efficacy of a belief that God is and that "he is
a rewarder of them that diligently seek him" in pro-
ducing a "pure heart and clean hands" is conclusively
evidenced by the fact that it moves one to repent of his
sins and obey the principles and ordinances of the celestial law.

The significance, power, and indispensability of such a faith in the Lord Jesus Christ have been repeatedly declared from the beginning. It was declared to them of the first dispensation by Adam, to whom the Lord said:

If thou wilt turn unto me, . . . and believe, and repent . . . and be baptized . . . in the name of mine Only Begotten Son, . . . Jesus Christ, the only name which shall be given under heaven, whereby salvation shall come unto the children of men, ye shall receive the gift of the Holy Ghost (Moses 6:52).

Such was the message of all the Old Testament prophets.

It was likewise the message of all the Nephite prophets.

As the Lord God liveth [said Nephi], there is none other name given under heaven save it be this Jesus Christ, of which I have spoken, whereby man can be saved (2 Nephi 25:20).

In the meridian of time, Jesus said to the Jews, as he taught them in the temple treasury: "If ye believe not that I am he, ye shall die in your sins" (John 8:24).

When Peter and John were being questioned by the Jews concerning the power by which they had healed the impotent man at the gate of the temple, Peter answered:

Be it known unto you all . . . that by the name of Jesus Christ of Nazareth . . . doth this man stand here before you whole. . . .
Neither is there salvation in any other: for there is none other name under heaven given among men, whereby we must be saved (Acts 4:10, 12).

In this last dispensation the Lord has repeatedly declared this truth. Through the Prophet, he said to Oliver Cowdery and David Whitmer: "Behold, Jesus Christ is the name which is given of the Father, and there is none other name given whereby man can be saved" (D&C 18:23).

I have quoted these several scriptures which emphasize the preeminent role of faith in the Lord Jesus Christ and in the plan of salvation because of my desire to teach, with all the power at my command, and bear witness to the truth that Jesus is the Son of God, our Savior and our Redeemer, and that a vital, moving faith in him is an indispensable prerequisite to forgiveness of sins, which forgiveness, as above indicated, is the catalyst which heals the sinner and creates in him a pure heart and clean hands.

To me, one of the most direct and persuasive lessons on this point is given in the book of Enos. He begins by saying, "I will tell you of the wrestle which I had before God, before I received a remission of my sins."

Then he recounts how, as he sought food in the forest,

the words which [he] had often heard [his] father speak concerning eternal life and the joy of the saints, sunk deep into [his] heart.

And [he continues] my soul hungered; and I kneeled down before my Maker, and I cried unto him in mighty prayer and supplication for mine own soul; and all the day long did I cry unto him; yea, and when the night came I did still raise my voice high that it reached the heavens.

And there came a voice unto me, saying: Enos, thy sins are forgiven thee, and thou shalt be blessed.

And I, Enos, knew that God could not lie; wherefore, my guilt was swept away.

And I said: Lord, how is it done?

And he said unto me: Because of thy faith in Christ, . . . wherefore, go to, thy faith hath made thee whole (Enos 2-8).

So much for faith in the Lord Jesus Christ, the first provision of the law which brings a pure heart and clean hands. We come now to repentance, the second provision.

One who has faith, and the desire which comes with it, to "look up to God at that day with a pure heart and clean hands" will repent, for the commandment as stated by the risen Lord himself to the Nephites is:

Repent, . . . and come unto me and be baptized in my name, that ye may be sanctified by the reception of the Holy Ghost, that ye may stand spotless before me at the last day (3 Nephi 27:20).

He early renewed this commandment in this dispensation in the revelation recorded in the 19th section of the Doctrine and Covenants.

To repent indicates a "godly sorrow for sin," which produces a reformation of life. It "embodies (1) a conviction of guilt, (2) a desire to be relieved from the hurtful effects of sin, and (3) an earnest determination to forsake sin and in the Lord's appointed way seek forgiveness" (Talmage, *Articles of Faith*, p. 109).

After faith and repentance, the third principle and the first ordinance in the prescribed celestial law for obtaining a pure heart and clean hands is baptism by immersion in water for the remission of sins.

Baptism is symbolical. It symbolizes a cleansing, a washing away of sins. It also symbolizes a resurrection.

Know ye not [said Paul] that so many of us as were baptized into Jesus Christ were baptized into his death?

Therefore we are buried with him by baptism into death: that like as Christ was raised up from the dead by the glory of the Father, even so we also should walk in newness of life (Romans 6:3, 4).

Baptism is the "water" birth spoken of by Jesus when to Nicodemus he said, "Except a man be born of water and of the Spirit, he cannot enter into the kingdom of God" (John 3:5).

One evidences his faith in the Lord Jesus Christ and his repentance, by being so baptized, by covenanting in the waters of baptism to keep the commandments. Alma, instructing the people of Gideon, put it this way:

Yea, I say unto you come and fear not, and lay aside every sin, which easily doth beset you, which doth bind you down to destruction, yea, come and go forth, and show unto your God that ye are willing to repent of your sins and enter into a covenant with him to keep his commandments, and witness it unto him this day by going into the waters of baptism (Alma 7:15).

Jesus, being sinless, did not need to be baptized for the remission of sins, but nevertheless he insisted that he be baptized, saying unto John, "Suffer it to be so now: for thus it becometh us to fulfill all righteousness" (Matthew 3:15).

Nehi, commenting on the baptism of Jesus, explains what is meant by fulfilling all righteousness and introduces the fourth provision of the celestial law which purifies one's heart and cleanses his hands. He says:

And now, I would ask of you, my beloved brethren, wherein the Lamb of God did fulfill all righteousness in being baptized by water?

Know ye not that he was holy? But notwithstanding he being holy, he showeth unto the children of men that, according to the flesh he humbleth himself before the Father, and witnesseth unto the Father that he would be obedient unto him in keeping his commandments.

Wherefore, after he was baptized with water the Holy Ghost descended upon him in the form of a dove.

And . . . the voice of the Son came unto me, saying: He

that is baptized in my name, to him will the Father give the Holy Ghost, like unto me; wherefore, follow me, and do the things which ye have seen me do.

Wherefore, my beloved brethren, I know that if ye shall follow the Son, with full purpose of heart, . . . repenting of your sins, witnessing unto the Father that ye are willing to take upon you the name of Christ, by baptism—Yea, by following your Lord and your Savior down into the water, according to his word, behold, then shall ye receive the Holy Ghost; yea, then cometh the baptism of fire and of the Holy Ghost (2 Nephi 31:6, 7, 12, 13).

This "baptism of fire and of the Holy Ghost" here spoken of by Nephi effects the great change in the hearts of men referred to by Alma. It converts them from carnality to spirituality. It cleanses, heals, and purifies the soul. It is the sealing and sign of forgiveness. It is the spiritual rebirth spoken of by Jesus to Nicodemus. Faith in the Lord Jesus Christ, repentance, and water baptism are all preliminary and prerequisite to it, but it is the consummation. To receive it is to have one's garments washed in the atoning blood of Jesus Christ.

Alma was trying to arouse his hearers at Zarahemla to a realization that their being able to look up "to God at that day with a pure heart and clean hands" would depend upon their experiencing the mighty change wrought in men's hearts by the baptism of fire and the Holy Ghost.

Reminding them that his father had accepted the words of Abinadi and that

according to his faith there was a mighty change wrought in his heart. . . .

And [that he had] preached the word unto [their] fathers, and a mighty change was also wrought in their hearts,

he continued,

And now behold, I ask of you, my brethren of the church,
have ye spiritually been born of God? . . .

Have ye experienced this mighty change in your hearts?
(Alma 5:12-14).

It was against this background that he put the
question: "Can ye look up to God at that day with a
pure heart and clean hands?" (Alma 5:19).

This "mighty change" wrought by the baptism of
fire and the Holy Ghost should and does, if the prose-
lyte is prepared to receive it, occur when he is baptized
by immersion for the remission of sins and receives
the laying on of hands for the gift of the Holy Ghost—
the two required ordinances for being "born of water
and of the spirit."

Alma gave his son Helaman a most graphic account of his being born again.   As he

went about with the sons of Mosiah seeking to destroy the
church of God [he was called to repentance by an angel who
said unto him] . . .

If thou wilt of thyself be destroyed, seek no more to
destroy the church of God.

[Whereupon, said Alma] I fell to the earth; . . .

And . . . I was racked with eternal torment, for . . .

I did remember all my sins and iniquities, for which I was
tormented with the pains of hell; . . .

Oh, thought I, that I could be banished and become extinct
both soul and body, that I might not be brought to stand in
the presence of my God, to be judged of my deeds.

And it came to pass that as I was racked with torment,
while I was harrowed up by the memory of my many sins,
behold, I remembered also to have heard my father prophesy
unto the people concerning the coming of one Jesus Christ, a
Son of God, to atone for the sins of the world.

Now, as my mind caught hold upon this thought, I cried
within my heart: O Jesus, thou Son of God, have mercy on me,
who am in the gall of bitterness, and am encircled about by
the everlasting chains of death.

And now, behold, when I thought this, I could remember

my pains no more; yea, I was harrowed up by the memory of my sins no more.

And oh, what joy, and what marvelous light I did behold; yea, my soul was filled with joy as exceeding as was my pain! . . .

Yea, methought I saw . . . God sitting upon his throne, surrounded with numberless concourses of angels, in the attitude of singing and praising their God; yea, and my soul did long to be there.

But behold, my limbs did receive their strength again, and I stood upon my feet, and did manifest unto the people *that I had been born of God.*

Yea, and from that time even until now, I have labored without ceasing, that I might bring souls unto repentance; that I might bring them to taste of the exceeding joy of which I did taste; that they might also be *born of God, and be filled with the Holy Ghost* (Alma 36:6, 9, 10, 12, 13, 15, 17-20, 22-24; italics added).

In the following three verses of the 4th chapter of Mosiah we have an account of a whole multitude experiencing a new birth.

And now, it came to pass that when king Benjamin had made an end of speaking . . . that he cast his eyes round about on the multitude, and behold they had fallen to the earth, for the fear of the Lord had come upon them. . . .

And they all cried aloud with one voice, saying: O have mercy, and apply the atoning blood of Christ that we may receive forgiveness of our sins, and our hearts may be purified; for we believe in Jesus Christ, the Son of God, . . .

And it came to pass that after they had spoken these words the Spirit of the Lord came upon them, and they were filled with joy, having received a remission of their sins, and having peace of conscience, because of the exceeding faith which they had in Jesus Christ (Mosiah 4:1-3).

Every one who complies with the prescribed conditions is born again. As Alma sought to impress this great truth on his recreant brethren at Zarahemla, he sought also to teach them that being born again does not guarantee one a pure heart and clean hands at the final judgment.

> If ye have experienced a change of heart [he said to them],
> and if ye have felt to sing the song of redeeming love, I
> would ask, can ye feel so now?
>
> Have ye walked, keeping yourselves blameless before
> God? Could ye say, if ye were called to die at this time, . . .
> that ye have been sufficiently humble? That your garments
> have been cleansed and made white through the blood of
> Christ? (Alma 5:26, 27).

The implication of these questions is in strict harmony with the teachings of all the prophets and of the
Lord himself. They all proclaim that he who can at
that great day look up to God with the "pure heart and
clean hands," which will qualify him for eternal life,
is he who so lives as to retain to the end of his life the
forgiveness received through "baptism of fire and of
the Holy Ghost." The Savior said it in these words:

> Whoso repenteth and is baptized in my name shall be
> filled [that is, filled with the Holy Ghost]; and if he endureth
> to the end, behold, him will I hold guiltless before my Father
> at that day when I shall stand to judge the world.
>
> And no unclean thing can enter into his kingdom; there-
> fore nothing entereth into his rest save it be those who have
> washed their garments in my blood, because of their faith,
> and the repentance of all their sins, and their faithfulness
> unto the end (3 Nephi 27:16, 19).

If time permitted, a proper sequence to the foregoing remarks would be a consideration in depth of the
things to be done to retain a remission of sins. To
know what they are and do them is as important as
obtaining remission of sins in the first place. Since,
however, we do not here and now have time for such
a consideration, I shall close by quoting Nephi's summary on this important matter:

> And now, my beloved brethren, after ye have gotten into
> this straight and narrow path, I would ask if all is done?
> Behold, I say unto you, Nay; . . .
>
> Ye must press forward with a steadfastness in Christ,
> having a perfect brightness of hope, and a love of God and

all men. Wherefore, if ye shall press forward, feasting upon the word of Christ, and endure to the end, behold, thus saith the Father: Ye shall have eternal life (2 Nephi 31:19, 20).

He who is born of the spirit, and continues to live in a state of repentance from the time he is thus "born again" to the end of his mortal life, will have retained the remission of his sins. After death he will be free from the powers of evil and he will be able to look up to God with "a pure heart and clean hands" and he will hear the great Judge say, "Come unto me ye blessed, for behold, your works have been works of righteousness upon the earth" (Alma 5:16).

That it may be so with each of us, I humbly pray.

And now, we can behold the decrees of God concerning this land, that it is a land of promise; and whatsoever nation shall possess it shall serve God, or they shall be swept off when the fulness of his wrath shall come upon them. And the fulness of his wrath cometh upon them when they are ripened in iniquity.

For behold, this is a land which is choice above all other lands; wherefore he that doth possess it shall serve God or shall be swept off; for it is the everlasting decree of God. And it is not until the fulness of iniquity among the children of the land, that they are swept off.

And this cometh unto you, O ye Gentiles, that ye may know the decrees of God—that ye may repent, and not continue in your iniquities until the fulness come, that ye may not bring down the fulness of the wrath of God upon you as the inhabitants of the land have hitherto done.

Behold, this is a choice land, and whatsoever nation shall possess it shall be free from bondage; and from captivity, and from all other nations under heaven, if they will but serve the God of the land, who is Jesus Christ, who hath been manifested by the things which we have written.

Ether 2:9-12

AMERICA
RESERVED FOR A RIGHTEOUS PEOPLE •

An address delivered at general conference April 1952.

I come to you representing a people for whom the inscription on our national coin "In God We Trust" has real significance. For we know that an effective relationship persists between God and this land and its people.

Centuries ago the Lord designated America a goodly land, choice above all others, to be reserved for righteous people. While it was yet unknown to

Eurasians, he decreed that it should be discovered only under his guidance and promised its inhabitants from that time henceforth and forever that they should "be free from bondage, and from captivity, and from all other nations under heaven" (Ether 2:12) if they would serve him. On the other hand, he warned that if they would not serve him, "they should be brought down into captivity, and also into destruction both temporally and spiritually."

Preceding the advent of Columbus, two mighty peoples dwelling upon this land prospered in obeying God's commands and, rebelling against them, sank into oblivion. Their records are eloquent proof of the certainty in God's warning and promise.

The builders of modern America, though without knowledge of the divine decree, have been aware of God standing within "the shadow keeping watch upon his own."

Columbus, not knowing it had been given, yet witnessed to the truth of the declaration that the discoverers of America should be led by divine inspiration. "God gave me the faith and afterwards the courage so that I was quite willing to undertake the journey," he said to his son, and in his will he wrote:

In the name of the most holy trinity, who inspired me with the idea and afterwards made it perfectly clear to me that I could navigate and go to the Indies from Spain, by traversing the ocean westward.

The early settlers of the Atlantic seaboard testified that they were led and sustained by the power of God. The colonists, rejecting the tyranny of King George, appealed "to the Supreme Judge of the world for the rectitude of" their intentions and "with a firm reliance on the protection of Divine Providence" struck for freedom.

At a critical point Franklin thus addressed the Constitutional Convention,

> We have been assured, sir, in the sacred writings, that "Except the Lord build the house, they labour in vain that build it." I firmly believe this; and I also believe that, without his concurring aid, we shall succeed in this political building no better than the builders of Babel (*Documentary History of the Constitution of the United States* 3:235-37).

In his 1789 Thanksgiving Proclamation, Washington made seven separate references to the Almighty, whom he acknowledged as the source of all the nation's blessings, including victory in the Revolution and "opportunity to establish a form of government for" our "safety and happiness."

Perhaps no American, save the prophets only, has put such implicit trust in God as did the Great Emancipator. Out of his personal experiences he testified he was as certain that God acts directly upon human affairs as he was of a fact apparent to the senses, such as that he was in the room where he was then speaking. He said:

> I have had so many evidences of his direction, so many instances when I have been controlled by some other power than my own will, that I cannot doubt that this power comes from above. I frequently see my way clear to a decision when I am conscious that I have not sufficient facts upon which to found it. But I cannot recall one instance in which I have followed my own judgment founded upon such a decision, where the results were unsatisfactory; whereas, in almost every instance where I have yielded to the views of others I have had occasion to regret it (John Wesley Hill, *Abraham Lincoln—Man of God*, p. 124).

A marked diminution of our trust in God has taken place in America since the days of Lincoln, the effect of which is everywhere apparent. We and our beloved country are today at the crossroads in our efforts to maintain our glorious American heritage of political, temporal, and spiritual freedom won and bequeathed to us by the fathers who had inscribed in their hearts, as well as on their money, "In God We Trust." In every hamlet of our land arises a plaintive cry for a return to that trust in God by which the fathers built our nation. I believe we are approaching almost an unanimity in our feeling that the great and imperative need of this hour of decision for America is to vitalize our trust in God.

I believe we can do it. I know we can do it if we are but willing to pay the price. Possessing a sure knowledge of the truth of what I say, I point out two prerequisites to the realization of this, our great need: First, we must in humility seek the God in whom we trust in earnest prayer; second, we must dedicate ourselves to the keeping of his commandments.

"Seek ye the Lord while he may be found, call ye upon him while he is near," counseled Isaiah (Isaiah 55:6).

"Evening, and morning, and at noon, will I pray, and cry aloud: and he shall hear my voice," sang the psalmist (Psalm 55:17).

"Watch and pray, that ye enter not into temptation" (Matthew 26:41), taught Jesus. And in his perfect life he set the pattern. He prayed (Luke 3:21) and fasted forty days (Matthew 4:2) at the beginning of his public ministry; he prayed in the wilderness (Luke 5:16); he prayed at the beginning of the day (Mark 1:35); he prayed a whole night preceding his selection of the twelve apostles (Luke 6:12); he prayed for strength in Gethsemane; and finally, on the cross in the hour of his death, he prayed (Ibid., 23:34).

All men who "under God" have advanced the cause of righteousness in America have been praying men.

Who has not heard Isaac Potts' account of Washington
on his knees in the snow in prayer at Valley Forge?
Lincoln's sublime trust in God came after he had many
times been driven to his knees in prayer. He thus explained to General Sickles the reason for the serenity
he experienced while the outcome of the battle of
Gettysburg hung in the balance:

> In the pinch of your campaign up there, when everybody
> seemed panic-stricken and nobody could tell what was going
> to happen, oppressed by the gravity of affairs, I went to my
> room one day and locked the door and got down on my knees
> before Almighty God and prayed to him mightily for victory
> at Gettysburg. I told him that this war was his, and our
> cause his cause, but we could not stand another Fredericks-
> burg or Chancellorsville. Then and there I made a solemn vow
> to Almighty God that if he would stand by our boys at Gettys-
> burg, I would stand by him, and he did stand by our boys,
> and I will stand by him. And after that, I don't know how
> it was, and I cannot explain it, soon a sweet comfort crept into
> my soul. The feeling came that God had taken the whole busi-
> ness into his hands, and that things would go right at Gettys-
> burg, and that is why I had no fears about you (*Abraham
> Lincoln—Man of God*, pp. 339-40).

If we would vitalize our trust in God, we—you and
I—must get down on our knees and pray to him as
Lincoln prayed, with all the energy of our souls. And
we must do so, as did the psalmist, at evening, morning,
and noon. We cannot leave it for the other fellow;
we must do it ourselves, and we must do it now. If
we will begin and close each day by praying unto our
Father in heaven in secret, as the Savior admonished,
thanking him for our lives, his protection over us, our
loved ones, our material comforts, and the freedom we
enjoy in this glorious land; if we will plead with him
to guide us in the paths of righteousness that we may
merit a continuation of his mercies; if the head of
every household will daily call his family about him
and, praying with them and they praying with him,

truly worship the Lord, the first long and sure step will be taken toward vitalizing our trust in God.

To take the second step, we must learn that in the relationship between God and ourselves both parties have obligations. We must stand by the Lord, as Lincoln promised to do, for he has promised to give us protection against temporal and spiritual bondage, and against all other nations under heaven, only if we serve him. Praying is one way to serve him, another way is to keep his commandments. There are numerous ways in which we are violating them in America today.

On many points the Lord has given us specific guidance with respect to the conduct of our lives; for example, he has said,

Thou shalt not take the name of the Lord thy God in vain; for the Lord will not hold him guiltless that taketh his name in vain (Exodus 20:7).

In harmony with this command Washington issued the following order in 1776:

The General is sorry to be informed that the foolish and wicked practice of profane cursing and swearing, a vice heretofore little known in an American army, is growing into fashion. He hopes the officers will, by example as well as influence, endeavor to check it, and that both they and the men will reflect that we can have little hope of the blessings of heaven on our arms if we insult it by our impiety and folly. Added to this, it is a vice so mean and low, . . . that every man of sense and character detests and despises it.

What respect is today being paid to this prohibition against profanity? If you hear what I hear, you know we have not placed the Lord in our debt through its observance.

"Remember the Sabbath day to keep it holy" (Exodus 20:8) is another familiar command.

That it was revered by the great Lincoln is evidenced by a general order to the army and the navy, signed by him November 15, 1862. From that order I quote:

> The President, commander-in-chief of the army and navy, desires and enjoins the orderly observance of the Sabbath by the officers and men in the military and naval service. . . . The discipline and character of the national forces should not suffer, nor the cause they defend be imperiled, by the profanation of the day or name of the Most High (Carl Sandburg, *Abraham Lincoln, The War Years*, 3:374).

How do we, as a nation, stand upon this matter today? Is it not rather noted in the breach than in the observance?

"Thou shalt not commit adultery" (Exodus 20: 14), spake the Lord amidst the thundering and lightning of Sinai, against one of the most debasing of sins, a practice which has preceded the disintegration of every fallen civilization. Paul's pronouncement that our bodies are the temples of God, that "If any man defile the temple of God, him shall God destroy" (1 Corinthians 3:17), is an eternal principle still in force. Much of our sorrow and distress stems from a violation of this divine command.

We might continue with other divine commands. "Thou shalt not steal," "Thou shalt not bear false witness," "Thou shalt not covet" (Exodus 20:15-17), but we now have in mind enough to persuade us of many ways in which we may improve, if we really, in truth and without hypocrisy, are committed to keeping the commandments of God.

I plead with you, my friends, for a vitalization of our trust in God through earnest prayer and a careful keeping of the Lord's commands. Every substitute we have tried has left us deeper in the mire. Our integrity, our liberties, our treasures, are slipping like sand through our fingers. Our cynicism and godless learning lead us ever farther from the truth. Why should we not put to test the one untried plan of self-disciplined conformance to the plain and simple commands of the God in whom we profess to trust? Doing this, turning not to the right hand or to the left, we shall become strong and of a good courage. The Lord will be with and prosper us, whithersoever we go. Our trust in him being thus vitalized into an all-powerful present reality, the strongest bulwark in all our defenses, we shall sing with strong conviction,

> Our fathers' God, to thee,
> Author of liberty,
> To thee we sing;
> Long may our land be bright
> With freedom's holy light;
> Protect us by thy might,
> Great God, our king.

That we may do so, I humbly pray in the name of Jesus Christ. Amen.

RESPONSE TO A CALL •

An address delivered at general conference October 6, 1951, in response to a call to the Council of the Twelve.

My beloved brothers and sisters, coming to this stand and speaking to you is not a new experience. This is the twenty-second time I have climbed up here in the last ten and a half years. I am not a stranger to you. Many of you know me—some of you may know me too well. This call has set up a tremendous emotional reaction in me. I didn't think there could be such a big tempest in such a little teapot. I suppose that I need the help of the Lord now more than I ever needed it in my life. Will you please ask him to give me strength to make a few remarks appropriate to this occasion.

RESPECT FOR OFFICE

The great respect I have always had for the office to which I am now called contributes greatly to the emotional strain I am experiencing. Men who held these offices were godlike men in the eyes of my parents. When they came to Old Mexico where I lived as a little child, I almost thought they were of a different race.

I remember what we thought of President Joseph F. Smith when he came. I don't remember any of the brethren who are now living coming down.

I have always thought of this office as the office of a special witness of the Redeemer of the world, and when I think about the Redeemer of the world, I think about the great council in the spirit world when he undertook to be the instrument and make the sacrifice to put into operation the gospel of redemption. I understand that God the Eternal Father was the author of the plan. I get that from President John Taylor. Jesus sponsored it.

"I will go," he said. I believe Brother Whitney put it in these terms: "Mine be the willing sacrifice, the endless glory thine."

Events in Life of Redeemer

Next I think of the Redeemer on the mount with the brother of Jared twenty-two hundred years before he was born in the flesh, as the infant child of Mary. There I get the idea of what I think a spirit looks like. The brother of Jared thought he had beheld flesh and blood, but the spirit spake to him, saying, "Thou hast seen that I shall take upon me flesh and blood" (Ether 3:9).

Then he said, "Seest thou that ye are created after mine own image? Yea, even all men were created in the beginning after mine own image.

"Behold this body" (which appeared to the brother of Jared to be a body of flesh and blood and bone), said the spirit Jesus Christ, "which ye now behold, is the body of my spirit; and even as I appear unto thee to be in the spirit will I appear unto my people in the flesh" (see Ether 3:15, 16).

And then I think of the Redeemer, that great spirit who created the world under the direction of God, our Eternal Father, entering the body of a tiny infant in a manger in Bethlehem.

I think of him in the temple at the age of twelve already somewhat conversant with his mission, when he said to his mother—I don't think in any sense of disrespect when she chided him a little about being there without her knowledge: "Wist ye not that I must be about my Father's business?" (Luke 2:49).

I think about him through his ministry. I could mention many cases, but I shall not take much time. I think about his baptism as the beginning of the pattern that we must follow. I think about him at the well with the Samaritan woman when he said that whosoever would drink of the water that he would give would never thirst again, because that water would be a well of living water, springing up into eternal life.

I think about him when Lazarus passed away, and Mary and Martha came out to meet him. I don't remember the conversation exactly, but I believe Martha said, "Lord, if thou hadst been here, my brother had not died," and Jesus said, "I am the resurrection and the life: he that believeth in me, though he were dead, yet shall he live: And whosoever liveth and believeth in me shall never die" (John 11:21, 25, 26).

I think of him in the temple during those last days of his mortal life. I think of him in Gethsemane. I will pass the scene. It moves me too deeply. He suffered for me there, and for you. I think of him on the cross. I think of him in the grove with the Prophet Joseph, and the Father, his Father, the Father of that spirit of his which appeared to the brother of Jared, the Father of my spirit, as President Clark has just explained, the Father of the spirits of all men.

When I think about being a special witness of him, and I remember that Peter, James, and John could not stay awake through his last suffering in Gethsemane, I think of some who have failed. I don't want to fail.

I think of those who have given their lives for the witness. I have counted that. If it should be necessary, I hope I will not falter to give my life for the testimony of Jesus. I know he lives. I doubt if I will know it better when I meet him.

LOVE FOR THE BRETHREN

I shall not go further. I would like to pay my respects to these men. I know President McKay holds the authority that the Prophet had, and I know the Prophet held the authority that Peter held. I have loved President McKay for a long, long time. He doesn't remember when I first fell in love with him. I guess he doesn't remember when you did, either.

It was down in Los Angeles in the winter of 1912 and 1913. We were known then as Mormon refugees. We had lost our home in Mexico—invited out down there. Brother McKay came to Los Angeles; he came to Sunday School, and he took a glass of water. He had a pen in his hand. He showed us how clear and beautiful the water was, and then he dropped a drop of ink in the water, and it clouded it all through, and he said to us little fellows, "That is what sin does to a life," and I have ever since then, President McKay, been trying to keep that sin out of my life.

I met him over in Australia. I got frightened of him over there. I was president of the conference. They used to call districts "conferences." I was conducting, and when he looked at his watch, he said, "Brother Romney, I believe it is thirty seconds late."

So the next time we started a meeting, we weren't late, and Brother McKay looked at his watch and said, "Brother Romney, I believe it is fifteen seconds early."

Then he didn't take me with him when he went up to visit the Genolean Caves; he took Elder Bischoff. I remember when he came back and taught us a lesson, telling us how those great stalagmites and stalactites in the caves were made by infinitesimally small deposits from drops of water.

Then he told us that was how a life was built. Every thought we thought, every word we spoke, every deed we did, registered on our character. I never have forgotten that, either.

I have always loved President Richards since I knew him. I went out with him in my early work as an Assistant, and I remember how he conducted conferences. He did it with the skill with which an artist paints a picture. I think everything he does is done beautifully. I sustain him with all my heart.

Then this great man, President Clark, has been closest to me of all the Presidency, in the administrations of President Grant and President Smith and now President McKay, because he has been directing for the Presidency the work that I have been assigned to. I don't think there is a man in the world who loves righteousness and is acquainted with Brother Clark who doesn't love him. He has been to me as a father. I love you, Brother Clark, with all the strength of my life.

I love Brother Smith, President Joseph Fielding Smith. He has been most kind and thoughtful of me. I thought he treated me especially good until I got talking to the other brethren about him and found out that he treated them all the same.

Now I love all the brethren, every one of them. I won't go down through the Twelve, except to mention Brother Lee and Brother Moyle. They are my closest associates. Brother Lee is a seer. I know I'll never go wrong if I'm with him, and I know I'll never go hungry if I'm with Brother Moyle because he is so liberal.

I love the brethren I have worked with, Thomas and Clifford and Alma, and Nicholas who passed away, the Patriarch, the Seventy, the Bishopric, and these new men who came in. Some of them I have been close to.

GRATITUDE FOR HERITAGE

Now I would just like to say I am grateful for my heritage. Both my families are of longstanding in the Church, the Redds and the Romneys. I am claimed by both of them. The Redds claim I am a Romney, and the Romneys claim I am a Redd, but I am proud of them both. I am very grateful for my father, the late George S. Romney, and my sainted mother who sits here today in tears. I am grateful for the righteous home they reared me in—Mother, I tell you I am grateful.

I am grateful for my own family and their support of me; my sons and daughter-in-law, my sixteen-month-old granddaughter who gives me lots of joy, and last, but not least, my beloved companion, the sweetheart of my youth, and the mother of my children. They have never put a straw in my way. We had been married seventeen years when I became an Assistant to the Twelve, and I had only been away from home, leaving Ida alone two nights. When I first started traveling around the Church, it was hard for her. She used to cry every time I left and every time I came back. Now she cries only when I come back.

LOYALTY OF MEMBERS

I am very grateful to you, my brothers and sisters. I love every one of you. I know some of the contributions you make. As I go about the Church and see you come to the meetings the brethren authorize me to call, I learn your hearts and your loyalty.

I sat in a meeting this morning with two regional councils, and I saw them yield to the decisions that have been made by these great men of the Presidency with the finest spirit of unity that I have ever beheld. I love you for what you have done for me as you have received me into your homes.

I will do everything I can to serve you, and I will do everything I can to honor this high calling. God bless you, and God bless me, and will you please pray for me that no enemy shall dent the small sector of the line which I am assigned to defend, I pray in the name of Jesus Christ. Amen.

INDEX •